DAILY GRACE
FOR TEACHERS

DEVOTIONAL REFLECTIONS TO
NOURISH YOUR SOUL

HONOR HB BOOKS

Inspiration and Motivation for the Seasons of Life

COOK COMMUNICATIONS MINISTRIES
Colorado Springs, Colorado • Paris, Ontario
KINGSWAY COMMUNICATIONS LTD
Eastbourne, England

There is nothing but God's grace. We walk upon it;
we breathe it; we live and die by it; it makes the nails
and axles of the universe.

ROBERT LOUIS STEVENSON

Dear Reader:

Daily Grace for Teachers: Devotional Reflections to Nourish Your Soul has been written and compiled with much love and care. As you read through these pages in the days, weeks, and months ahead, it is our prayer that the revelation of the riches of God's grace will abound in your heart and mind.

We've designed this book with you in mind, combining the wonderful truth of God's Word with devotional readings relevant to the everyday life of a teacher. A variety of writers were chosen—people from divergent backgrounds and seasons of life—to give each daily reading a fresh, unique perspective. And a "grace principle" has been included, so you will have a bit of God's grace to carry with you throughout your day—both in the classroom as well as in your life away from school. For the weekend entries, we've taken from the works of classic and well-known writers and added a prayer to help you take hold of these remarkable insights and principles.

We pray that God will bless you as you read, fill your heart with grace and peace, and draw you closer to the God who gave His all to meet your every need.

The Publisher

HANDS-ON SAVIOR

Jesus said to them, "Come and have breakfast."

JOHN 21:12 NIV

A popular elementary science teacher was a hands-on guy. He taught his most powerful lesson in paleontology by burying a life-sized skeleton model of a T-Rex three feet deep in a field. Carefully and methodically, but always with a heightened sense of discovery, he taught his students how to conduct an authentic dig.

For an examination of outer space, this same teacher helped his students build a shuttle command-and-control center in the classroom.

And for a unit on microbiology, he let his students make and consume their very own batch of root beer.

Lessons in faith resulted in some of Jesus' most powerful object lessons. Whether He was feeding a multitude from a few loaves and fishes, or turning water into fine wine, He was always careful to bring His followers along, patiently and compassionately teaching them to trust, to expect, to dig a little deeper into what it meant to believe in the Father. All of their senses were engaged, whether Jesus taught in the temple or wrote in the sand.

> ### GRACE FOR TODAY:
> **Because Jesus is a hands-on Savior, He can teach us to rediscover the joy of grace in our lives.**

So many religious leaders of that day failed to move the people because their religion was haughty and unapproachable, their message one of condemnation. But Jesus, the carpenter's son, was the hands-on Messiah. Because He welcomed His disciples to eat with Him, pray with Him, and touch His scars of sacrifice, He got through to them. For a child to retain most of what he's taught, the teacher must engage all of that child's intelligence. Hands-on experience leaves a lasting impression. When your students work alongside you, see the joy on your face, and hear the excitement in your voice, you will get through to them in new and wonderful ways.

LAUGH TO LEARN

A cheerful heart is good medicine.

PROVERBS 17:22 NIV

A South Carolina judge told the story of the day his three-year-old daughter's beloved pet turtle died. Knowing she would be heartbroken, the judge's wife asked him to break the news.

"Sweetheart, I know you're going to be sad, but your turtle died," the judge said, as he knelt and put his arms around his daughter.

"What's that mean, Daddy?"

"Well, I'm afraid it means he's never coming back."

The judge promised that they could go down to the pet store and get another turtle just like him, but his daughter knew there could never be another turtle exactly the same. Looking at her crestfallen face, the judge tried again.

GRACE FOR TODAY:

Take delight in your students.

"But we could have a funeral for him if you'd like," he said.

"What's a funeral?"

Seeing his chance to cheer up his daughter, the judge chose to embellish the definition of funeral.

"It's kind of like a party to remember someone who's died," he said. "All the children in the neighborhood could come and play—all because your turtle has died."

"Could we have cake?"

"I guess so," he said.

"And balloons for me and my friends?" She was obviously warming to the idea.

"Sure, honey."

At that ill-timed moment, the "dead" turtle slowly began to crawl away. The judge looked at it with relief—his daughter with consternation.

"Daddy," she said, "let's kill him."

WORTHY OF HONOR

Let every soul be subject to the governing authorities.
For there is no authority except from God, and the authorities that exist
are appointed by God.

ROMANS 13:1 NKJV

One of the principle ways in which school prepares young people for the "real world" is in its development of respect for authority. In a society where children are bombarded through the media, and too often at home, with images of the ineptitude of grown-ups, you have a chance to be an all-too-rare role model: an authority figure worthy of respect and honor.

When you think of your parents or of teachers who had a positive influence on your life, what qualities come to mind? You likely think of mutual respect, compassionate honesty, a solid work ethic, and a willingness to take responsibility, or to be the bottom line.

Exhibiting those types of qualities as a teacher will both earn your students' respect and also set an example of a successful, influential professional working within the structure of the system. As a Christian, you're fulfilling the call to be in the world but not of it, to be a citizen of a kingdom yet to come while still giving proper respect both to those in authority over you and to those under your authority.

In doing so, it's the little details that count. Lecture all you want about respect for governing bodies, but it's in how you address them—when your students hear you refer to "Monotone Jones" the civics teacher as Mrs. Jones, or when you call the custodian Mr. Clemmons—that they really see you mean what you say.

When you're deciding what you want students to call you, consider what will help them offer you due respect. If you can accomplish that while going by your first name, that's terrific. What matters most is that you establish a learning environment built on the idea that God sets those in charge in their places, not to intimidate, but to rule wisely.

GRACE FOR TODAY:

God sets us in charge not to intimidate, but to rule wisely.

God's Grace Instructs

The grace of God . . . has appeared to all men. It teaches us to say "No"
to ungodliness and worldly passions, and to live selfcontrolled,
upright and godly lives.

Titus 2:11–12 NIV

Melodie, an independent young woman of twenty, was finally living on her own and attending the University of Mississippi. The first few weeks flew by, and she reveled in her freedom—nobody telling her what do or when to do it! But by the time Halloween rolled around, Melodie's bubble had burst, and the real world in which she lived had her spooked. Most of her friends didn't go to church, and many spent the night with their boyfriends. And she was shocked that so many students cheated on tests. Thoughts and opportunities were tempting Melodie to compromise in ways she'd never anticipated. She needed help. When she called her mother at one A.M., her mom quickly answered the phone.

"Mom, I gotta talk to you." Melodie's voice was troubled. "Some things are really eating me up, and I need you to pray with me."

Hopefully, you can still remember your own days of transitioning into adulthood as you help your kids discern right and wrong in the classroom. Melodie's dilemma is a candid reminder that there is a world of distractions to pull you, as well as your students, away from God.

Like Melodie's revelation, God wants you to recognize areas in which you may need to change, saying no to temptation or yes to spending more time with Him, so that you can be an example at your school. His still small voice will instruct you, whether your need is learning to relate better to your students or walking away from gossip. Take time to listen.

Grace for Today:

God's grace takes us as we are, then instructs us to be
all that we can.

POWERFUL IN PATIENCE

Wild Asian elephants don't know their own strength. They heedlessly trample through cultivated fields and wreak havoc with the slender trees of rubber plantations. For those who must bear the damage, the reckless pachyderms are an expensive cost of doing business.

Those who log the forests of India and Thailand, however, have learned to direct elephant power. They teach the giants patience—to move in moderation. So effective is the training that the worker elephants glide gracefully about the forest, carefully wrapping their trunks around only those logs marked for removal.

Jesus possessed all power in Heaven and on earth, yet He did not use it as a weapon. He came to minister, to seek and to save the lost, to point the way to God. Though Scripture tells us He could have called down His angels to save himself, He did not. Instead of destroying those who plotted His demise, He prayed for their forgiveness. He knew His own strength. With divine precision, He directed His power at sin and death and by His mercy redeemed His own.

Do you ever experience the raw power of untamed anger or injustice? Or perhaps you've felt just the opposite—powerless and unappreciated. We all know those times when the school board is unfair, parents are too demanding, and your students resist learning. It is in those dark and disappointing moments that you can ask God to quell your frustrations and put a damper on your temper. He delights in making you strong in your weakness. Trust Him by His strength to bring you calm and rational thought. Tomorrow's another day. Power under control is sweet victory!

GRACE FOR TODAY:

Our all-powerful God gives us calm and rational thought.

I pray that out of his glorious riches he may strengthen you with power through his Spirit in your inner being.

EPHESIANS 3:16 NIV

HIS JOY

By Evelyn Christenson

It was pouring rain. Three miles from home, a truck, a compact car, and I stopped for a red light, but the car behind me didn't. Crunch. All four vehicles accordioned into one. I recovered from the jolt to my nervous system, but as I drove during the following week I kept my eyes as much on the rearview mirror as I did on the road ahead of me!

The next weekend I was to drive to a northern Minnesota retreat. I couldn't. I felt nothing but apprehension and fear at the possibility of being hit from behind. And the theme for the retreat was to be J-O-Y!

Just before I was to drive to the retreat, God gave the answer I needed as I was reading in the Psalms. A smile spread over my face as I read: "But let all those that put their trust in thee rejoice: let them ever shout for joy, because thou defendest them: let them also that love thy name be joyful in thee" (Psalm 5:11 KJV). Immediately I saw my problem—failing to trust Him! At that moment He exchanged my fear for His joy. The apprehension disappeared, and I drove, a changed woman, to that J-O-Y retreat, really experiencing what I was to preach.

My spiritual barometer has been 1 John 1:4 NKJV: "These things we write to you that your joy may be full." I can always measure the amount of time I'm spending in the Scriptures by how much joy (not superficial happiness, but deep-down abiding joy) I have. When I find a lack of joy in my life, the first thing I check is how much time I'm spending in God's Word.

—∿∿—

HEAVENLY FATHER, THANK YOU FOR THE JOY THAT I RECEIVE BY SPENDING TIME IN YOUR WORD. YOUR GRACE INCLUDES EVERYTHING I NEED TO LIVE A LIFE THAT RADIATES YOUR JOY TO MY STUDENTS AND THE WORLD. USE ME TO BLESS THEM. AMEN.

Be glad in the LORD and rejoice, you righteous; and shout for joy, all you upright in heart!

PSALM 32:11 NKJV

THE TEACHER'S NEW YEAR

In the morning, O LORD, you hear my voice; in the morning I lay my
requests before you and wait in expectation.

PSALM 5:3 NIV

A blank slate.
A new page.
A clean plate.
A fresh beginning.
A reinvention.

For those who teach, the New Year is not rung in to the sound of horns, the clink of toasting glasses, and the soft whisper of confetti on a chilly winter evening. Resolutions are not made in the front pages of a brand-new calendar, binding still stiff. Anticipation of new adventures doesn't begin only after the excitement of the holidays has faded into just another memory for the scrapbook.

Rather, for those who teach, the new year begins in September. It begins slowly when a few yellow leaves fall prematurely in July. It surges in mid-August when the urge to design a new bulletin board and rearrange a classroom is nearly unbearable. It peaks in September when yellow school buses roll, leaves are on fire with autumnal splendor, and new backpacks, sharpened pencils, and colorful notebooks abound.

> **GRACE FOR TODAY:**
>
> **When God asks us to serve Him in the classroom, He will give us a new beginning each day.**

For teachers, resolutions are made in the front of gloriously crisp blank pages of a plan book. Oh, the ideas we can't wait to try out on this year's crop of students! In the neat rows of apple-red grade books, we vow, "This year I'll write legibly all the way to June!" It's the school bell that rings in our new year. We know the adventures are daily, and they have just begun.

Make your mark.

Write on your page.

Begin again.

Reinvent yourself. This is your year. Dream. Imagine. Build. Wait in expectation of the adventures God has for you this term. This could be the best year yet!

BEING THERE

The LORD is gracious and full of compassion,
slow to anger and great in mercy.

PSALM 145:8 NKJV

Having taught for any length of time, you know what it is to feel heartache for one of your kids. It might be the challenge of a learning disability, or a rough situation at home. It's hard to cut through the way those problems manifest themselves to get to the heart of the matter.

What looks like, and sometimes is, your sophomore's antisocial behavior is actually loneliness or having missed breakfast or her move to a new house. What seems to be laziness or apathy in that third-grader is actually frustration because the letters keep flip-flopping in his head.

When you first realized you wanted to be a teacher, it wasn't all about spreading the wonders of the quadratic equation, or ensuring the next generation's proper use of semicolons. It was also about having relationships with young people, about being a positive influence in their formative years.

You wanted to teach because you'd had some great teachers yourself, or sometimes because you'd had a few too many poor ones. Either way, you wanted to make a difference, to guide, to impart knowledge, to listen, and even to help when things were going wrong. You felt compassion.

More than just "being nice" to people, compassion is about "being there" for them. A literal breakdown of the word compassion means "to suffer with someone else." In other words, you share their difficulty and distress, desiring to help alleviate it.

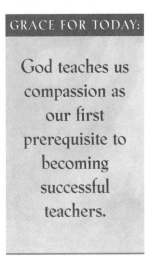

GRACE FOR TODAY:

God teaches us compassion as our first prerequisite to becoming successful teachers.

Think of all the times Jesus reached out to the most needy, the most desperate people He encountered. Consider how He looked beneath your veneer to find the child of God for whom it was worth suffering death on the Cross. It's that love, inspired and demonstrated by the divine, that will allow you to demonstrate the compassion that your students need so desperately from you.

TALK OF THE TOWN

You're a fountain of cascading light, and you open our eyes to light.

PSALM 36:9 MSG

Joycelyn, one of Southwest High's younger teachers, casually strolled through the front entrance with an air of sophistication, her long blonde hair bouncing with each step. As usual she was decked out in designer clothes from head to toe.

"Look! She's carrying a Louis Vuitton bag!" said Emilie, another teacher. "I can't believe she dresses like that to teach."

As Joycelyn passed by, Amanda couldn't help but stare. "Well, that's nothing. Check out the Versace suit! Did you notice her boots? She told me yesterday, they're Armani!"

"Must be nice," Emilie replied in an envious tone. "I'd die for a wardrobe like hers! If only I had her money. But on my teacher's salary, I can't even afford an imitation handbag."

"She sure turns heads around here . . ." Amanda's remark faded as she walked into her classroom.

Have you ever envied someone the way Emilie and Amanda were jealous of Joycelyn? It creates a hunger for material possessions, rather than things of lasting value. God reminds us in Scripture that clothes are only temporal, but those things which can't be seen are eternal.

The truth is, if you are a believer in Jesus Christ, you have the same potential to create a stir among your peers as Joycelyn. You are a joint-heir with Christ, and if you really believe that, you'll shine with an inner light that people will notice immediately. You won't be wishing for designer clothes. No, you'll be walking the hallways, creating a desire in others to know Jesus because of how you're spiritually decked out. God desires that the light in you would make the world envious to know Him. If you will dare to live like this, you'll definitely be the talk of the town.

GRACE FOR TODAY:

If we want to make a lasting difference, God can give us eternal values that will never fade or wear away.

IT TAKES TIME

Remain in me, and I will remain in you.

JOHN 15:4 NIV

Does it often seem that the bulk of your teaching time is consumed by lesson preparation, grading papers, and progress reports? All are necessary tasks in their own way, but when do you get time to actually teach?

Less than 10 percent of Christ's life was devoted to public ministry. Ninety percent of His time on earth was spent growing, learning, and communing with the heavenly Father. For three decades, the Son of God grew in stature and wisdom before He ever taught the multitudes. In the printing trade, this preparation time is known as "make ready" time, the time required to get a project on the press and ready to run. For Jesus, the years of preparation were God's provision to get Him ready for the brief but critical three years to follow.

It was in those first thirty years of His life that Jesus learned the importance of abiding, or remaining, in the Father, of maintaining that essential link with the source of all power. In 1 John, the idea is expressed in the phrase "continue in Him." Why would that be to our benefit? Jesus says that it's so we can bear fruit and experience the fullness of the love of God.

Noah learned to abide when he spent many years building the ark. Mary learned to abide when she was told by an angel that in nine months she would bear the Son of the Most High and be blessed among women to raise the Messiah. Maybe those nine months provided her with an opportunity to get used to the whole stunning idea!

View the time when you're not teaching as God's way of getting you ready. And when you do teach, thank Him that He is in you and beside you giving you the power to speak the truth. What an awesome gift to give any child!

GRACE FOR TODAY:

If you spend time communing with God, He will give you plenty of time to love others.

THE CANDLE

Imagine you are standing in a dark room. However, in the room are placed five straight white candles—simple in design and purity—ensconced in plain, functional pewter holders. When lit, their soft whispering flames softly illuminate and bring hope to that dark place.

Now imagine that each candle is lit by a phrase of enthusiasm, curiosity, or wonder that you might hear in any classroom:

Candle #1: "Look, Teacher! I colored my sky purple and my grass pink!"

Candle #2: "Sir, I was just wondering why it is that we have to sit in alphabetical order."

Candle #3: "Mrs. Smith, I had to work late every night this week. I'm afraid my assignment isn't finished."

Candle #4: "I wrote a poem! Let me read it to you! See, there's a picture to go with it!"

Candle #5: "When I grow up, I want to be just like you!"

Now picture each flame being extinguished by the cruel breath of realism, responsibility, and well-meaning platitudes.

"Now, you know that the sky isn't purple! And grass is just green."

"That's what we always do so I can get to know your names."

"I'm sorry, but you know the rules—no late assignments, no exceptions. Period."

"Later. Please sit down, we have to get started."

"That's very nice, but you need to grow up and be your own person."

Rarely can we change the interruptions or circumstances that will inevitably come our way, but we always have a choice about our response. Take a deep breath, count to ten, and before you blow out a candle, make your response a shining light reflecting His love.

> **GRACE FOR TODAY:**
>
> ## God's light encourages us daily so that we can light other candles with our encouragement.

May the God of steadfastness and encouragement grant you to live in harmony with one another.

ROMANS 15:5 NRSV

LIVING AND ACTIVE

By Evelyn Christenson

The beach at Lake Michigan is my favorite place to read God's Word and let Him speak to me. Every day while we are on vacation, I rise early and, weather permitting, take my Bible down to the edge of the lake and read until He speaks. One morning I read such a great psalm about our God that I found myself skipping down the beach instead of doing my usual hiking. God had changed an ordinary, run-of-the-mill vacation day into one of exhilaration and exploding joy, joy that could not be contained in ordinary steps. The thrill that sent my body soaring like an eagle blurt out in impromptu songs of praise as I adored Him for who He is and praised Him for what He is. Changed by a psalm? Yes, changed!

Fifty-nine years of underlining answers for actual situations have proven to me that the Bible truly is a living Book, "living and active" as Hebrews describes it. Yes, it is alive. It has answers in the midst of our knowledge explosion today—or tomorrow—on this planet and in outer space. And precept upon precept as I let it renew my mind, my attitudes, and wisdom to live by, I am changed. Changed into what is His perfect will for me to be.[2]

—◆—

FATHER, THANK YOU FOR YOUR LIVING WORD THAT CHANGES MY LIFE BY YOUR GRACE. IT IS ENCOURAGING TO KNOW THAT I DON'T HAVE TO REMAIN AS I AM, BUT I CAN GROW AND BE TRANSFORMED AS YOUR WORD BECOMES PART OF ME. LEAD ME IN YOUR WORD NOW, SO I CAN MAKE THE MOST OF THIS DAY. AMEN.

The word of God is living and active and sharper than any two-edged sword, and piercing as far as the division of soul and spirit, of both joints and marrow, and able to judge the thoughts and intentions of the heart.

HEBREWS 4:12 NASB

KEEP THE LINES OPEN

I try to find common ground with everyone so that I might
bring them to Christ.

1 CORINTHIANS 9:22 NLT

Perhaps the greatest challenge of effective communication comes from being a good listener. As a teacher you're used to having the answers, not only in your area of expertise, but also when it comes to the general issues surrounding education.

After all, there are times when you've had your fill of communication—all day interacting with students, then a faculty meeting, parent conferences, and let's not forget your department committee to improve communication within the department. It's kind of overwhelming, and the end result can be resorting to pat answers in order to save time. When your sanity is at stake, that's understandable, but the challenge is not letting it become a habit.

GRACE FOR TODAY:

When God proclaims His message, He often uses us.

In order to reach people with the gospel, Paul made it his primary goal to be a servant, to strive to understand people where they were in their lives. He understood that, more than the message itself, communication was how that message of peace and truth and love had a power beyond his words to cut through all boundaries and forms of resistance in a way that he himself never could. It was God's message that he was proclaiming, but it was Paul's life, his speech, his listening, his habits, through which God communicated.

When those around you see that you're about more than your subject matter, that you listen and go through good times and bad just as they do, the lines of communication will be opened in ways you've never envisioned, and God can use your words speak to into waiting hearts.

IN LOSING—YOU WIN!

A man's discretion makes him slow to anger, and it is his glory
to overlook a transgression.

PROVERBS 19:11 NASB

With arms struggling to balance a half-spilt briefcase, Ms. Regouby made a beeline for the dean's office. Slowing her pace and calming her irritation, she approached the dean's half-opened door and asked, "May I have a word with you?"

"Sure! Come on in," the dean said, swinging around in his chair.

"Something's really wrong here," she said. "For eleven years, I've had morning classes!" Her voice continued to escalate. "I have seniority and tenure, so why am I assigned two evening classes when an adjunct's listed with morning classes?" she demanded.

"Have a seat, Ms. Regouby," the dean said softly. "You can bump Ms. Jacobs from the morning classes, but first allow me to explain."

After she gave the dean a chance to talk about the assignments, she backed down and could see the wisdom of his decision.

Ms. Regouby's dilemma represents a situation most teachers will face in one form or another—when they have the right to control. Like her, most people's propensity is to get angry and demand what's rightfully theirs, but often it may not be God's best for them. Benjamin Franklin aptly put it when he quipped, "Remember not only to say the right thing in the right place—but far more difficult still—is to leave unsaid the wrong thing at the tempting moment."

GRACE FOR TODAY:

When our anger burns bridges, God can rebuild them with His love.

How to react in a difficult situation is your choice. Is anger your first reaction, or can you walk away from such tempting moments in exchange for more of God's grace and trust Him alone when it appears you have been treated unfairly?

Today, keep track of your emotions moment by moment. Are you allowing God to rule your heart?

EMPTY YOUR POCKETS

There is nothing concealed that will not be disclosed, or hidden that will
not be made known.

LUKE 12:2 NIV

When Abraham Lincoln was shot, he was carrying seven items, including
two pairs of spectacles and a lens polisher, a pocket knife, a watch fob, and
a monogrammed linen handkerchief. The seventh item was perhaps the most telling: a
brown leather wallet containing a five-dollar Confederate note and nine newspaper
clippings, including several favorable to the president and his policies.

What do the wallet's contents tell us about perhaps the greatest leader the free
world has ever known? Was he insecure and in need of reassurance that people liked
him despite his handling of the war? Or did they provide encouraging signs that the
Union could indeed be preserved?

What do the contents of your desk or your classroom say about you? Does the
yo-yo in the top drawer reveal your fun side? How about the antique Remington manual typewriter keeping the encyclopedias from sliding off the shelf? And what's the
story behind that stuffed rattlesnake in the corner, the one wearing the doll-sized baseball cap and a goofy grin?

As colorful and telling as these objects might be, nothing reveals the story of the
teacher in you quite like the walking, talking contents of your classroom—your students. When they move on, they carry a piece of you with them. They will miss you
and never forget the time you said, "I'm so proud of you; you're my shining star!"

Your job is never more important than when affirming a child, bringing him out
of his shell, and believing in his ability to succeed the way God does. God sent His
Son so that you might know forgiveness now and in eternity. By showing your students the same degree of mercy, you put them on solid ground. What do the lives of
your students say about you?

GRACE FOR TODAY:

God's grace flows through us to affirm our students.

THE LEAST OF THESE

[Jesus said,] "And the King shall answer . . ., Inasmuch as ye have done it
unto one of the least of these my brethren, ye have done it unto me."

MATTHEW 25:40 KJV

Her name was Linda. She was in the seventh grade of Mrs. D's first class ever,
and she smelled worse than rotten cantaloupe left on a roadside curb for three
days. Breathtaking would have been the kindest word said about her. Strands of
unkempt hair hung in greasy ropes, often hiding her eyes. Her teeth were crooked and
discolored.

None of the kids at the small rural school liked her. Even if they had gotten past
her clumsiness and painful shyness, the smell would have gotten to the best of them. A
month into the school year, the situation reached crisis proportions.

The rumors drifted in after lunch, and on the playground. "Someone tied a
deodorant bottle to Linda's locker. You'd think she'd get the hint!" "That's nothing. Day
before yesterday, we all put a bunch of those potpourri stick-ups all over her locker
door." "She stinks!"

In desperation, the teacher met with Linda after school. "Why do they all hate
me?" she sobbed into the teacher's shoulder as Mrs. D plotted to burn her clothes later.
They discussed personal hygiene, and the teacher discovered that there hadn't been
electricity at Linda's house for several months and, therefore, no washing machine.
Arrangements were made for her to use the locker-room showers at school and the
athletic department's washer and dryer.

The first day she came to class in clean blue jeans with clean hair was a banner
day for everyone. One student gave her a barrette and showed her how to pull her hair
away from her face. And when Linda smiled, it was a different kind of breathtaking.

Chances are, you'll have a "Linda" in your classroom one of these days. Who
knows how much hope there is in a hug or a hair barrette given in Jesus' name?

GRACE FOR TODAY:

God builds our character one day at a time.

BEHIND CLOSED DOORS

It takes a lot of hard work to be a successful teacher, from the time you put in hitting the books and going to seminars, to the prep work for each day's lessons, to the actual daily dealings with kids, colleagues, and parents—and, oh yes, the grading.

If you've ever gone into a classroom unprepared, you know what it's like. At best, God's grace washes in like a welcome tide, and you have a productive work session, even if it's a repeat of yesterday's work. At worst, your attempts to wing it fall flat, and you lose a day of potential for learning. Either way, you're inspired to come back ready the next time.

The most important aspect of your preparation, however, comes in a way that your students won't ever see directly, but will be affected by each and every day: your personal time with God. When you have that regular, daily time reading the Bible and praying, all of your other preparations will fall into place.

After all, most days bring at least a little something for which you can't prepare—a technological glitch that spikes your whole presentation, a conflict between students that needs your immediate attention, a phone call on an urgent family matter. In some cases, you can have that backup plan ready, going to the library instead of surfing the Internet or showing a video when the lab equipment goes awry.

Situations arise, however, for which there is no possible anticipation except the peace and grace that come to you as a believer in Christ, when you have grounded yourself in God's Word and you trust Him to help it all work out. That is essential preparation for which there is no substitute.

GRACE FOR TODAY:

If we keep our tools sharpened, God will provide us with work.

We can make our plans, but the final outcome is in God's hands.

PROVERBS 16:1 TLB

A SISTER OF JESUS

By John MacArthur Jr.

The Bible says that God's will is that men be saved, and that is where it all starts. Jesus made this clear in Mark 3:31–35. He was already teaching inside a building when His brothers and mother arrived. The multitude was sitting on the inside, and it was so crowded that His family could not get to Him. Someone said to Him, "Jesus, Your mother and brothers outside seek You."

He answered, "Who is My mother, or My brothers?" (v. 33, NKJV).

I am sure the crowd's reaction was something like: "What kind of question is this? Everybody knows His mother and brothers!"

If Jesus' first reaction did not shock them, His next words did. "He looked around in a circdle at those who sat about Him, and said, 'Here are My mother and My brother!'" (v. 34).

Each person probably looked at the others and thought, Who, me?

Then He qualified it: "For whoever does the will of God is My brother and My sister and Mother" (v. 35 NKJV).

What was Jesus saying? He was teaching that in order to be related to Him, one has to do the will of God. Turn it around. To do the will of God one has to be related to Jesus.[5]

—◊◊◊—

HEAVENLY FATHER, TO BE CONSIDERED THE SISTER OF JESUS IS ALMOST MORE THAN I CAN COMPREHEND, YET IT IS TRUE. THE ONLY QUALIFICATION IS THAT I OBEY YOU AND DO YOUR WILL, WHICH IS MY HEART'S DESIRE. AT THOSE TIMES WHEN I FIND THAT DIFFICULT, I ASK YOU TO GIVE ME AN EXTRA DOSE OF GRACE. I'M WILLING TO BE MADE WILLING. AMEN.

[Jesus said,] "They who have my commandments and keep them are those who love me; and those who love me will be loved by my Father, and I will love them and reveal myself to them."

JOHN 14:21 NRSV

A "PANEL OF ROSES"

See, the Lord your God has given you the land. Go up and take possession of it. . . . Do not be afraid; do not be discouraged.

DEUTERONOMY 1:21 NIV

The American painter John Sargent once painted a panel of roses that was highly praised by critics. It was a small picture, but it approached perfection.
Although offered a high price for it on many occasions, Sargent refused to sell. He considered it his best work and was very proud of it. Whenever he was deeply discouraged and doubtful of his abilities as an artist, he would look at it and remind himself, "I
painted that." Then his confidence and ability would return.

GRACE FOR TODAY:

The beauty of God in our lives far outweighs the prick of a few thorns.

Most teachers, at one time or another, find themselves in similar seasons of discouragement as did the
painter John Sargent. And just as Sargent did, you need
to have your own "panel of roses" to remind you of
your own unique giftedness. As Sargent had a call on
his life as an artist, remember that you also have a call
on your life as a teacher. You may serve as a teacher for
only a short time in your life, but it is still just as
important in God's plan as being the President of the
United States. Besides, that failing student you coax
along the way, all the while feeling your hair daily
graying, may just one day turn out to be the President.

So if you are experiencing a down time—a little
discouraged or a lot—let this be a reminder to find your
own "panel of roses" and set it on your desk. It could be a picture, a student's well-
deserved "A" paper, or a note from a grateful parent. Then reflect on it when the need
arises to remind you that "you did that," and you will discover on those trying days
that your confidence will quickly return.

STAYING THE COURSE

Now it is required that those who have been given a trust
must prove faithful.

1 CORINTHIANS 4:2 NIV

Remember how trustworthy Joseph proved to be when Potiphar, captain of Pharaoh's guard, left the young man in charge of the king's household? Potiphar's confidence in Joseph to look after every detail in both house and field was so strong that Scripture tells us the official concerned himself with nothing but the food he ate.

Joseph's master saw a rare quality in his attendant—fidelity. It speaks of loyalty and devotion, a strict and continuing faithfulness to an obligation, trust, or duty that remains steadfast in the face of any temptation to renounce, desert, or betray. Joseph's faithfulness is even more remarkable in the face of his jealous brothers' terrible betrayal of him and their ensuing attempt to cover up the fact that they had sold him into slavery.

At the end of the day, you may not always feel that you have measured up to the teaching ideal. You might occasionally feel like quitting and hiding out in Bora Bora. But the fact that you are there at your post day in and day out may be the most stability some of your students ever see in their lives. Divorced or disinterested parents, uncertain living conditions, and domestic abuse are sad realities. To hear your greeting in the morning, to experience the warmth of your smile and acceptance, are bright lights of hope in the surrogate "family" of your classroom.

If those feelings of misgiving crowd in when you lay your head down at night, tell the Lord you tried and thank Him for His measure of success—faithfulness. It's not what you own, not even what you accomplished, but how firmly you stood for what is good and true and wise that counts. Listen for His words of reassurance, "Well done, good and faithful servant! You have been faithful with a few things; I will put you in charge of many things."

GRACE FOR TODAY:

God usually provides us with faithfulness when we pray for success.

ON YOUR KNEES

[The Lord said to Solomon,] "If my people, who are called by my name,
will humble themselves and pray and seek my face . . . then will I hear
from heaven . . ."

2 CHRONICLES 7:14 NIV

braham Lincoln, sixteenth president of the United States, once remarked, "I
have been driven many times to my knees by the overwhelming conviction
that I had nowhere else to go. My own wisdom and that of all about me seemed insuf-
ficient for that day."

Astounding, isn't it, that so great a man, who seemed to possess such wisdom,
faith, and determination, found himself inadequate for the task without God's help? And
yet, we find that a far greater Man, Jesus—God's own Son—found solace in the same
places: a boat, a garden, a withdrawal from the crowds, a circle of friends, and prayer.

You don't yet know what you will face today. A cranky principal. An irate parent. A needy student. An anxious colleague. A lay off due to state budget cutbacks. An
overwhelming workload. Perhaps a new lesson that you aren't quite sure how to
approach. Or the unthinkable—a Columbine-like tragedy.

God knows exactly what you will face, and He has promised that His grace is sufficient for all your needs and in your weakness. Perhaps it's as simple as the popular
advertising campaign for milk—Got Milk? Got prayer? It's for even more than healthy
teeth and bones. It's got all you need for spiritual muscle and supernatural strength.
Perhaps at the top of today's plan book you should pencil in, Appointment with God,
7:30 A.M.

GRACE FOR TODAY:

When we need spiritual strength, God first asks us to
go to Him in prayer.

A TEST OF CHARACTER

We also glory in tribulations, knowing that tribulation produces perseverance; and perseverance, character; and character, hope.

ROMANS 5:3-4 NKJV

Much recent effort in public education has been devoted to the concept of character. You've no doubt seen some version of a list of qualities that engender
character, and perhaps you've seen positive results as a result of implementing such
programs.

Indeed, character development is well worth system-wide attention. Of course,
you also know that unless students see their teachers and administrators living out
these principles, no amount of catchy slogans or flashy T-shirts will bridge the gap
between where they are and where they need to be.

True character results from passing life's tests, from overcoming the temptation to
be less than you were made to be. From your own experience, you know that the best
way to develop the character necessary not just to survive but to thrive is to accept
those trials as tests of who you are and who you are becoming.

Your students are always watching, and you never know when the way you handle a challenge thrown your way will affect their development. It's okay to let them see
how you handle hard times.

When trials come, you endure through faith. James said that trials produce
endurance when we face them with faith, with our eyes fixed on God (James 1:2-3).
Trials are a part of how God works in your life, to strengthen you and draw you closer to Him. As you endure, He gives you what you need to keep going, to take the next
step. That's character, and the result of character is hope.

You don't necessarily know how the situation will turn out, but with faith in
Christ's love and strength—He has overcome the world, after all—you can hope for the
best with the solid assurance that the best is what God wants for everyone involved.

GRACE FOR TODAY:

Because our characters are forged in the trials of life,
God can strengthen our ability to endure them.

LONELINESS—DON'T PARK THERE

Susan and Sarah stood talking in the shade of a large oak tree as they watched their classes play during recess.

"My birthday's next week," Susan sighed, "and I don't even want to party."

"Why not?" Sarah asked. "Birthdays are meant to be fun."

"I'm turning thirty, and I don't even want to think about it. I'm tired of living alone, and I'm sick of not being able to find a decent guy to date. What's to celebrate? Being over the hill? The bottom line is that I'm just so lonely."

Sarah could have come back with some quip like "bloom where you are planted," but the truth is that whether married or single, everyone at sometime in life goes through seasons of loneliness.

> **GRACE FOR TODAY:**
>
> God teaches us to conquer our loneliness by looking outward—not inward.

Maybe you're even sitting at your desk reading this before your class starts, and with all the busyness around you, inside you still feel lonely. Loneliness may be an accurate description of how you feel right now, but God is pouring out His grace on you so that can know He is always with you. You are not alone.

Today, instead of dwelling on your loneliness, why not consider your class the family that God has set you in for this season? Thank Him for each unique student He's surrounded you with, and instead of looking inward, look outward and pay special attention to those kids who are feeling lonely and rejected. As you minister to their loneliness, it's a pretty sure bet that God will take care of yours!

Turn to me and be gracious to me, for I am lonely and afflicted. The troubles of my heart are enlarged; bring me out of my distresses.

PSALM 25:16–17 NASB

HIDDEN TREASURE

By Evelyn Christenson

I was going to speak at a retreat on the subject of "God's Living Word." I packed my three Bibles and headed for the plane in Minneapolis, where the security guard started systematically to check my carry-on luggage. When he pulled out the first Bible, he gave me a "that's-a-nice-lady" smile. The second one produced a puzzled expression on his face. But, at finding the third, he was sure I had hidden something valuable in those Bibles, and proceeded to search each one diligently. He even held one up to its binding and shook it vigorously.

That guard never discovered the treasure I had hidden in those three Bibles. The omniscient Lord Jesus Christ, "in whom are hidden all the treasures of wisdom and knowledge" (Colossians 2:3 NIV), had given it to me. Underlined and marked on those pages was all the direction I had needed for a "chaste and reverent" lifestyle since I was eighteen years old. Line upon line,

precept upon precept, God had taught me how to change.

When I have needed direction for my life, has He ever left me groping in the dark, trying to find my way? Oh, no! He has given me His Word as a "lamp unto my feet, and a light unto my path" (Psalm 119:105 KJV). And, as I have obeyed His instructions, He has changed me, step by step, into the person He wants me to be.[4]

—⁓—

HEAVENLY FATHER, THANK YOU FOR THE TREASURE OF YOUR WORD! IT IS MORE TO BE DESIRED THAN GOLD, AS THE PSALMS TESTIFY. IT IS A GIFT OF GRACE TO ME BECAUSE IT LEADS ME, TRANSFORMS ME, AND GIVES ME THE POWER I NEED TO FACE EACH DAY. HELP ME DISCOVER PEARLS OF WISDOM TODAY.

I rejoice at Your word
as one who finds great treasure.

PSALM 119:162 NKJV

BEAUTIFUL—AT A DISTANCE

The testing of your faith produces endurance; and let endurance have its full effect, so that you may be mature and complete, lacking in nothing.

JAMES 1:3-4 NRSV

B allet dancers, figure skaters, and Shakespearean actors fill us with awe for their grace and beauty of movement or conviction of speech. We applaud their leaps, marvel at their speed, relish their nuanced phrasing. And should they achieve the pinnacle of performance, we might rise to our feet and cry, "Encore!"

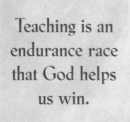

GRACE FOR TODAY:

Teaching is an endurance race that God helps us win.

But were we up close and backstage, we would pick up other, less savory details—the heavy breathing, the rivers of sweat, and the running makeup.

Teaching is a lot like that. From a distance—a safe distance—it looks like a beautiful dance of learning, and sometimes it is exactly that. When you "click" with your students, when a critical parent lightens up and tells you what a good job you're doing, there's nothing like it. The truth is that there are glorious days like that, and thank God for them.

There are also days when you may suffer from a lack of wit and wisdom, days where little seems to work, moments of self-doubt when you seriously question your calling. Think of them as "backstage days," when your feet are killing you and you feel about as graceful as a rhino on a trampoline. Tell the Lord your troubles and lean on His understanding. Jesus didn't always get through to everyone all the time, either. Remember the night His disciples fell asleep in the garden when He most needed them to pay attention? Some lessons they got; others they completely missed.

God wants you to do well and to be effective. He also wants you to be honest when it's not working. Talk it out, rest in His love, and you will hear the heavenly shouts of "Encore!"

THE LEGACY

[The Lord said to the prophet Joel,] "Tell it to your children,
and let your children tell it to their children, and their children to the
next generation."

JOEL 1:3 NIV

A few years ago, a chain e-mail made the rounds. It was a quiz that put forth some interesting questions:

- Name the five wealthiest people in the world.
- Name the last five winners of the Miss America contest.
- Name the last dozen Academy Award winners for best actor and actress.
- Name the last decade's worth of World Series winners.

Perhaps you had a bit of trouble coming up with some of those answers. Fortunately, the quiz didn't end there.

- List the teachers who aided your journey through school.
- Think of several people who have taught you something worthwhile.
- Name three friends who have helped you through a difficult time.
- Think of five people with whom you enjoy spending time.

Bet those names were easier to recall.

Very often we make the mistake of assuming that in order to be influential we need to be wealthy, or a politician, or a celebrity, or someone else whom the world would deem important. Nothing could be farther from the truth. In fact, most of us have the potential of wielding far more influence because we are more accessible. We don't have bodyguards, palatial estates, or yachts on the Riviera. What we do have is time. What we can do is spend out time on those things that outlast this life.

Every day you have the chance to make somebody's list. A kind word. A compassionate moment. An encouraging smile. Time to listen. To spark enthusiasm. To explain clearly. Why not today?

GRACE FOR TODAY:

When we let God influence our lives, He can influence our students through us.

EVERYTHING IN ITS PLACE

I discipline my body and make it my slave, so that, after I have preached
to others, I myself will not be disqualified.

1 CORINTHIANS 9:27 NASB

No one needs to tell you that today's students, by and large, lack discipline. More and more, you've seen the results of permissive parenting, of so-called positive discipline—I can't let you throttle your sister but here's a doll you can choke—and you've probably even seen it creeping into the educational philosophy of entire school districts.

The idea of saying "No" or "Don't" has become anathema, but the result is a student population with growing contempt for the adults in their lives. How can you maintain your own self-control in such a setup, much less guide these kids to a modicum of self-restraint?

Start by taking a look at the root of the word discipline itself, the Latin *discipulus*, or pupil. It's the same word we get the term disciple from. Now there's something you can sink your teeth into! Discipline is all about teaching and learning.

As a Christian, you know what being a disciple is all about. According to Jesus, you're His disciple if you obey His teachings (John 8:31), love your fellow believers (John 13:35), and bear fruit (John 15:8).

Discipline, then, works on two levels: first, in regard to your relationship with God, as you strive to become more like His Son; and next, in regard to your other relationships, as God works through you to reach the people in your life.

The same principles that apply to your training to become a better Christian are also true in your work as a teacher. Even if you are the only adult in a kid's life who sets a firm standard for moral excellence, trust God to make your efforts worthwhile.

GRACE FOR TODAY:

God disciplines us so that we might
discipline others His way.

GOD IS IN CONTROL

Hope never disappoints or deludes or shames us,
for God's love has been poured out in our hearts.

ROMANS 5:5 AMP

Rachel was so glad that recess had finally arrived—thirty whole minutes to herself. She had doubts she'd even make it through the whole day. Spreading her windbreaker on the ground, Rachel sat down and leaned back against a barren tree. Frustrated and bordering on despair, she heaved a deep sigh and called out in prayer, "God, are You there?"

What was the use in trying so hard? This was the fourth straight time she'd come in second for "Teacher of the Year."

What am I doing wrong? she asked silently, looking heavenward. *I give up; I don't know what else to do. If I could just do better; if I could somehow measure up.*

I want you to know it's a far higher goal to believe you're complete in Me, came the answer.

I guess I'll just have to try harder next year.

The victory, Rachel, is not in doing . . . it's in being.

God, You just don't get it—I need this; I've worked hard—harder than Ms. Gilpin.

Rachel, you just don't get it. Rest in Me! Trust wholeheartedly in Me; don't lean on your own way of thinking about things. My timing is perfect, and I will accomplish My plan in you. Awards or no awards, always remember: I love you.

Have you ever battled with God when disappointments have come? Most of us have, but He doesn't mind. In fact, He wants you to tell Him your complaints, share your disappointments, and run to Him in your times of need. Your heavenly Father wants a close relationship with you—not just a Sunday—morning friendship.

Fellowship with the Father is the secret to pleasing Him—not service.

GRACE FOR TODAY:

With God's grace, He makes our efforts successful.

THE HUNTER OF HEARTS

Explorers on a hunting expedition to Madagascar for a fragrance company captured the hidden essence of a waterfall. By using special silicone probes in the spray, they were able to capture the precise combination of vegetation and minerals that, when mixed with water, give off the fresh, clean aroma we associate with waterfalls.

Finding what makes a particular child tick is a lot like that search for the scent of a waterfall. The hard-to-reach kids in your classroom require you to follow a mysterious trail of clues deep into unknown territory. The route demands that all your senses be attuned to swings in mood, snatches of conversation, and body language. By sticking with it and taking your discoveries to God in prayer, He will help you find the keys to unlock those precious hearts and minds.

When you do this for a child—bring his real personality to the surface, allow him to shine despite the negatives and doubts in his life—you show him what he's really made of. Jesus worked one-on-one with His pupils, His disciples, in this same way. He knew Thomas was "from Missouri" and had to be shown the scars. He knew that despite Peter's denial, the headstrong fisherman loved his Master very much. Jesus probed the heart in a way unique to each disciple.

We know that not every child learns in the same way or at the same speed. Thank God that He, the knower of all secrets, knows and understands that very same thing is true of every believer.

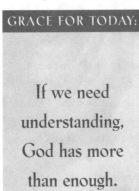

GRACE FOR TODAY:

If we need understanding, God has more than enough.

He opens up the depths, tells secrets, sees in the dark—light spills out of him!

DANIEL 2:22 MSG

SALVATION FOR ALL

By John MacArthur Jr.

Talking about sin and salvation is offensive to some people. Who wants to hear about sin? Most people mask it. Sin is not sin. Oh, no. Sin is "a prenatal predilection," psychologists tell us. Sin is an "idiosyncrasy of individuality." Sin is "poor secretion of the endocrine glands"!

But God's will is that people be saved! And basic to salvation is the recognition of sin. This lays it right at your feet. Either you are not saved from your sin and you need to come to Christ because that is God's will, or you are saved and need to reach others with the message of salvation. There is a world out there that needs Jesus Christ. God wants them to be saved, and you and I are the vehicles for the transportation of the gospel. That is God's will.

You say you do not know what God's will is, but I'll tell you what it is: first, that you know Christ, and then that your neighbors hear about Christ. So often we sit around twiddling our thumbs, dreaming about God's will in some far distant future when we are not even willing to walk down the street and do God's will right now.

God so desired that men be saved that He gave the One whom He loved most, His Son, and sent Him to die on a cross. That is the measure of His love, and that indicates how much He wills that men be saved![5]

—⁂—

FATHER GOD, YOUR WORD SAYS THAT YOU WANT ALL TO BE SAVED AND YOU'VE ASKED US—ME—TO SPREAD THIS GOOD NEWS TO EVERYONE. LEAD ME TO THOSE WHO ARE READY TO RECEIVE SALVATION, AND BY YOUR GRACE, GRANT ME THE BOLDNESS I NEED TO BE AN EFFECTIVE WITNESS.

[God] longs for all to be saved and to understand this truth: *That God is on one side and all the people on the other side, and Christ Jesus, himself man, is between them to bring them together.*

1 TIMOTHY 2:4–5 TLB

UP ALL NIGHT

[Jesus said,] "Who of you by worrying can add a single
hour to his life?"

MATTHEW 6:27 NIV

Richard Carlson, author of the renowned *Don't Sweat the Small Stuff* series, tells the story of a time when he was worried, stressed−out, and overscheduled. He unloaded on a friend of his, fully expecting some sympathy and commiseration. Instead, his friend looked at him and remarked, "Why should you be any different than the rest of the world?"

GRACE FOR TODAY:

**God wants us to
lay our worries
at His feet.**

What about you? Ever wet your pillow at night with the frustrated tears of not knowing how your needs will be met? Ever worry the frayed edges of a ragged notebook with restless fingers that wonder if any dreams recorded there will come true?

Have you groused at a faculty meeting? "They keep us here too late after school; I have too many papers to grade; lesson preps; I hate bus duty/bathroom duty/playground duty; open houses; final exams; career ladder; club sponsorships; fieldtrip organization; com−mittee meetings." And that's just school! Never mind our other obligations of family, spouse, kids, church, friends, and home maintenance. Our never−ending to−do lists can all too easily turn into a litany of complaints.

Instead of counting our blessings, we nurture our hurts. Testiness replaces thank−fulness, and we begin to think that worry might actually help! *Well,* you're thinking, *it must be effective; most of what I worry about doesn't happen anyway.* There's a far better way—it's so simple, but it's not easy. Lay your worries at the feet of the One who is up all night anyway. Surrender your long lists to God's plan, punch your pillow, roll over, and go to sleep. That beats worry for extending life any day.

A Time to Laugh

A cheerful look brings joy to the heart,
and good news gives health to the bones.

PROVERBS 15:30 NIV

How important is a good sense of humor? Think of it this way: Given two teachers of equal skill and knowledge, which would you choose, Sergeant Rigorous or Captain Crackup? After all, what's better than someone who can impart the value of a certain topic while engaging your funny bone?

You may be thinking that certain subjects don't lend themselves to a comedic approach—what's funny about calculus or Westward Expansion? But humor isn't really about cracking jokes or clowning around (depending on your students' ages).

Humor is about not taking yourself or your content area so seriously that you and/or it lose all relevance to your students.

Some things aren't funny—the Battle of Shiloh, for instance, or AIDS. Bottom line, you're not a comedian, you're a teacher, and that means covering certain topics and issues with grace and sensitivity.

As a human being, however, you've no doubt experienced the value of well-timed levity. Especially after covering a heavy matter, it's all right to let the kids know the sun is still shining, that the value of going over such a hard subject is in learning how to make themselves and the world slightly better.

GRACE FOR TODAY:

God invented humor so that we could laugh at ourselves.

As with so many things, you're the model for learning about life, so strive to find the up side in the unexpected and the difficult. Humor is God's idea, so it's no surprise that sharing laughter or a smile bridges almost every gap known to mankind—culture, religion, socioeconomic status, age, or gender. As Solomon noted, a cheerful heart is good medicine (Proverbs 17:22).

GOD'S KALEIDOSCOPE

Those who receive God's abundant provision of grace . . . reign in life
through the one man, Jesus Christ.

ROMANS 5:17 NIV

Twisting, turning, shaking, looking. Kaleidoscopes—beautifully colored views of illuminated reflections of tiny pieces of glass, no two ever the same—are fun no matter what your age. God's grace is like that—a kaleidoscope of changing perspectives of His wisdom and love. Now put your eye up to your own inner kaleidoscope; twist it and shake it! Wow, what a different image! In this view perhaps you are the student, and the students are the teacher.

Have you ever noticed how students expect their teachers to know everything and have all the answers? Most are so trusting of their teachers that they take what they say at face value. Often they tend to set their teachers on a pedestal, defending their words as truth: "Well, Mrs. Johnson said . . ."

Such simple observations can bring fresh grace into your life. In the perspective of a student, apply their childlike faith to your relationship with God. Hold that view! Let His grace reflect on the many aspects of your life. What if you truly expected Him to have all the answers to your problems, waiting expectantly, as your students do, to see what He has to say about them? What would your life be like if, as you read His Word, you took it at face value?

Do you set God high on a pedestal, as your students do you, defending His words as truth? When trouble comes your way, do you think, *Well, God said when trials come my way to consider it pure joy, so that's just what I'm going to do!*

Sometimes simple, but profound, lessons can be learned from your students. Looking through the kaleidoscope of their perspective today, you can experience new depths of His grace by simply taking God at His Word, just as they do yours.

GRACE FOR TODAY:

As we look into God's kaleidoscope, He can change
our perspective on life.

No Fear

Strengthen the feeble hands, steady the knees that give way; say to those
with fearful hearts, "Be strong, do not fear. your God will come."

ISAIAH 35:3-4 NIV

Teachers can be thankful that arithmophobia (fear of numbers), scriptophobia
(fear of writing in public), or testophobia (fear of taking tests) are as rare as they
are. To be afflicted with phobophobia, though, might be the worst. It's the fear of pho-
bias.

As rare as intense, irrational fears such as these may be, we do struggle against
insecurities and anxieties in the classroom. For some, it's the fear of not being liked by
the students. For others, it's the fear of failure, of not measuring up as a teacher. Perhaps
you stress over never "getting through" to that girl who dislikes reading. Or maybe it's
that principal who makes unfair demands of your time who has you in knots.

Isaiah's message to Israel was, fear not the drought, fear not the oppressors, fear
not the unrighteous. Why? Because God Almighty was coming to the rescue, and there
was healing in His wings. Our salvation is just that: God is on the way. Nothing to
fear. Abide in Him.

He has not forgotten you. "Cast your cares on the Lord," says the psalmist, and
He will never let you fall. He is our burden-bearer, our Jehovah Jireh, the great
Provider. He calls us His children, delights in caring for us, and wants us not only to
call Him Father but to make our requests known. Jesus is our reminder that God is all
about giving good gifts to His children.

If that's music to your ears, then you're definitely not euphobic (afraid of hearing
good news)!

GRACE FOR TODAY:

God asks us to cast our cares on Him and He will
provide for us.

THE FAILURE

Winston Churchill was one of the worst students in his class, yet he single-handedly bolstered the morale of England during the German blitz, leading his nation to victory in World War II. He also won the Nobel Prize for Literature in 1953.

While novelist William Faulkner was enrolled at Ole Miss, he received a "D" in English, yet now his novels are taught in nearly every high school and college literature class.

Woodrow Wilson did not learn to read until he was eleven, yet he became a strong leader in World War I as a U.S. president and was instrumental in forming the concept of what would later become the United Nations.

Michael Jordan was cut from his high-school basketball team his junior year, but fortunately, the Chicago Bulls decided he could play.

Lucille Ball's first drama teacher failed her, citing that she "had no talent." Tell that to the millions of fans in reruns who are still laughing at her impeccable comic timing and versatile roles.

Abraham Lincoln's 1863 Gettysburg Address was criticized as a shining example of mediocrity, yet today it is one of the most beloved, memorized, and modeled speeches in American history.

Many factors affect our perception of whether a person is a success or a failure—personality conflicts, jealousy, maturity, comparisons, ambitions, mood. But God's plans supercede all of our petty concerns and self-doubt.

Today, encourage a student in a special way. You may have a future president, star, leader, or writer in your classroom. The support you give could make all the difference.

> **GRACE FOR TODAY:**
>
> God casts the deciding vote when our success is on the ballot.

"I know the plans that I have for you," declares the LORD.

JEREMIAH 29:11 NASB

FORSAKEN FOR US

By Evelyn Christenson

Jesus knew that He would be forsaken. He had already told His followers, "You will leave me all alone." But He added, "Yet I am not alone, for my Father is with me" (John 16:32 NIV). That fact is also true for all of us as followers of Jesus—we are never alone, for the Father is with us.

But it was while suffering on the cross that Jesus had a sense of being forsaken that will never be experienced by any true follower of His. The Father was always with Him—until that excruciating moment when Jesus cried with a loud voice, "My God, my God, why hast thou forsaken me?" (Matthew 27:46 KJV). As Jesus hung on that cross, the Father had to turn from His Son so that the Son could experience and bear our sins in His death.

That forsakenness will never be ours. We who deserve to be forsaken by the holy God will never be—because Jesus, who had never sinned, undeservedly bore that sin for us. We will never be forsaken as Jesus was—for us.

—m—

MY DEAR JESUS, MY HEART IS BROKEN BECAUSE, WHILE WE CHRISTIANS WILL NEVER BE FORSAKEN BY THE FATHER, YOU WERE. AND IT WAS BECAUSE OF US. WHEN YOU WERE TAKING OUR SINS UPON YOURSELF, YOU WERE FORSAKEN BY THE FATHER SO THAT WE, CLEANSED, WOULD NEVER HAVE TO BE. THERE'S NOTHING I COULD EVER DO TO DESERVE THIS; IT IS BY YOUR GRACE.

NO DOUBT, SOME OF MY STUDENTS HAVE BEEN FORSAKEN BY ONE OR BOTH OF THEIR PARENTS. HELP ME TO BE SENSITIVE TO THOSE STUDENTS AND GIVE ME OPPORTUNITIES TO SHARE YOUR LOVE WITH THEM. AMEN.

[Jesus said,] "I am with you always, even to the end of the age."

MATTHEW 28:20 NKJV

IT STARTS WITH YOU

The wise will inherit honor.

PROVERBS 3:35 NRSV

You are working with the second generation of students who are growing up in a system that has taught them that they are, generally speaking, no more than cosmic accidents, descended from primates and of no more value than the chemicals from which they're composed. No wonder it's so hard to create a culture of respect! What really matters?

Respect has become synonymous with relativism—whatever works for you is great, just stay out of my business. As a child of God, however, you know there's more. Your worldview teaches that each individual person is a life precious to its Creator, worthy of the shed blood of God's only Son. Respect for each other is honor to God, whose very image is integral to our existence.

GRACE FOR TODAY:

God set the standard for respect and expects us to follow it.

You love because He loved you first. Your relationships, your work, are all part of His perfect plan, His good will towards you. Seen through that lens, life is sacred and respect is critical.

You even know how it's supposed to work. Because God, omnipotent and all-knowing, sees fit to give you free will, you extend that courtesy to others. Because God, merciful and tender, loves you too much to let you get away with being a slave to sin, you set a standard of excellence in your relationships, knowing that no one is perfect but all may reach for Heaven.

As an authority figure, you may demand respect, but you know that you will have to earn it every day, and so you set the example by extending it first, confident of its return. So many have given up on respect as a futile attempt to tame the monkeys in the zoo. You see the potential of God's plan in every life and know that respect is the currency of that hope.

God Will Carry You

When you go through deep waters and great trouble, I will be with you.

ISAIAH 43:2 NLT

L auren was late and barely made it to her classroom as the first bell rang. A moment later, the principal paused at her door, giving Lauren a knowing glance, as the young teacher corralled her unruly third graders. With the children finally seated, the announcements began over the P.A. system, and Lauren moseyed to the back of the room, intending to use those few minutes to collect herself.

Lord, I don't know how I can go on. I don't think I can pull it together to teach today, she silently prayed. *Why, God, why? Couldn't You have stopped it? How can I keep going when Michael's having an affair, and today of all days, he announces he's filing for divorce? God, help me.*

Her prayer was interrupted by the ending of the announcements. With glassy eyes and holding back tears, Lauren noticed little Madison tugging at her hand, "Teacher, can I please go to the bathroom?"

Like Lauren, overwhelmed with problems, have you ever faced your classroom and thought you'd never make it through the day? It might be a divorce, a terminally ill parent, financial troubles, a pregnant daughter—no matter what your problems might be, God sees and God cares.

Gideon also had problems, and he came from a pretty messed-up family. He vacillated in faith and

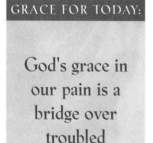

GRACE FOR TODAY:

God's grace in our pain is a bridge over troubled waters.

could even be accused of trying God's patience. But despite Gideon's difficulties, God stuck with him, and His grace brought him through his many dilemmas. Gideon was real with God, and God made allowances for His reluctant warrior, right where he was. The angel of the Lord gave Gideon some powerful advice that could benefit you as well: "Go in the strength you have. . . . Am I not sending you?" (Judges 6:14 NIV).

Meditate on these words in your heart; and you'll discover renewed hope, no matter what problems you're going through today!

TAKE A HIKE

He said to them, "Come with me by yourselves to a quiet place
and get some rest."

MARK 6:31 NIV

Have you ever sought the wilderness? You know, that wild place where the paths are faint, the signposts are few, and dangers—imagined or real—are heightened. In North America, "wilderness" conjures up images of thick forest, towering mountains, and rushing rivers. But the "wilderness" of the Bible was more often thousands of square miles of empty, parched, and lonely expanse.

Jesus often sought solitude in the wilderness, especially in times when He needed to commune with the Father or to gain some quiet time and personal space from the multitudes that followed Him. Scripture says He went up into the hills or out along the Sea of Galilee to pray or be alone with His thoughts.

Between classes, parent–teacher conferences, school events, and administrative meetings, you are with others a great deal of the time. Remember to take time to get apart with God to pray and soak up His presence. For Jesus, too, it was time to listen to the Father; to pray for those with whom He traveled and to whom He ministered; to retreat and refresh; to be still and rest.

Just before the feeding of the five thousand, Jesus was keenly aware of the press of people. So great were the demands on His time, writes Mark, there was not even time to eat. He expressed concern for His disciples and devised an escape plan in a boat to a wilderness place. But the people saw them go, ran ahead, and waited for the Shepherd. It was because the crowd was caught so far out without food that the Lord took mercy and miraculously fixed lunch for them all.

Escape with God, and you will be fed.

GRACE FOR TODAY:

When we need rest, God asks us to retreat with Him.

WHY WE DO THIS

Pursue a godly life, along with faith, love, perseverance, and gentleness.
Fight the good fight for what we believe.

1 TIMOTHY 6:11-12 NLT

It's February—the longest short month of the calendar year, especially for teachers. It's hard to get out of bed at the alarm's shrill insistence when it's so dark outside. The days are short, except in a classroom whose four walls seem inadequate for containing the strange mix of unharnassed energy and growing lethargy. Even the snow is a gray, dirty mix of salt and car exhaust. The excitement of the holidays is long past, and spring break seems out of reach. On such days, we find ourselves unequal to the task. Perhaps we even question our choice of professions.

Such queries are not unlike the questions we ask ourselves in those dark hours before dawn, stumbling around to comfort, feed, soothe, and walk the floor with a tiny newborn. Can we do this? Are we equal to the task? The questions surface because parenthood and teaching both involve sacrifice.

We teachers enter this profession knowing full well that we will never be paid according to the real hours we spend preparing, reading, grading, and creating. We know that sometimes our best efforts will not meet with success and that our grandest ideas will sometimes be met with a hoot of rejection—guffaws even—especially as the students grow.

But what keeps us coming back at the ungracious hour of 7:30 A.M. is that tenacious superhero quality that all teachers share—the unshakable faith that this could be the breakthrough day. We might change a life. It's the thrill of having a "lightbulb" moment when you are keenly aware that your students understand and are interested! It's having a former student write or visit your classroom and say, "Thanks for caring. You made a difference."

GRACE FOR TODAY:

When we persevere in our profession, God helps us
make a difference in the lives of our students.

TIME WELL SPENT

When time gets tight, the first thing you tend to sacrifice is your time with God. Parents' Night was last night, or you just finished grading a huge stack of papers, or you wrote the last twenty-five report cards—that extra half-hour of sleep this morning might just get you through the day. You've got to eat breakfast, after all, and you can't be late for work because that's where the money for breakfast comes from. God will understand, won't He?

Put yourself in His shoes, from a teaching standpoint. You've gone to a lot of effort and even expense to provide useful materials for your students. You've told them a test is coming, but you've provided the study topics, guides, and reference materials. You've led study sessions and set up tutors. You've even made yourself available at all hours, should they need to call for help.

> **GRACE FOR TODAY:**
>
> Since time is a servant of God, He always has enough for us to accomplish His desires.

You've done everything you can to ensure their success, except for one small but vital detail. They've still got to study. Why won't they open their books, peruse their notes, or give you a ring? They know the test is important, so why are they spending all their time talking on the phone, watching TV, or playing videogames?

God loves you and is there for you at all times and in every situation, and more than your daily bread, He has the bread of life for you, critical to your growth as His child.

When you make that sacrifice to spend time with God, all of the other time-constraining challenges you face will be put in their proper perspective, and He will give you what you need to finish the job. When it's all said and done, you will never say that such time with your loving Father was time wasted.

There is a time for everything, and a season for every activity under heaven.

ECCLESIASTES 3:1 NIV

YIELDED TO THE SPIRIT

By John MacArthur Jr.

A Fizzie is a small tablet used to make a soft drink; it's sort of a flavored Alka-Seltzer. Put it in a glass of water and its flavor is released throughout the water. This concentrated, compact power pill is no good as long as it sits on the bottom of the glass. It has to release its energy to fill the glass, and then it turns the water into something new.

If it is a grape Fizzie, you get a glass of grape drink. The flavor of the tablet determines the flavor of the water.

In a measure, that pictures how the Spirit of God operates in a human life. As a Christian, you have Him inside of you all the time as a compact, concentrated, powerful force of divine energy. The question is, has He ever been able to release that power, to fill your life so that you can become what He is? A Christian not yielded to the Spirit does not manifest the Christ-life. The Spirit of God has to permeate a life if that life is to radiate His power, glory, and love.

We cannot do anything apart from being filled with the Spirit.

If I say to a glove, "Play the piano," what does the glove do? Nothing. The glove cannot play the piano. But if I put my hand in the glove and play the piano, what do I hear? Music! If I put my hand in a glove, the glove moves. The glove does not become pious and say, "Oh, hand, show me the way to go." It does not say anything; it just goes. Spirit-filled people do not stumble and mumble around trying to find out what God wants. They just go![7]

—⁓—

HEAVENLY FATHER, IT IS SO GOOD TO KNOW THAT I DON'T HAVE TO LIVE THE CHRISTIAN LIFE ON MY OWN. YOU HAVE FILLED ME WITH YOUR SPIRIT. TEACH ME TO RECOGNIZE HIS PROMPTING, AND SHOW ME HOW TO YIELD MYSELF COMPLETELY TO HIM.

They were all filled with the Holy Spirit, and they spoke the word of God with boldness.

ACTS 4:31 NKJV

GRACE TO INSPIRE

From where the sun rises to where it sets, you [O God] inspire.

PSALM 65:8 NLT

Have you ever become bogged down in the humdrum routine of teaching? Most of us have. But God has a remedy—one He's eager to provide the inspiration for you to embrace.

If you're in a classroom today, it's by God's design. It may not be His will for the rest of your life, but it is for today. So grab hold of the bigger picture! Consider these words from Daniel Webster: "If we work on marble, it'll perish . . . temples, they will crumble . . . but if we work on [children's] minds, imbue them with high principles, with just fear of God . . . we engrave on those tablets something which time cannot efface, and which will brighten to all eternity."

> GRACE FOR TODAY:
>
> When we need inspiration, God expects us to go to Him first.

Consider this noble vision. God has placed each of your students in your classroom because He knew you'd make a difference and inspire them to fulfill His plan for their lives. The Holy Spirit is helping you.

Each child you inspire by God's grace is an investment in eternity. It starts with one small step—believing God's called you to be highly influential as a teacher. Believing brings more grace for you to walk out His calling in your classroom. As you receive His grace to inspire, you'll find God leading in the little things, empowering you to make a big impact.

You may not recognize the next Billy Graham, George Bush, Mother Teresa, or Dr. Phil sitting in the desks before you, but the potential for greatness is there. So take God's grace and pour it out, and you'll discover His inspiration working through you to affect eternity—one child at a time.

KEEP HEART

God is light, pure light; there's not a trace of darkness in him.

1 JOHN 1:5 MSG

Mrs. Hall was a teacher with great heart. You know the kind. Big, accepting arms. Strong hands, one minute patting the air of reassurance back into a deflated shoulder, the next tracing the path of each perfect letter of the alphabet on the handwriting chart at the front of the room. A multi-watt smile to light a city. A head that nodded encouragement and tilted with wisdom. A rich, hearty laugh that with one peal put the world right again.

Not one of her students knew if Mrs. Hall cried in secret. If she ever held her head in shaky hands of uncertainty. If she got discouraged or doubted her abilities or questioned authority. Everything about her was "can do," "give it a try," and "let's see about that." A great heart, indeed.

Her positive, reinforcing light was the spirit of the classroom. Her students knew they could do it because Mrs. Hall believed they could do it. What was the source of her greatness of spirit?

GRACE FOR TODAY:

God shines His light into our classrooms when we let Him shine through us.

Isaiah says those who hope in the Lord will have their strength renewed. They will soar with the wings of eagles, run and not grow tired, walk and not falter. Paul told the Corinthians they were not to lose heart because God was renewing them daily. The Holy Spirit in us keeps our warranty current.

Mrs. Hall was great because the God she trusted is the greatest. Her pupils were created in God's image and that was the end of the matter. She claimed the blessing of God in her life for the lives of her students. They couldn't help but be caught in the tractor beam from heaven that shone on their beloved Mrs. Hall.

THE MIND'S PAINTBRUSH

Paul said, "Have this attitude in yourselves which was also
in Christ Jesus."

PHILIPPIANS 2:5 NASB

The banner in the back of the classroom read: Attitude is the mind's paintbrush—it colors every situation. It's a powerful reminder that while we can't control our circumstances, we can control our attitudes. And as teachers, our attitudes help shape and color those of our students.

Walk back through your mind's youngest, most elusive corridors to your own grade school days. Remember your elation at holding that first box of Crayola's sixty-four crayons, with a built-in sharpener in the back and clean tips in myriad colors lined up like prismatic soldiers? You select a favorite color—cornflower blue, sea-foam green, periwinkle, or burnt sienna—intent on creating a masterpiece, and then it happens. SNAP! One over-exuberant press and in your hands, you hold just pieces.

What did you do then? Cry? Sulk? Refuse to color again? Demand a new box? Or did you peel back the wrapper, salvage the remains, and start again? The stakes might be bigger than crayons these days, but the choices aren't all that different.

We can color our days in bold, brilliant strokes of joy. We can shade them subtly with mellow contented tones. We can coat them in neutral bland hues of mediocrity. We can drench them in the cool colors of adventure. We might even want to share our colors with someone else. It all depends on what we choose from the box.

So how about it? What colors are you using in the classroom these days?

GRACE FOR TODAY:

God's presence colors our classrooms with sunshine.

HEARTS WIDE OPEN

"Comfort, yes, comfort My people!" says your God.

ISAIAH 40:1 NKJV

Along with several others from Javier's church in El Paso, he'd had the whole 2,000-mile trip to think about what awaited them in New York—destruction, smoldering ruins, chaos, and a whole city in need of God's healing touch. Last week's news of September 11 was still raw and unreal, and Javier wondered if all New Yorkers were as tough as they seemed on TV. It wasn't long before he found out. A group of orange-vested workers were taking a break near the site. They gratefully accepted the bottled water Javier extended to them. Timidly, he offered to pray with them. The men stared a second, then shocked him with their response: "Would you?"

In the course of your busy day at school, it's easy to forget that you are in a unique position not only to instruct but to comfort. In the midst of teaching and discussions and experiments and meetings, are real people who bring real troubles and real heartaches into the classroom along with their textbooks and backpacks. God has you where you are for a reason, and today that reason might be so that you can offer solace to someone in need.

It's important to remember that, as a Christian, you aren't able to comfort because you're strong and untouched by difficulty. You can comfort others because you have been comforted. You know that even though you love God, He loved you first, and that nothing can ever separate you from His love.

You can offer others God's love, and it often takes on the simplest of forms and gestures—making time to listen, a gentle touch, or sometimes just sitting there and sharing the pain. Because you never know what someone may be enduring, ask God to help you keep your heart open.

GRACE FOR TODAY:

God comforts us so that we can in turn
comfort others.

GOD'S COMPASS

Years ago, an old sailor repeatedly got lost at sea, so his friends gave him a compass. The next time he sailed he used it, but again he couldn't find his way back to land. Fortunately, the Coast Guard rescued him.

Irritated and disgusted with the old sailor, his friends demanded, "Why didn't you use the compass we gave you?"

The sailor explained, "I tried! That darn thing gave me so much trouble! I wanted to go northwest to get home, but hard as I tried, the needle kept pointing southeast."

The old sailor, so convinced which way was home, stubbornly imposed his own viewpoint upon his compass. When it didn't work, he pitched it overboard, failing to benefit from the safe guidance it would have provided.

How often as a teacher do you get stuck in your own way of doing things? Do you ever resist changes the administration wants you to apply in the classroom? Do you ever persist down your own path in teaching or in attitude rather than just following the Holy Spirit's promptings?

God doesn't want you walking through the school year alone. His grace has given you a compass that will provide direction at every turn, for every need. As the sailor, there'll be times you won't understand His directions, and at these times, it's vital to hold tight to the compass and resist the lure of mankind's most universal flaw—doing it my way!

You will find that following God's grace compass gives you the ability to trust God more, receive His direction, and experience His very best in your classroom. His grace always provides smooth sailing and will fill you with peace and joy to boot!

> **GRACE FOR TODAY:**
>
> **When we follow God's compass, His grace will guide us safely through the school year.**

Listen for GOD'S voice in everything you do . . . he's the one who will keep you on track.

PROVERBS 3:5–6 MSG

KEEPING STATISTICS OF EVIL

By Evelyn Christenson

Are you aware that each of us has an internal "bookkeeping" system? We have one column in the ledger where we record the good things that happen to us, and another where we keep track of the wrongs leveled against us. Year after year, these accumulated statistics tip the balance one way or the other. The side outweighing the other has a strong effect on our whole being. If it is the "bad" side, it can affect us adversely.

I heard of a woman who actually has a little book with a page for each acquaintance. She makes an entry each time they say or do something against her. Then when she comes to a predetermined number, she draws a dark diagonal line across that page—slashing her off her list of friends! Statistics of evil.

But forgiving does a strange thing to the forgiver's column of hurts. It wipes clean the evil statistics, which have been hoarded in the internal ledgers. In 1 Corinthians 13:5 NEB, that great love chapter, we read, "Love keeps no score of wrongs." In other words, as in the Phillips translation, "It does not keep account of evil."

We may feel there is a personal gain in the satisfaction we derive from exercising our "right" to refuse to give up our angry, negative, accusing, wounded spirit. But in reality, just the opposite is true. We are the losers. The emotional and physical gains come when we take our spiritual eraser and wipe the ledger clean—by forgiving.[8]

—⁓—

DEAR GOD, HELP ME REALIZE THAT I AM THE LOSER WHEN I KEEP TRACK OF THE WRONGS DONE AGAINST ME. GIVE ME THE GRACE TO SINCERELY FORGIVE THOSE WHO HAVE HURT ME AND TO ERASE ALL THOSE COLLECTED HURTS EATING AWAY AT ME. I RELEASE THEM ALL TO YOU. AMEN.

Be kind to one another, tender-hearted, forgiving each other, just as God in Christ also has forgiven you.

EPHESIANS 4:32 NASB

HIGH HOPES

Hope deferred makes the heart sick, but a longing fulfilled is a tree of life.

PROVERBS 13:12 NIV

Hope is a beautiful thing. You enter your classroom from day one positively brimming with it. You hope for growth in your students. You hope the light will come on for those who struggle to grasp difficult concepts. You hope for discoveries of new worlds, new ideas, new understanding. Of course, there are those days, too, when it is all you can do to cling to the hope that someone, who knows how, made the coffee in the faculty lunchroom.

Children are the offspring of passionate hopes. Conceived in hope, they come bundled in all manner of family expectations—or lack of them. Overlaid with your hopes for them, they arrive at school each day shaped, burdened, and challenged by the hopes and disappointments of others. That their own individual dreams have any hope of blossoming depends in no small measure on how eagerly and hopefully you garden their tender shoots.

> **GRACE FOR TODAY:**
>
> If we need hope, God's abundance can fill our cups to overflowing.

Jesus knew how to restore hope in the sin-sick heart. Sometimes, the language He used was firm and unyielding: "Stop doubting and believe." At other times, He was free with terms of endearment, calling His followers His "chicks," "lambs," and "little ones." And how often He encouraged His own to anticipate the future through words ripe with hope: "I go to prepare a place for you" (John 14:2 NKJV).

Our job as teachers is to be Christlike purveyors of hope. Such teachers instill an eager anticipation of what that day's learning holds. And soon, your students will watch for knowledge and wisdom as keenly as you do. They may or may not be primed to learn at home, but in their time with you, they will rise above their circumstances and travel a world bursting with possibility.

THROUGH HIS EYES

[The Lord says,] "I have loved you with an everlasting love."

JEREMIAH 31:3 NIV

The errant Southern states pulled away from the Union like so many spoiled children. Fine! We can't keep slaves? We don't get States' Rights? Then we quit. We'll just take our toys and go home! We'll make up our own nation!

A beleaguered but committed President Lincoln saw things differently. In an address to the Confederate States, he announced, "I can only see through Constitutional eyes; so I can't see you." To him, their rebellion didn't exist. He acknowledged only the plan, the way it was supposed to be.

God is exactly the same. He doesn't see what we are; He sees what He created us to be—what we can become through Holy Spirit transformation. Although He remembers that we are but dust, we stand before Him redeemed. When we pester Him about our sins, flaws, and shortcomings, flogging ourselves with past guilt, He can't remember. His Son, Jesus, came, once and for all. Because of that, we are not condemned.

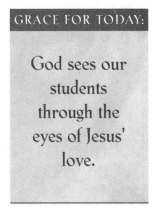

GRACE FOR TODAY:

God sees our students through the eyes of Jesus' love.

It is important that we learn to see ourselves and others through God's eyes. It is perhaps especially important that we see our students as God sees them. The child in the second row that irritates us like a bit of sand underneath a contact. The self-appointed class clown who disrupts our every effort. The clingy child. The ragged kid. The gifted student who has everything but parental attention. The loner.

Jesus made them all. They all bear some of His image. He died for them, too. He has lent them to you for a season. Love them through His eyes. It's a lesson they'll never forget.

REWARDS

[Jesus said,] "Be thou faithful unto death,
and I will give thee a crown of life."

REVELATION 2:10 KJV

raise.

* A bonus.
* A card of encouragement.
* A note of thanks.
* A new book.
* A night out with the girls.
* Fishing with the guys.
* Dinner and a movie.
* An awesome dessert.
* The perfect steak.
* A dream vacation.
* A new outfit.
* A student who finally grasps that difficult concept.
* An excellent evaluation.
* A phenomenal compliment.
* A surprise party.
* A plaque inscribed with gratitude, accomplishments, or achievements.

How we look forward to, revel in, such rewards. And yet, in far too short a time they seem empty, devoid of what we thought was fulfillment. Look at the list again. Add to it. What is it that captures your attention? What is it that holds your heart? Who or what motivates what you do, what you think, and how you spend your time? Did Heaven make your list, or were you, like many of us are sometimes, just too busy or too shallow to give that reward much consideration?

Now, look at this list: Eternal life. No pain. No sorrow. No tears. A Savior who greets you at Heaven's gates with open arms, saying, "Well done, good and faithful servant." There's no comparison, is there?

Have you ever wondered if what you do is worth it? If it's making a difference? See your students as a mission field, ripe for seed-planting. Keep your reward in mind, but remember the harvest belongs to God. Then there is no question.

GRACE FOR TODAY:

We can keep our rewards in mind, but God wants us to give Him the credit.

HIS SOVEREIGN HAND

In returning and rest shall ye be saved;
in quietness and in confidence shall be your strength.

ISAIAH 30:15 KJV

His critics said Michael Chang was too small, too weak, to cut it on the men's professional tennis tour. Imagine their surprise when he won the French Open in 1989 at the age of seventeen, just two years after turning pro. What they witnessed was the result of hard work, incredible resilience, and unerring professionalism and confidence. If they'd asked, they also would have learned that Michael Chang was able to rise to such heights and weather the fame and money that accompanied them because of his relationship with Jesus Christ.

As Michael did, you've worked hard at your chosen profession. You've put in the hours of study, endured the bureaucracy of teacher certification, and are constantly seeking ways to get better at what you do. Informed by experience and diligence, you keep your students learning not only about your subject area but also about life. Maybe you've even been officially recognized for your efforts by your administrator or the district. You've every reason to be confident.

What is it, then, that keeps everything in perspective? It's your relationship with God. You know that God has given you the talents and abilities that you demonstrate in the classroom, and that it isn't about being recognized for what you do by anyone other than God. It's great to be acknowledged by your fellow professionals for being successful, especially when they know that you're in it to have a positive effect on people's lives, not to win prizes.

Your ultimate confidence is in knowing that God loves you. He is in control of your life, and all of the things that others call coincidence or chance, you know are in the hands of your Creator. No matter what happens, God is with you and for you. Now, there's confidence.

GRACE FOR TODAY:

When we need confidence,
God expects us to draw on His.

IT TAKES ONLY ONE

Are there days when you feel like you've run out of grace and provision? Ever wondered, *Am I really making a difference?* Well, God wants to expose one of the biggest lies that Satan tries to pull on teachers—telling them, "You aren't important." Don't fall for that!

Just as the military has its marching orders from the President down to the lowest-ranking private, each person plays a significant part in securing our nation. Even so, in God's army you're important and appointed to a role that no one else can fill! He wants one of His people assigned to every classroom in America. Providence has placed you there.

Never think, *I'm just one teacher; what could I possibly do?* There was just one Noah, one Deborah, one Moses—but each believed, as one Esther, that they were called to "such a time as this" . . . and God views your teaching role likewise.

It takes only one person's obedience to the still small voice of the Holy Spirit. It only took one David to kill Goliath. It only took one Noah to build an ark. It only took one Martin Luther King Jr. to turn the tide of racism. It only took one Mother Teresa to change the course of Calcutta. Few ever realize the scope of how God uses them until they get to Heaven.

You are more than a teacher. You're not there by chance. In God's plan and with His grace, you are the difference in the spiritual war between light and darkness. When you're tempted to shrug off your importance as a teacher—stop, consider those who've gone before you, and lay hold of His providence to counteract those lies. God's counting on you in that classroom, and one teacher walking in grace can make a powerful difference.

> **GRACE FOR TODAY:**
>
> God's providence empowers us to make a difference in our students' lives.

You gave me life and showed me kindness, and in your providence watched over my spirit.

JOB 10:12 NIV

WHY DO SO FEW PRAY?

By Evelyn Christenson

The Bible clearly says one of the main reasons we don't have solutions to our family problems is that we have not asked God for them. We have not prayed. "You do not have because you do not ask" (James 4:2 NASB). But when you do pray, God releases His divine power into the lives of your family members. Our prayer groups at our church joined a devastated mother and father praying persistently for their son. He had left his family's Christian lifestyle for one of organized crime. But prayer did work. Today he is the father of a fine family and on the board of a good church.

Another family had a daughter who was breaking their hearts. She rebelled at the Christian leadership lifestyle of her parents and many times refused to even go to high school. She ended up running away from the family, on drugs, and in a very godless lifestyle. But our prayer groups joined her praying parents also— praying almost daily. And now she and her husband have a successful ministry in Hollywood reaching those in the movie industry for Jesus.

Are you praying for your family?⁹

—ᴍ—

DEAR LORD, I DON'T UNDERSTAND WHY YOU USUALLY CHOOSE TO WAIT FOR ME TO ASK BEFORE YOU ACT, BUT YOU DO. FORGIVE ME FOR ALL THE TIMES I HAVE BEEN NEGLIGENT OR TOO PROUD TO ASK FOR YOUR HELP. I NEED YOUR HELP NOW AND ASK YOU TO INTERVENE IN THE SITUATION THAT IS TROUBLING ME. NOTHING IS IMPOSSIBLE WITH YOU, AND I TRUST YOU TO RESOLVE THIS ISSUE. AMEN.

[Jesus said,] "All things for which you pray and ask, believe that you have received them, and they shall be granted you."

MARK 11:24 NASB

ALWAYS PREPARED

I waited patiently for the LORD; he turned to me and heard my cry.

PSALM 40:1 NIV

How much of your classroom prep time is time spent with God? Yes, the lessons need preparing, the materials need gathering, the papers need grading, and your teaching clothes need regular washing and pressing. Presentation is important. But frustration and dissatisfaction are built in if "getting ready" to teach excludes time with the Master Teacher, renewal time spent listening to that which He considers most important.

A good teacher is a good listener. God tells us to "seek My face," that He will patiently make time to hear from us whatever is on our hearts, be it praise (hopefully), complaints (undoubtedly), petitions, confession, argument, and even cloudbursts of anger. Jesus urges us to go to Him to find rest for our weariness. Likewise, the apostle Peter says we are free to "cast our cares upon Him" (1 Peter 5:7). Praise God His door is always open.

> **GRACE FOR TODAY:**
>
> God wants us to prepare for class by first spending time with Him.

But just how good are we at going to Him with no agenda, only open hearts and open hands to receive His comfort and instruction? Can the teacher in you be taught?

Sometimes that word from the Lord will come via the principal—sometimes the school custodian. Because Scripture teaches that "a little child will lead them," don't be surprised if God's instruction or chastisement or encouragement for you comes special delivery from one of your students.

But to neglect a time of stillness before the Lord is to shortchange yourself, your teaching, and ultimately, your students. He desires "alone time" with you to teach you to recognize His voice. There's power in quietude. Make it an essential key to getting yourself together for the day.

THE STAND

So be strong and take courage, all you who put your hope in the LORD!

PSALM 31:24 NLT

K evin stood alone at midfield, holding his helmet. The stadium lights shone down on the capacity Friday-night crowd. He'd anticipated a major case of nerves but instead felt only peace as he spoke, "Our Father, who art in heaven . . ." The crowd hushed temporarily, many of them recalling the recent Supreme Court ruling against another school that had given permission to a student to pray before a game. Kevin wanted to find a legal way to do what was on his heart. ". . . Thy will be done on earth . . ." Hundreds in the crowd stood and joined him.

When you consider the very real persecution that so many of your Christian brothers and sisters endure in the hostile regions of the world, it's hard to lend any weight to the kinds of challenges to your faith that you face at school. Nevertheless, it takes courage to teach for the reasons that you do it.

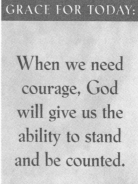

GRACE FOR TODAY:

When we need courage, God will give us the ability to stand and be counted.

You teach in a society that cries out for a higher standard for education yet won't acknowledge that the only true standard comes from God. Especially in the public schools, you have to choose your words carefully when expressing your beliefs. You've seen the apathy that results from your students not having any real bottom-line beliefs, and you know it's important for them to see you stand strong on yours.

Careful and prayerful consideration is required when you feel you have to take a stand because of your faith. That's not necessarily presenting the gospel or making a specific statement of faith, but there will be times when God puts you in a situation where what you believe will be made known by what you do. God, the source of your courage, your strength, and your shield, will protect you when you make that stand.

UNEXPECTED GRACE

When all kinds of trials and temptations crowd into your lives, my brothers, don't resent them as intruders, but welcome them as friends!

JAMES 1:1 PHILLIPS

Students whispered and stared as Mr. Brodt, obviously infuriated, stomped toward his classroom. Unbeknownst to them, while driving to school, he'd been pulled over for speeding and received a hundred–and–twenty–dollar ticket. Reaching his room, he dumped his satchel on the floor and slumped into his desk chair, holding his head in his hands. Then the P.A. system blared, "Mr. Brodt, the principal wants to see you in his office . . . immediately!"

The principal met Mr. Brodt at his office door, quickly shutting it behind him. "Mr. Brodt, we've serious business to discuss. I haven't received your professional development hours—due two weeks ago! Do you realize that this could compromise your position at Southwest High?" Mr. Brodt instinctively dreaded where the conversation was headed, even if it was for his own good.

Ever had a morning like Mr. Brodt's? Everyone has, but the question is: Where do you find God's grace at such times?

Grace isn't always a pat on the back. It comes in varying forms, always blessing you and keeping you on the right path. When a parent spanks a child for playing in the street—that's grace! When a police officer pulls you over for going twenty–five miles per hour over the speed limit, that's grace too. He might have just saved your life or someone else's! An attitude that embraces correction will always keep you in the center of God's grace.

The next time you're in a situation like Mr. Brodt's, be encouraged. You're in a position to receive more grace. In such moments, God may send you special messengers. Receive them with gratefulness, appreciate their wisdom, and follow their direction. No one likes correction, but if you see it as a messenger of God's grace, you'll come out on top every time!

GRACE FOR TODAY:

As God corrects us, He also pours out His grace on us to change.

ALL THAT GLITTERS

The quiet words of the wise are more effective than
the ranting of a king of fools.

ECCLESIASTES 9:17 MSG

In 1898, gold seekers by the tens of thousands poured into Skagway and Dyea, Alaska. They were the jumping-off towns for the treacherous ascent from the ocean up and over the icy mountain passes leading to the Yukon gold fields. Most of the fortune hunters found only heartache and disappointment, and many lost their lives in the attempt.

One woman, however, made her fortune not by prospecting for gold, but by prospecting the prospectors. Harriett Pullen decided to forego the deadly Trail of '98 in favor of providing the hordes of men in Skagway with a commodity in pitifully short supply—homemade apple pie.

"Ma" Pullen, as she was known, imported Red Delicious apples from Washington state, hammered tin cans into pie pans, and charged a healthy five dollars each for her heavenly baked creations. In demand for their taste, prized for staving off scurvy, the apple pies soon earned the busy baker enough money to order dairy cows to supply her customers the milk to go with the pie. And start a freighting company and open a hotel. Ma quickly banked more than a million dollars from her enterprises without the risk of bankruptcy or death.

Whoever sought wealth by becoming an educator? And yet, how often have we heard an accomplished person give credit to a single teacher who, by force of inspiration and high expectations, helped that pupil achieve the pinnacle of personal success?

Like Ma Pullen's apples and milk, good teaching is rarely showy or newsworthy, but oh, what a difference it makes! There will probably never be a stampede on teachers' colleges, but make no mistake. There is a fortune to be made in teaching, one measured in lives blessed by God and forever changed.

GRACE FOR TODAY:

God gives us eyes to see and thoughts to think that no
one else has discovered.

SNOW DAY

It's been a tough week. You're behind on grading. A special department report is due Friday, and you're not yet done typing the test to give your students tomorrow.

A quick glance takes in a sputtering fire, a carpet that needs vacuuming, an inviting mug of hot cocoa, and a stack of schoolwork spilling from a bulging briefcase. Nothing brief about that, you think. The disparate mix of sights and smells is the daily composition of choices: work or rest, clean or relax, do something or simply be.

The cozy places beckon us to be still—to curl up on the couch in front of that fire, drink the cocoa, and let the work wait. You want quality in life; you want to make a difference; you want to do what you want to do for a change. But somewhere a hundred other voices proclaim urgency and need. Grade me. Get ahead. Work harder. Volunteer more.

You glance out the window, briefly stopping your inner philosophical debate. Like a benediction ending the argument, God's answer appears in the form of snowflakes. Great chunks of pristine whiteness piggyback on smaller feathery flakes. The down of a gigantic comforter soon covers the ground.

Despite yourself, you grin, reach for the remote, and tune in to the weather. "Six to nine inches of snow," the weatherman predicts. "Stay tuned for school closings as we receive them." Every kid in the county is cheering! And so does the child you've buried deep within the confines of a grown-up mind and schedule.

It will be a day of unexpected grace. A day for one of God's best gifts—rest. Refreshment. Recharging. You can unplug the alarm. Work can be done at a more leisurely pace. And yes, you might just fit in a good book in front of the fire after crafting the neighborhood's best snowman! Thank You, Lord, for the gift of slowing down to rest.

> **GRACE FOR TODAY:**
>
> **When our work is done, God wants us to rest and recharge.**

[God] rested on the seventh day from all His work which He had done.

GENESIS 2:2 NASB

THE PEACE THAT GUARDS OUR HEARTS

By John MacArthur Jr.

John Bunyan's allegory *The Holy War* illustrates how God's peace guards the believer's heart from anxiety, doubt, fear, and distress. In it Mr. God's-Peace was appointed to guard the city of Mansoul. As long as Mr. God's-Peace ruled, Mansoul enjoyed harmony, happiness, joy, and health. However, Prince Emmanuel (Christ) went away because Mansoul grieved Him. Consequently, Mr. God's-Peace resigned his commission, and chaos resulted.

The believer who doesn't live in the confidence of God's sovereignty will lack God's peace and be left to the chaos of a troubled heart. But our confident trust in the Lord will allow us to thank Him in the midst of trials because we have God's peace on duty to protect our hearts.

During World War II, an armed German freighter picked up a missionary whose ship had been torpedoed. He was put into the hold. For a while he was too terrified to even close his eyes. Sensing the need to adjust his perspective, he tells of how he got through the night: "I began communing with the Lord. He reminded me of His word in the 121st Psalm: 'He that keepeth thee will not slumber. Behold He . . . shall neither slumber nor sleep' (vv. 3-4 KJV). So I said, 'Lord, there isn't really any use for both of us to stay awake tonight. If You are going to keep watch, I'll thank Thee for some sleep!'" [10]

He replaced his fear and anxiety with thankful prayer, and the peace of God that resulted enabled him to sleep soundly. You, too, will enjoy peace and rest when you cultivate the habit of looking to God with a grateful heart. [11]

—⁓—

HEAVENLY FATHER, BY YOUR GRACE YOU HAVE PROVIDED PERFECT PEACE FOR MY TROUBLED AND CHAOTIC HEART. I THANK YOU FOR YOUR UNINTERRUPTED, WATCHFUL CARE THAT ALLOWS ME TO REST PEACEFULLY. AMEN.

The peace of God, which transcends all understanding, will guard your hearts and your minds in Christ Jesus.

PHILIPPIANS 4:7 NIV

NEVER GIVE IN

God is not unfair. He will not forget the work you did or the love you
showed for him in the help you gave and are still giving.

HEBREWS 6:10 GNT

Female loggerhead turtles often swim thousands of miles from feeding areas to
nesting grounds along the beaches of the world. If they survive the sharks,
storms, and shrimpers, they lay their eggs in a single night and return to the sea. The
hatchlings emerge at night, using light as a visual cue to guide them to the water, where
a week-long, foodless sojourn to natural sargasso "rafts" determines their survival and
the continuation of the reproductive cycle.

There are days throughout the school year when time seems to crawl, when your
lesson plans seem stale, and your students are disinterested. It's difficult to make something positive happen,
and your efforts to do so may fall flat. As with the loggerhead turtles, getting through the day seems like a
monumental task.

You can be sure, though, that God has something
instructive for you each and every day. He will ultimately make the struggle worth the hardship. He wants
you to look beyond circumstances—spring fever, bored
students, a particularly challenging topic—and find your
ultimate motivation: serving Him.

Failure is a part of everyday life, and the fear of
failure crippling. You've seen it in your students and
you've experienced it yourself, but failure isn't the end.
God is the God of second chances and third chances and so on. When you're trusting
God to redeem the hard times, you're planting seeds of faith.

Learning to get up, dust yourself off, and move on is critical to any form of success. When your students see your determination to forge ahead despite setbacks, even
to fail spectacularly, they will witness God's grace at work in you. The value of that is
well worth your best efforts.

GRACE FOR TODAY:

When we need
to forge ahead,
God's grace will
give us
determination.

STANDING IN THE SHADOWS

May the God who gives endurance and encouragement give you a spirit of unity among yourselves as you follow Christ Jesus.

ROMANS 15:5 NIV

D o you ever feel like your life's in the shadows and wonder if you're making a difference? Teaching can seem that way when every nine months your class moves on and you get a new one that will move on again in another nine months! Year in-year out, you seldom hear from those to whom you devoted your heart and soul.

If that's you, consider Bronson Alcott, an innovative and exceptional teacher. Ever heard of him? Maybe not, but you've most likely heard of his famous daughter, Louisa May Alcott.

Bronson Alcott was a man of passion, devoted to teaching; however, he engaged in very unconventional teaching methods, believing school must be electrifying to stimulate a true educational experience. Although many proper sorts of parents didn't agree with his unorthodox teaching methods, Louisa May (and the few privileged to continue in his schools) flourished under his tutelage. Why? Because he inspired them to believe in themselves, encouraged them to discover

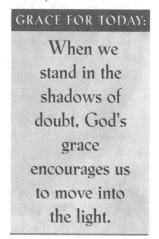

GRACE FOR TODAY:

When we stand in the shadows of doubt, God's grace encourages us to move into the light.

their own creativity, and convinced them that learning was the ultimate adventure. How fortunate that he didn't surrender his passion, lest the world would have gone without the wonderful books authored by Louisa May Alcott.

Bronson Alcott may be considered by some as a mere teacher who stood in the shadow of his famous daughter, but would Louisa have been so famous without her father's encouragement?

If you feel as if you're standing in the shadows today, God's grace is shining in to reveal truth and encourage you to keep on keeping on. Only God knows the end of your efforts. Receive His encouragement today to stand confidently in the shadows, and then trust His grace to accomplish the results.

THANKS, BIG AND SMALL

Thanks be to God for His indescribable gift!

2 CORINTHIANS 9:15 NASB

Have you ever wondered what the administration is thinking when they assign more students to a classroom that is already beyond recommended capacity? How about when art and music are the first programs to go in a budget crunch? And whoever decided over summer break that lizard-green walls were conducive to study?

Many of the decisions that most irritate and make teaching harder are made with little or no input from you. Often, you are certain, those decisions had to have been made by people who couldn't possibly have taught a day in their lives.

Isn't it interesting how the acid of injustice can give you ulcers without any noticeable effect on the decision-makers? Pretty soon, you're convinced that while you stew, they scheme more ways to make life difficult. Nothing sours the sweet taste of teaching faster than dwelling on the politics of education.

Better and more productive for you to practice gratitude for the incalculable benefits of teaching. The smile on the face of a child who gets it. The essay answer that reveals an ability to reason beyond the young essayist's years. The fervent hand thrust into the air by a student who knows you will be pleased with his newfound knowledge—a gift from you.

The apostle Paul warned the Roman believers about people who knew God, but neither glorified Him as God nor gave Him thanks. He speaks of their foolish hearts and futile thoughts. They squandered their time and talents on making and worshiping silly wooden idols when they could have been walking with almighty God.

The most capable teachers invest their energies where they can make the most difference—in the heads and hearts of their kids.

GRACE FOR TODAY:

If we ask, God will fill our hearts with gratitude.

THE PRAYER CHAIRS

He hears the prayer of the righteous.

PROVERBS 15:29 NRSV

In the quiet twilight between the lazy days of summer and the bustle of back-to-school supplies, bright yellow buses, crisp notebooks, and sweater sales, there are the first days of August.

Teachers emerge from summer cocoons of hibernation and blink at the sight of class lists, a few straggling staples and bent paperclips peeking from beneath their desks, and the first of an endless stream of memos on brightly colored paper.

Slowly we stretch and begin to prepare. Files full of ideas, gleaned from a summer of easier living, are opened and perused. Student desks are dusted. A plant is rescued from the back porch and haphazardly secured on a classroom windowsill. Lesson plans are jotted down. Calendars are filling up. Some of us will even practice reading the names on our student rosters so that the "First Day" might be error free.

But maybe we should add something to this year's ritual preparations. Perhaps as we formulate seating charts and begin to commit our students' names to memory, we could also commit to praying for their lives.

As you arrange desks for this year, why not place your hands on each chair and pray for the student that will sit there? Pray for his home life. Pray for the choices she will make. Pray that your influence will reach beyond this grade, this subject, or this year. Pray for him to make good friends and to come to know the Best Friend. Pray for her to focus easily. Pray for him to rise above the reputation you've heard about in the teachers' lounge. Pray that you won't listen to that reputation, but will give each student a chance on his own merit. Intercede for these lives. With your hand on each chair, lift each occupant to the throne of Heaven. Wait in anticipation of the answer.

GRACE FOR TODAY:

God wants us to lift our students to His throne in intercessory prayer.

GET A GRIP

Freshly beheaded chickens make quite a flap. The final half-minute of their lives is fueled by a final burst of adrenaline through the muscle tissues, resulting in wildly flapping wings and even a mad sprint for several feet before they finally expire. These convulsions give the appearance of life and have also birthed the common metaphor that describes frenzied, disorganized behavior in people.

Almost every classroom, at one point or another—whether intentional or not—resembles a corral of stampeding wildlife. While there is such a thing as controlled chaos (allowing loud voices and the kinds of physical activity normally reserved for recess), such a situation happens by your design, as a part of your lesson plan. Of course, your students don't know that unless you tell them; they'll just think the cat has checked out and the mice are going to play.

GRACE FOR TODAY:

When we give God control of our emotions, He will steer us through the chaos.

What happens, though, when circumstances arise that are out of your control? Out of nowhere, there's a conflict between students, or a serious rules infraction, or an injury, and it needs your immediate attention. How will your students see you react? Having a contingency plan in place helps, but beyond that, will the adrenaline of the moment force you into "headless chicken" territory, or into a position of calm authority?

The key to choosing the latter option is making sure that you acknowledge God's control of every situation. Jesus is described as the head of the body—His Church—and that takes the load off of you. When you spend time each morning in God's Word and in prayer, it prepares you for the day's events. The rest is in God's hands, and He will give you what it takes to stay on top of life in the chicken coop.

The fruit of the Spirit is love, joy, peace, patience, kindness, goodness, faithfulness, gentleness, self-control.

GALATIANS 5:22-23 NASB

WHEN WE DON'T KNOW HOW TO PRAY

By Evelyn Christenson

There are those times when we don't know how to pray for our families. But God has provided the solution to that problem. The Father gave us the Holy Spirit to live in us—who prays to Him whatever is the Father's will—when we don't know how to pray.

Our daughter Nancy called recently saying that her five-year-old Kathy was going through a stage—arrogant, bossy, and aggressive. Remembering her older sister's similar attitude and the spiritual-warfare prayer against Satan that changed her completely, I started to pray the same for Kathy. But somehow it wasn't right.

Finally, kneeling in the living room, I prayed, "O Holy Spirit, I don't know how or what to pray for Kathy. Please take my 'not knowing how to pray as I ought' to the Father according to His will."

What a relief! The pressure to figure out just what to pray left me. I knew God knew exactly what Kathy needed—and the Holy Spirit would take my inadequate prayer to the Father exactly according to the Father's will.

Talking to Nancy the next day, I asked about Kathy. A little surprised, she said, "Oh, she seems so much better." I thought, *I wonder how God answered my prayer of not knowing what to pray?* Well, I don't need to know as long as God knows—and answers![12]

—⁂—

FATHER, THERE IS NO WAY I COULD HAVE EARNED THE RIGHT TO PRAY; IT IS A GIFT OF YOUR GRACE. BUT OFTEN I DON'T KNOW WHAT TO PRAY. THANK YOU FOR GIVING ME THE HOLY SPIRIT TO PRAY ACCORDING TO YOUR WILL, FOR THEN I KNOW I CAN EXPECT THE ANSWER YOU HAVE FOR ME. I ASK FOR HIS ASSISTANCE IN PRAYER TODAY. AMEN.

We do not know how to pray as we should, but the Spirit Himself intercedes for us with groanings too deep for words; . . . He intercedes for the saints according to the will of God.

ROMANS 8:26–27 NASB

CHRIST'S AMBASSADOR

[The Lord said,] "Indeed for this purpose I have raised you up,
that I may show My power in you, and that My name
may be declared in all the earth."

EXODUS 9:16 NKJV

Have you ever needed extra grace or motivation to handle negative influences in your classroom? Often subtle, they may creep in with stone-faced, difficult students, and it's important to recognize this when it happens. Be prepared in Christ to impact your classroom positively and help fulfill God's purpose for your students.

God doesn't want these negative influences to be an irritation or a distraction to you, but rather He wants to give you power to stand before your class as His appointed ambassador, receiving and communicating His love.

> GRACE FOR TODAY:
>
> Since God has appointed us ambassadors of Christ, He will show us how to fulfill His higher purpose.

Isn't it exciting that God assigned you to a "covert mission" like a classroom to accomplish His purpose? Just as our Heavenly Father selected the Virgin Mary to be the mother of Jesus, He must have servants today as His agents in the earth to accomplish His plans.

As God's ambassador, He's graced you to be His authority in your classroom (see Luke 10:19). He wants you to be so in tune with Him that you'll feel His heart of compassion for students who come to class having been exposed to negative influences—those who have been abused, neglected, molested, or traumatized at home. God's grace is actually making its appeal through you to fulfill His purpose in those hurting and hopeless students.

Being Christ's ambassador is serious business, but He provides daily grace to those He's appointed. So receive help from Him, and be attentive to listen to His Spirit throughout the day while instructing your class. He'll show you how to pray for this one, give a word of encouragement to that one, or gently impart confidence to the kids who don't seem to fit in.

You'll quickly discover that God has higher purposes for your teaching than you ever imagined. You're His appointed ambassador!

HAVING FAITH IN FAITH

Without faith it is impossible to please God.

HEBREWS 11:6 NIV

I n Latin, *uberrima fides* means "super abounding faith." It is the faith of a badly out-numbered army that the victory is theirs. It is the faith of a mother that seven pounds of helpless newborn could one day become the president. It is the faith in God that He can move mountains.

It is also the faith that you carry with you into the classroom every day. Faith in your students to learn. Faith that despite all the brokenness in the world, love is the greatest motivator and healer of all. Faith that contrary to the news reports, kindness and compassion will prevail.

Without the rudder of faith demonstrated by your faith, your students will floun-der. The Bible speaks in Deuteronomy of an entire generation of faithless children lost to disobedience and opposition to righteousness. Spare your students so ugly a fate. They need your super-abounding faith in God, in them, in the stability that learning affords, and in the ability to see beyond them-selves and their circumstances to better lives and a stronger future.

Small wonder, then, that Solomon called sound teaching "a light," and David extolled God for teachings so effective that "to this day I declare your marvelous deeds" (Psalm 71:17 NIV). Though both men suffered from spiritual crises, we know from their writings that at times they possessed super-abounding faith so far-reaching that we—and generations to come—will continue to learn from them the pattern for joyous lives well and faithfully lived.

GRACE FOR TODAY:

Have faith in your students.

By countless means bold and subtle, you are imparting "a way of life" to your stu-dents. They see by your faith and actions what nourishes and satisfies the soul. From you, they develop a hunger for learning and a thirst for understanding. Never discount the strength they gain from the faith you place in them.

BEGIN WITH ME

No discipline seems pleasant at the time, but painful. Later on, however, it produces a harvest of righteousness and peace for those who have been trained by it.

HEBREWS 12:11 NIV

The pulpy sphere of a soggy paper wad arced through the air and stuck to the teacher's elbow. She was understandably furious and marched straight to her desk to pull out a yellow slip for detention and a pink one for a visit to the principal's office.

Then she reconsidered. Yep, there was a better way. She finished teaching the class and motioned the offending student to stay after. Smiling sweetly, she explained that the paper wad was poorly made, thus offending her standards of excellence. The boy would be spending his lunch time with her, filling a shoe box with properly made spit wads. She promised to demonstrate the technique.

Midway through lunch time, the formerly swaggering student was slouching and parched. "Too dry," the teacher instructed. "Nope, that one actually uses too much saliva." The student asked for a break to get a drink of water. "Sorry. I really want to use this time to teach you something."

As lunch ended and the paper count mounted, the student turned sheepish. He understood the lesson—and his teacher had learned one as well.

God, she prayed, Please let me lead by example. I am so quick to notice the faults of others. I know discipline is part of my job, but begin with me. Let my life be sifted, so that what remains are the qualities that would best reflect You. Fill my shoe box with good things.

That would be an excellent prayer for all of us: Lord, begin with me.

GRACE FOR TODAY:

Before we discipline our students, God wants us to apply His discipline to our own lives.

A POWERFUL LEGACY

We know that in all things God works for the good of those who love
him, who have been called according to his purpose.

ROMANS 8:28 NIV

A study once compared the lives of two seventeenth-century men: Jonathan
Edwards, a preacher, and Max Jukes, an avowed atheist. Mr. Jukes, an alcoholic, married a woman of low character, and among 540 of their descendents were 300
paupers, 150 convicts, 7 murderers, almost 200 prostitutes, and hundreds of drug and
alcohol addicts. His family cost the state more than one million dollars.

Mr. Edwards married a woman of strong Christian character, and the study of
more than a thousand of their descendants revealed a list of over 300 preachers, dozens
of authors and professors, 7 congressmen, 3 governors, and 1 vice president. They
never cost the state a penny.

If you've ever wondered what the impact of one person's decisions can be, look no
further than the case of Edwards and Jukes. Every teacher experiences times of doubt—
times when it seems as if nothing really matters in the long run, or even right now. You
want to play a role in producing a legacy like that of Jonathan Edwards, but it seems so
hard to do when you keep getting Jukes' progeny in your classroom!

When you believe in the sovereign Lord of the universe, you're placing your trust
in the one Being who actually knows how it's all going to turn out. So make it a habit
to consult God in prayer, read the Bible, and seek advice from trusted counselors of
like mind before you make a decision.

The choices you make today will have repercussions down the road, not just for
you, not just for your students' lives, but for the entire nation and even the world. If
that sounds heavy, it is. But don't worry: When you're making sound, godly decisions,
you're really acknowledging God's ability and desire to have an impact on people's
lives.

GRACE FOR TODAY:

God helps us choose what is good, even when both
options seem wrong.

THE BLESSING OF INFLUENCE

It's been reported that years ago the Chinese communist government hired a disparaging author to write a distorted account of Hudson Taylor's life with the intention of presenting him in a negative light. Their aim—to discredit the gospel. Most unexpectedly, as the writer did his research, he was touched by Taylor's godly life and found it impossible to complete his assignment. After months of observing Taylor as he went about his daily tasks—and knowing he could be put to death for his beliefs—the author renounced communism and received Christ as Savior. Unquestionably, Hudson Taylor had an eternal influence on this author, the scope of which won't be known until Heaven's roll is called. What an amazing picture of influence!

In Webster's 1828 Dictionary, the word influence is defined as: "referring to substances spiritual . . . in the sense, influence denotes power whose operation is invisible and known only by its effects." This illustrates how diluted influence has become in the twenty-first century! However, today, as you walk the halls of your school, God wants to pour out His grace for you to possess His spiritual substance (the Holy Spirit) to operate in His invisible power and to influence others for Him.

Sometimes, God's grace moves us to take a spiritual inventory in order to be more effective for Him. It's helpful at times to contemplate whether you're being influenced more by your peers or by God's Holy Spirit. If it's a challenge to take a stand for Christ, God is eager to give you courage. He delights in providing grace for such a desire. If you already are influencing others at school, make it your passion and prayer for more grace and more opportunities to be used by God.

> **GRACE FOR TODAY:**
>
> God gives us the courage to influence our students for Him.

Let your light so shine before men.

MATTHEW 5:16 KJV

SALT AND LIGHT

By John MacArthur Jr.

I f we Christians would live the kind of life the Bible describes, we would knock the world right off its pins. But sometimes the world can't distinguish us from itself. The apostle Paul calls us who are Christians working for non-Christian employers to give them an honest day's work for a day's pay, and to show them that is the norm for a Christian. (See Ephesians 6:5–8.)

If you are the citizen of a certain state, obey the laws of that state so that people might know that your faith is real, that it reaches and influences every area of your life. You may ask, "Am I supposed to obey every law in the land?" Yes, every law. If you do not agree with them, that doesn't change the matter. Obey them. If you know a way to work politically to change poor laws, fine; but until they are changed, obey them.

The only time a believer is ever to violate the law of the land is when the law either forbids him to do what he has been told to do by direct command from God or commands him to do what God forbids.

God wants us to be the kind of citizens in the world who will draw the attention of the world. We need to have the qualities of salt and light (Matthew 5:13–16). That involves submission, which is clearly commanded in the Scripture.[5]

—∞—

HEAVENLY FATHER, PLEASE FORGIVE ME FOR THE TIMES WHEN I HAVEN'T OBEYED THE LAWS OF THE LAND. IT IS A PRIVILEGE TO LIVE IN OUR FREE COUNTRY—A GIFT OF GRACE—AND I WANT TO UPHOLD THE LAWS SO THAT WE CAN ALL ENJOY PEACE. HELP ME TO SET A GOOD EXAMPLE AND BE THE SALT AND LIGHT THAT THIS WORLD NEEDS. AMEN.

Remind your people to submit to the government and its officers. They should be obedient, always ready to do what is good.

TITUS 3:1 NLT

CAN YOU HEAR ME NOW?

Since the creation of the world His invisible attributes . . . have been
clearly seen, being understood through what has been made.

ROMANS 1:20 NASB

God gave us five senses for exploring this amazing world. How often do you employ all five with your students?

In a unit on the ocean, for example, you might:

- Listen to a recording of the sea.
- Look at favorite student photos of past trips to the seashore.
- Handle seashells and comment on their different textures and shapes.
- Take veggies to dip in salt water for all to taste.
- Write a class poem describing the aroma of the sea (helped along by the seashells, salt water, and seaweed from an Asian food store).

> **GRACE FOR TODAY:**
>
> **When we learn to perceive God in the details, He will teach us how to pass on His gift of creativity.**

The life of Helen Keller provides us with a stimulating springboard from which to celebrate the senses. Few of those in possession of all their senses have ever examined the wonders of "alive-ness" to the degree she did despite being blind, deaf, and mute. She could tell the difference between the cornets and the strings by merely placing her hands on a radio from which music played.

One of Keller's pet peeves was people "whose eyes are full of light but who see nothing." She equated such indifference to our surroundings with ignorance. Scripture treats spiritual receptivity in similar fashion. The phrase "he who has ears to hear" in older Bible versions is rendered, "Are you listening to me? Really listening?" in *The Message*. God has sought to gain our attention since day one in Eden.

Using all five human senses is one way in which we can perceive God in the details. There's no greater joy than in helping yourself and your students read the signs of God in the designs of God.

THE RUSH

They will run and not grow weary.

ISAIAH 40:31 NIV

If someone asked us about our priorities, most of us would spout off the correct answer: God, spouse, children, work, church, friendships, service, hobbies. In other words, we know what to say, but our life choices don't always reflect what we know.

A wise observer of the human condition once said, "Your date book is your creed; what you believe in, you have time for." Ouch! All of our modern time-saving devices—Blackberries, Palm Pilots, cell phones, e-mail, fax machines, microwaves—have, ironically, not given us more time. Instead, we have merely stuffed any and all empty spaces with more stuff. More stuff to clean, to repair, to dust. More committees on which to serve, more extracurricular activities, more worthless pursuits disguised as opportunities.

"Yes, but you don't understand," we protest. "This busy season is just for a while. It will slow down after (fill-in-the-blank): vacation/school/this semester/this obligation/this sport/the children are older/I'm tenured/the remodeling is finished." The trouble is, if we're honest, we know it won't. There will always be something taking its place.

> GRACE FOR TODAY:
>
> God wants us to set priorities so that our lives can be lived, not just endured.

Recently, one woman—an energetic soul who wanted to serve on endless committees in order to make a difference—chaired yet another early-morning meeting. Puzzled, she inquired of the group as to why they were increasingly arriving at 8:00 A.M. instead of the stated 7:30 A.M. "I can answer that," piped up one brave soul. "I've been complaining to my workout buddy about the exhausting pace of my early schedule. She asked me who was responsible for making this schedule. I told her that I was. Her answer to me was as simple as it was profound: Stop it! So I am!" The group agreed to push back the meeting time and cash in the extra minutes toward sleep.

Sound familiar? Maybe it's time for you, too, to just "stop it!" Life must be lived, not endured.

WORDS OF LIFE

Out of the overflow of the heart the mouth speaks. The good man brings good things out of the good stored up in him.

MATTHEW 12:34-35 NIV

James Coughlin had been in the teaching game for a long time. He'd stayed in the barrack north of the cafeteria for thirty-three years, even after the new building was completed, preferring his trusty electric fan to the refrigerated air. His students associated its steady hum with American history, with constitutional articles and westward expansion, with the most challenging projects, toughest tests, and deepest feelings of accomplishment they'd ever known.

Mr. Coughlin, they said, knew how to get the best out of you. When asked how he managed this, the answer was simple and uniform, an oft-repeated quotation: "I've provided the framework and the tools; now you paint the picture."

Who among the finest teachers of your recollection did not at some critical moment provide you the spark of encouragement? They opened a door into a new realm and invited you to pass through it. They took the seeds of your imagination and carefully watered them. After a moment of censure, they put a hand on your shoulder and told you the only true failure was in refusing to get up and try again. Through their caring touch, you felt God's loving hand.

Perhaps one of God's most wondrous and mysterious habits throughout the history of His interactions with humanity is that of using people to accomplish His will. As His dear child, you are a part of that tradition. Without the trials He allows, His consolation would not seem as sweet.

In a cultural and educational landscape rife with challenges, your words of encouragement are oxygen to those around you, just as God's words are the breath of life to you. Draw them in, make them a part of you, and then breathe them out to a world gasping for direction and a nod of approval.

GRACE FOR TODAY:

When we pray for opportunities to encourage others, God will encourage us first.

UNLEASH THE FRUIT OF THE SPIRIT

The Spirit helps us in our weakness.

ROMANS 8:26 NIV

Justin slid out from behind his desk. Looking back over his shoulder, he gave the teacher a menacing stare and rushed out of the classroom.

"Excuse me, class," Ms. Peterson muttered, obviously irritated, as she darted to the classroom door. "Justin Rogers, get back in this classroom right this minute or . . ." Her words trailed off as Justin rounded the corner at the end of the hallway.

I can't stand that kid, Ms. Peterson thought, struggling to hold her temper as she walked back to her desk.

Does this scenario strike a chord, reminding you of a "Justin" in your class—a difficult student, a bully, a troublemaker who causes problems or interruptions? Today, God is pouring out His grace on you to consider such situations in a different light.

After all, He's given you the fruit of the Spirit, and it's not just a lackluster list of suggested character qualities to improve your disposition. No, the fruit of the Spirit is spiritual power residing within you, and God wants to unleash that power through you to your students—especially to the Justins.

So today, receive His grace for each student. Start by asking God to forgive you for those toward whom you've had a bad attitude or maybe even hated.

Next, prayerfully receive fresh grace from God's Spirit to flow through you to your students. Love never fails. Patience can't be thwarted. Long-suffering can transform even the most difficult person. As you come into class each day, believe that the fruit of the Spirit is being released through you.

Finally, expect those kids to change! As you receive God's grace to release the fruit of the Spirit, the problems that you've experienced with troublesome students will be problems no more, but opportunities to help them change into vessels fit for the Master.

GRACE FOR TODAY:

God pours out the fruit of His Spirit on us when we reach out to help difficult students.

CLOSE ENCOUNTERS

Leviathan is both awesome and terrible in size and strength. We go whale watching in the hope of seeing these incredible mammals of the deep, yet should the boat venture too close, our hearts quake at the nearness of the encounter. We back away from beasts measured in tons, and federal regulations mandate that we keep our distance from creatures so huge and wondrous.

Yet God most powerful and uncontainable, He who made leviathan, is unimaginably approachable! Jesus used marvelous language to describe our access to the Father. He explained that through the Holy Spirit, He abides with you "and will be in you." Further, Jesus said that if anyone keeps His word, "My Father will love him, and We will come to him and make Our abode with him" (John 14:23 NASB).

Teaching can at times feel like the most impossible task on earth. There's too much to do, too little time in which to do it, and before you know it, it's time to prepare for next year's class. How often have you felt that the best you've done in a young person's life is the equivalent of a pat on the shoulder, when all your good intentions meant to embrace that person with the fullness of life and learning? Welcome to a very crowded club.

But don't let the fact you are spread so thin keep you from rising with a hallelujah every school morning. Lay claim to the fact that you have a divine Teacher's Aid who will teach you all things and bring to your remembrance how much you are loved. Boldly start your engine, confidently head out to sea, and watch for the most beautiful sights any teacher ever beheld.

> **GRACE FOR TODAY:**
>
> When we approach God's throne of grace humbly, He will make sure we depart the throne of grace enabled.

[Jesus said,] "But you know Him because He abides with you, and will be in you."

JOHN 14:17 NASB

PONDERING OR PRAYING?

By Evelyn Christenson

Much of what we think is prayer is actually only pondering. Even when we are on our knees in our prayer closets, it is easy just to roll our own thoughts and our own answers around in our minds, not really including God at all. This is not prayer; it is only pondering.

My dictionary defines ponder like this: "to consider something deeply and thoroughly; to meditate over or upon, to weigh carefully in mind; to consider thoughtfully; to reflect, cogitate, deliberate, ruminate." This is a healthy process as it helps us sort out whys, unravel perplexing puzzles, come to conclusions, and even put to rest hurtful events. But people frequently think they have prayed when they have only spent time pondering. Pondering is not prayer. Only when we involve God in this process does it turn into prayer.

In the supernatural battle for our classrooms, pondering is inadequate. It is powerless to change the problem that we are deliberating.

But when we include God, our pondering suddenly involves the omniscient, all–wise God of the universe. The God who never makes a mistake. The God who knows all the whys, all the outcomes, all the perfect things He intends to bring about through everything that happens in our classrooms. When God becomes personally involved in our pondering, there are accurate conclusions and correct attitudes in and for our students—supplied by a loving, caring, all–knowing God.[14]

—◈—

DEAR FATHER IN HEAVEN, WHEN WE INVOLVE YOU IN OUR PONDERINGS, WE DON'T GET ONLY OUR OWN INADEQUATE AND FREQUENTLY INCORRECT HUMAN ANSWERS, BUT WISDOM FROM YOU—THE OMNISCIENT, ALL–WISE GOD OF THE UNIVERSE. THE GOD WHO NEVER MAKES A MISTAKE AND WHO KNOWS ALL THE WHYS AND ALL THE OUTCOMES YOU INTEND. HOW COMFORTING; HOW SWEET. THANKS, DEAR GOD! AMEN.

Draw near to God and He will draw near to you.

JAMES 4:8 NASB

I WANT TO BE FIRST

[Jesus said,] "And the last [shall be] first."

MARK 10:31 KJV

Thomas was the smallest boy in third grade. Had he been a puppy, doubtless he would have been the runt of the litter. In every P.E. class and every playground game, he was picked last. Team captains rolled their eyes at each other in mute disgust. Thomas scuffed the toes of his shoes over and over, trying hard to look like he didn't care. *Just once I want to be first,* was his heart's cry.

Perhaps if we're honest, it is the cry of all our hearts. Wouldn't it be nice if our efforts were well-received and acknowledged with gratitude, or at least with a pay raise! Sometimes, despite knowledge to the contrary, we work at being first in destructive ways: being a know-it-all to a new teacher and disguising it with ill-motivated "mentoring."

Or working so publicly that our new principal will take notice and reward us. Grandstanding. Making sure we are appreciated for every act of service. After all, that's what gets us noticed, right? How else are we supposed to get ahead? Everybody needs a pat on the back every once in a while.

> GRACE FOR TODAY:
>
> God loves a heart turned to the service of others.

So is it wrong for us to want somebody to occasionally notice that we're doing a good job? To feel satisfaction after a lesson, conference, or meeting goes exceptionally well? No. In fact, Ecclesiastes tells us that this side of Heaven, a good day's work is about all there is. No, we can and should feel a healthy sense of pride in our accomplishments. However, we must always reflect the glory back to the One who blessed us with every gift and talent we possess.

Benjamin Franklin put it this way in *Poor Richard's Almanac:* "Humility makes great men twice honorable." Jesus modeled it. Remember the evening when the Creator washed the dusty feet of twelve other men? When's the last time you've done any foot washing or behind-the-scenes work, genuinely not caring if you got the credit?

What a difference it could make if we entered every classroom as though we were teaching Jesus when He was a small boy. If we greeted each student with His love. If we graded papers, helped dig paper jams from the guts of the copier, dispersed gossip in the teacher's lounge, and had a ready smile for even the most difficult of colleagues.

A WING AND A PRAYER

Wounds from a friend are better than kisses from an enemy!

PROVERBS 27:6 TLB

The cowbird lays its eggs in the nests of songbirds, its survival dependent on the care provided by the other species. Cowbird chicks, however, are usually larger than the other babies; they win more food, often starving out the other nestlings. This example of parasitism, wherein one species benefits at the expense of the other, is one of three forms of symbiosis.

Another form is commensalism, where neither species is harmed nor benefited. Buffalo and cowbirds share this type of relationship, as cowbirds eat the insects stirred up as the buffalo tramp through the grass. Mutualism is the third form of symbiosis, whereby both species benefit, as with sea anemones and clownfish.

Though people often seem to be of different species, we all share the common ground of being made in God's image. It's a part of who you are to desire an intimate, meaningful relationship with your Creator. He has also hardwired in us the need for relationships with each other, a form of symbiosis peculiar to Homo sapiens.

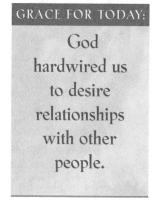

GRACE FOR TODAY:

God hardwired us to desire relationships with other people.

As a teacher, you're all about relationships. Much more than finger painting, grammar, and lab sessions, everything you teach points to relationships—to God's creative drive within each person, to being able to effectively communicate with others, to figuring out how all the pieces of the world around us interlock in an astonishingly unique environment.

In order to make sense of this huge network, you need to first focus on your primary relationship with God. Though you're definitely the primary beneficiary, God is glorified in the praises of His people. He enables mutualism in the best of your other relationships, with your spouse, family, friends, and church, and helps you root out the parasitic associations that vie for your time and attention.

THE PAWN TICKET

[He] redeems your life from the pit and corruption . . . [and] dignifies . . .
you with loving-kindness and tender mercy.

PSALM 103:4 AMP

M r. Santos was a well-liked and respected teacher at Halston High, even though he was an outspoken Christian. He lived to communicate values to his colleagues—especially Mr. Bunnelli—who always had financial problems. The man was always hocking something to gamble, hoping for the big score!

One day, Santos providentially ran into Bunnelli in the teachers' workroom. Slamming down the phone, Mr. Bunnelli cursed and said, "I'm in big trouble now!"

"What's the problem?" Santos asked.

"I hocked my wedding band, and it's too late to get it back! What a rip-off!"

The following day, Santos found Bunnelli alone and urged, "Let's talk. We've been friends for what . . . seven years? Has it ever occurred to you that maybe your problem's not the problem?"

"What do you mean?"

"The pawnshop gave you a redemption ticket for your wedding band," Santos said, "and you let it go for far less than it's worth. Now it's lost."

"Don't rub it in," Bunnelli said.

"Well, the pawnshop thing is like life without Christ. Problems develop, sin crowds in, you get lost, and sell out for less than God's best."

"And your point is?" Bunnelli asked.

"My point is that sometimes you gamble on what the world offers and lose—like what happened with your ring—but God longs to redeem you."

Santos reached into his pocket and pulled out a small paper envelope, dumping its contents into Bunnelli's hand. A gold ring tumbled out. Santos had paid a much higher price for the ring than Bunnelli had hocked it for.

GRACE FOR TODAY:

God paid the highest price to redeem our souls, so
that we could take His redemption to others.

SECOND WIND

The words of the wise prod us to live well.

ECCLESIASTES 12:11 MSG

D oes school ever get old? Has the teacher in you blown hot and cold? Ever wish you'd gone into the travel industry when you'd had the chance?

Second thoughts are nothing new. Christ's three days in the grave must have been the worst of times for His disciples. In addition to feelings of emptiness, confusion, doubt, and despair, second-guessing would have been a favorite pastime: "I gave up tax collections for this?" (Matthew) "At least when I fish for fish, I feed my family." (Peter) "Christ's dead, and now we're the scapegoats for a new religion that has no leader." (Andrew? James? Bartholomew?)

In fact, it wasn't until the disciples were cowering behind locked doors for fear of the religious rulers of the day that the resurrected Jesus materialized before them and their joy was restored. Faith has its moments—some great, others not so great.

Faithfulness, steadfastness, patience, long-suffering, endurance—all are qualities that teaching shares with faith in the race to a good finish that the apostle Paul says every believer runs. And if it's anything like a marathon, there are times when speed and style are called for. But the longest stretches are those in which a runner paces herself, finds that second wind, and goes the distance. It isn't always pretty, and the rewards of a race well run don't come until the end of the day.

But the rewards do come. You have chosen wisely. Teachers rank in people's esteem right up there with rescue workers and firefighters. To aspire to teach children the way that is good and right is ennobling and satisfying work.

When second thoughts assail you, seek a second opinion. God's Word speaks highly of teachers dedicated to the truth.

GRACE FOR TODAY:

When we have second thoughts, God wants us to seek His opinion first.

OUR LAST BEST HOPE

A preacher once officiated at two funerals during a single week-end. The first was for a courageous police officer, fallen in the line of duty; the other for a man who took his own life.

One had no idea that day would be his last; the other planned for this ending. Thousands attended the officer's services, with the celebration of his life on earth and that which is yet to come. Only a handful of people attended the other man's memorial service, and those mainly out of a sense of duty.

At the first funeral there were smiles through tears, laughter despite the pain. The service offered hope and the certain knowledge that this life is not the end. The second funeral was overshadowed by unrelieved pain because there was no future and the present made absolutely no sense.

What was the difference? In a word, hope.

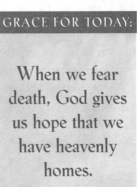

GRACE FOR TODAY:

When we fear death, God gives us hope that we have heavenly homes.

Those teachers and students who lost their lives, or were injured, or were forever affected by the tragic events at Columbine or Paducah or any number of sadly similar sites, probably never thought much about that particular day, either. There was likely no sense of dread or foreboding, no suspicion of anything other than ordinary daily routine. And then, with the screech of metal, or the fast click of a gun, life was snuffed out—suddenly, irretrievably, unplanned.

None of us knows which day will be our last. We can't afford the luxury of being so hurried that the sweet things in life pass us by. We can't know the last kiss, the last wave, the last dinner, the last day. But what we can know is that there is hope. And because of Jesus, our only hope, we can claim it as ours and begin to live, and yes, smile, again.

May our Lord Jesus Christ and God our Father, who loved us and in his special favor gave us everlasting comfort and good hope, comfort your hearts and give you strength.

2 THESSALONIANS 2:16-17 NLT

An Awesome Weapon

By John MacArthur Jr.

We ought to keep our bodies in subjection to insure that we are honoring God. That includes controlling the way we dress and the things we do with our bodies. This principle covers the whole area of the lust of the flesh, not just sexual things. A person can dishonor God by overdressing to attract attention to oneself. Gluttony also puts one in the position of dishonoring God and committing sin because it is obvious to everyone that the glutton cannot control the desire to eat. Nothing that gratifies the body to the dishonoring of God can have a place in the will of God.

Robert Murray McCheyne spoke at the ordination of young Dan Edwards in the 1860s. He said something like this: "Mr. Edwards . . . do not forget the inner man, the heart. The cavalry officer knows that his life depends upon his saber, so he keeps it clean. Every stain he wipes off with the greatest care. Mr. Edwards, you are God's chosen instrument. According to your purity, so shall be your success. It is not great talent; it is not great ideas that God uses; it is great likeness to Jesus Christ. Mr. Edwards, a holy man is an awesome weapon in the hand of God." (See 2 Timothy 2:21.) McCheyne was right, and God's will is that you be holy—sanctified.[15]

—⁂—

GOD, I WANT TO BE YOUR INSTRUMENT OF HONOR. BY THE POWER OF YOUR GRACE, HELP ME TO LIVE A HOLY LIFE, ONE THAT IS WHOLLY GIVEN TO YOU AND YOUR WAYS, SO THAT I CAN BE EFFECTIVE AS YOUR DISCIPLE—BOTH IN THE CLASSROOM AND THROUGHOUT THE REST OF MY LIFE. LET ME SHINE AS AN EXAMPLE OF THE GOODNESS THAT A HOLY LIFE IN YOU BRINGS. AMEN.

God did not call us to be impure, but to live a holy life.

1 THESSALONIANS 4:7 NIV

GUARD THE GATES

My lips will not speak falsehood, and my tongue will not utter deceit.

JOB 27:4 NRSV

A Hassidic story tells of a man who went about the village spreading lies about the rabbi. Finally, feeling remorse over his deeds, he went to the rabbi to ask forgiveness and seek atonement. The rabbi told him to take several feather pillows, cut them open, and scatter the feathers. The man completed this task and returned to the rabbi.

"Now what?" he asked. His mouth fell open as the rabbi instructed him to gather all of the feathers. "That's impossible!"

The rabbi nodded. "Though you may regret your words and seek to repair the damage done, it is as impossible to do so as it is to gather every single feather."

In most workplaces, gossip is a way both to bind the community in ties of common knowledge and to disrupt it through malicious rumors. Unfortunately, even the first approach opens the door to the latter, which is why Jesus mentioned in the Sermon on the Mount that even being angry with or cursing someone is tantamount to murder.

> GRACE FOR TODAY:
>
> God alone can help us control our tongues and refrain from gossip.

You've seen the damage rumors and hearsay can cause among your students. For some of them, the old game "Telephone" is a way of life! Naturally, you want to put an end to such practices as soon as you can, but it helps if your students (and colleagues) know that you don't engage in gossip yourself.

God desires you to bring every area of your life under His auspices, especially your words, seemingly simple things that actually hold the power of life and death. When you refrain from any form of falsehood, insincere flattery, and unnecessary dispute, you set a tone not only for your own life, but for your classroom, as well.

PRACTICE—DON'T PREACH

[God said,] "It's with lasting love that I'm tenderly caring for you.

ISAIAH 54:8 MSG

M rs. Gleason was walking her dog when she discovered ten–year–old Libby, sitting on the street corner, sobbing into her backpack. "Sweetie, what's the matter?"

In broken speech, Libby replied, "I got off the bus . . . the sheriff was here, puttin' all our stuff on the curb and locking our house. I'm scared! Nobody's home!"

Unfortunately, Libby's parents never came home. She went into foster care and was placed in a good home, but she had been wounded by her abandonment.

At school, Libby just existed. She didn't pay atten–tion, never turned in her homework, and refused to make friends. After four months of insolent behavior, Ms. Beadle sat the girl down for a heart–to–heart talk.

"Do you want to do fourth grade over?" Ms. Beadle asked.

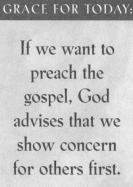

GRACE FOR TODAY:

If we want to preach the gospel, God advises that we show concern for others first.

"I don't care," Libby said indifferently.

"Well, we're going to do things differently until the end of the year," her teacher said. "I've talked with your foster mom and told her I want to help you. So no more dissin' your homework! I'm going to stay after school with you until it's done."

The next afternoon, the onerous task of tutoring began, and four weeks later not much had been accomplished. Libby was defiantly uncooperative. Then one afternoon, five–thirty rolled around, and still Ms. Beadle patiently worked with Libby.

"Ms. Beadle, how long you goin' keep doin' this?" Libby whined.

"As long as it takes," Ms. Beadle answered.

"Why?" Libby asked. "It don't seem worth it."

"No, but you are."

Oftentimes, teachers aren't privy to what's going on with students at home, but more than anything else, students need to know you care. Show godly concern. Let your students know that they are worth more than anything they can throw at you.

TRUE TALENTS

Each person is given something to do that shows who God is: Everyone gets in on it, everyone benefits. All kinds of things are handed out by the Spirit, and to all kinds of people! The variety is wonderful.

1 CORINTHIANS 12:7–8 MSG

Some of your students are bigger mysteries than others. What makes them tick? What will their collection of abilities and challenges lead them to become? Where do their true talents lie?

Some are early risers. A few are late bloomers. There are leaders, followers, and daisy pickers. There are jocks, cool dudes, timid Tillies, prima donnas, drama queens, gentle souls, kings of the jungle, and class clowns. Some mirror their parents to a tee, while others are as individual as snowflakes. Classroom DNA is a kaleidoscope of potential.

And like each twist of the kaleidoscope, each day in the classroom presents a new pattern of color and combination. Yesterday's scene was sweetness and light, Friday's was laughter and discovery, today's is stormy and taxing. Absences, fire drills, incoming transfer students, playground disagreements, divorce, or a death in your own or a student's family—life happens, and learning may veer across your carefully drawn map on strange and unexpected paths.

How well you manage the bright array of color chips that comprise the lives represented in your classroom can be a determining factor in the way your students' lives play out. They closely watch how you handle any and all situations. They interpret your body language. They listen to your words—and to your tone. All this happens even on those days when they seem about as receptive as bricks.

In the midst of these shifting—and occasionally colliding—classroom dynamics, you bring their gifts and talents to the top and afford them opportunities to shine. Thank God for the ability to make beautiful scenes with your kaleidoscope of kids.

GRACE FOR TODAY:

God celebrates the variety of students in our classrooms.

AN OUTBREAK OF JOY

Thou wilt shew me the path of life: in thy presence is fulness of joy; at
thy right hand there are pleasures for evermore.

PSALM 16:11 KJV

Any instructor who teaches vocabulary knows that sometimes confusion
results. Some spellings are so close; some words are separated by but a single letter or a shade of meaning. Add a surrounding concept, and the potential to misunderstand increases exponentially.

Teachers, indeed people, aren't immune, either. For example, how often we confuse joy with happiness. Happiness is utterly dependent on circumstances. Joy, however, is impervious, oblivious even, to the current situation.

Joy can be found walking hand in hand with crushing disappointment. Joy sits in the waiting room of the local cancer ward. Joy hovers above a heart that is literally cracking under the weight of sorrow.

How can this be true? It is true because Jesus is its source. Joy cannot be manufactured. It cannot be commanded. But, wonder of wonders, joy can be chosen.

Perhaps this is why the apostle Paul urges us to think about things that are lovely, excellent, and praiseworthy. The way we think affects our attitudes, our outlooks, and our joy quotient. Make no mistake—joy is not a false cheerfulness or a denial of pain when life is hammering against the shores of our faith. But it is a powerful antidote to unrelenting despair. Can we grieve? Yes. Can we question? Absolutely. Can we ever get the blues? Certainly. But we can't wallow there.

If you were able to know intimate details about every person you meet, you'd find that nearly every person on this earth has plenty of reasons to be miserable if they want to be. But those who trust that God is always good, no matter what they see or how they feel, have both hands wrapped tightly around joy.

God says in Proverbs 17:22, "A joyful heart is good medicine." Did you catch it? Joy is God's prescription for not living in the dreadful barren land of a dried-up soul. No matter what happens today, choose joy.

GRACE FOR TODAY:

When our souls dry up,
God's prescription is a dose of joy.

CANCELING THE DEBT

Chuck Colson tells the story of a Mrs. Washington who attended a graduation ceremony for inmates in a prison fellowship program. She stepped to the stage, memories and emotions flooding in—a murdered daughter, a dead husband, a son lost to drugs and AIDS. Overpowering all of these, however, her joy and pride centered on the man before her. She embraced him and declared to all present that this was her "adopted son." The poignancy resonated within the crowd as they beheld the bond between the woman and her daughter's killer.

Such an account of forgiveness is staggering under any circumstances, especially for those who haven't personally encountered Jesus. You're in on the truth, however: The world is populated entirely with sinners in desperate need of forgiveness. The grace you've experienced at the Cross is available for everyone, especially those who need it most.

GRACE FOR TODAY:

God's forgiveness levels the playing field for all of us.

When you're in the classroom, it can be easy to forget that simple truth. Your heart readily goes out to certain students and hardens to others, and it becomes a matter of rationalizing why it's like that. *Well, this poor child has psychotics for parents and deserves my understanding, while this kid has all the advantages and still acts like a big jerk—they should just go take their medicine.*

You have to act based on the behavior at hand. What you don't know, though, is the specific plan God has for each and every one of those students. Therefore, it makes sense to look into the heart of the matter, seeking God's counsel with each child. Leave yourself open to the possibility that God has more for them than their current course of behavior would suggest. Forgiveness is for everyone, even if only God can make it possible.

As far as the east is from the west, so far has
He removed our transgressions from us.

PSALM 103:12 NKJV

HOW CAN YOU BECOME CONFIDENT?

By John C. Maxwell

Establish your worth according to God's value system. God demonstrated our importance to Him in two great acts. First, He created us in His own image, and second, He—through Jesus Christ—died for our sins. God thought so much of you, believed in you, and saw you as a person of such worth, that He allowed His Son to die so that you could live. When we begin to see ourselves in light of God's actions on our behalf, then we immediately begin to have more confidence. There is nothing more humbling than the realization that if you were the only person on this earth, Jesus would have died for you. That makes you priceless.

Confidence is not the result of an absence of problems. It is very clear in Psalm 27 that the psalmist encountered many problems and difficulties. He mentions his enemies, evildoers who want to devour his flesh, adversaries, and a host encamping around him.

Confidence is a result of trusting God in our problems. In the midst of his difficulties, the psalmist kept focusing on God, and not on his difficult situation.[16]

—⁓—

FATHER GOD, I AM SO AWARE OF MY INADEQUACIES AND FAILINGS THAT IT IS OFTEN DIFFICULT FOR ME TO BE CONFIDENT OF OR TO REALLY GRASP MY WORTH. HELP ME TO COMPREHEND THE DEPTH OF YOUR GRACE AND WHAT MY WORTH IS IN YOUR EYES. CAUSE IT TO BECOME REAL TO ME SO THAT IT TRANSFORMS ME FROM BEING AN INSECURE BELIEVER TO A CONFIDENT-IN-CHRIST ONE. TODAY I CHOOSE TO FOCUS ON YOU AND EXALT YOU OVER MY NEGATIVE FEELINGS AND CIRCUMSTANCES. YOU ARE MY LIGHT AND MY SALVATION. I HAVE FULL CONFIDENCE IN YOU. AMEN.

The LORD is my light and my salvation; Whom shall I fear? The LORD is the defense of my life; Whom shall I dread?

PSALM 27:1 NASB

JUDGE NOT

[Jesus said,] "Judge not, that ye be not judged."

MATTHEW 7:1 KJV

One day when Jesus was in a crowd of people, a man stepped forward and requested that Jesus demand the man's brother to share his inheritance. Jesus' reply is worth pondering: "Friend, who made me a judge over you to decide such things?" (Luke 12:14 NLT). Jesus valued the man as a friend and realized it wasn't His place to pass judgment.

Sometimes we fail to be as tolerant as Jesus when a mistake has been made. Even though we might not dare speak our secret thoughts of judgment, we still judge others harshly.

GRACE FOR TODAY:

God tolerates our mistakes so that we can tolerate those of others.

Consider . . .

When was the last time you had a bad day?

When was the last time you missed a deadline?

When was the last time you were rude to a waitress?

When was the last time you yelled at your child?

When was the last time you didn't like a student?

When was the last time you drove over the speed limit?

Sometimes we can experience a complete change of heart by just slowing down and walking in someone else's shoes for a while. God is tolerant of our mistakes and usually gives us another chance, which is all the more reason we should be tolerant of others who make mistakes.

Spread God's grace around. The next time the secretary doesn't have copies ready for your class, consider what her day's been like. Or when the principal calls another meeting, consider the reasons for it, remembering that tolerance will keep you from passing judgment.

Since Christ refrained from being intolerant and condemning people for their mistakes, it's certain He's provided the grace for you to do likewise.

BLAZING THE TRAIL

In your unfailing love you will lead the people you have redeemed.

EXODUS 15:13 NIV

A young, short-term missionary's first impressions of Fiji were expressed in a vivid twenty-word snapshot: "Falling coconuts, piles of cow manure on the trails, time is not kept, and mosquito nets are gifts from God."

In the weeks that followed, Fiji proved much more than that, of course. For one thing, the warm-hearted Fijian people entered the picture. But the missionary's first impressions were necessarily framed by those signs that she was far from her familiar world.

Students entering your classroom for the first time also walk strange and unfamiliar trails. Hopefully, free-ranging cows have not passed that way first. But the way you do things, your expectations, what things cover the walls in your classroom, even the way the tables and desks are arranged are parts of an alien world. It will take a little time and adjustment for everyone before the class becomes a comfortable fit and begins to work together as a team.

GRACE FOR TODAY:

God blazed the trail for us to follow.

That in-between time of falling coconuts is your time to establish yourself. Your confidence, leadership, and balance steady everyone and help you chart the course for the year. Bless God for that wide-eyed time of adjustment when even the most assertive students take a wait-and-see attitude.

Notice how Jesus met His first disciples, fisherman brothers Peter and Andrew, on their own turf. He got right into one of their boats and gave them some fishing advice that established His Lordship and forever changed their lives. They were ready after that to quite literally follow Him anywhere. Show your students that you empathize with their need to succeed, and they will take whatever trail you blaze.

A SEVERE MERCY

For I reckon that the sufferings of this present time are not worthy to be compared with the glory which shall be revealed in us.

ROMANS 8:18 KJV

In his book *A Shepherd Looks at the Twenty-Third Psalm,* Philip Keller mentions that sometimes a shepherd has to take his staff and break the shins of a sheep that is continually running off to unsafe pastures. The breaking is for its own good. What a thought!

Joni Eareckson Tada, author, singer, disabilities advocate, and quadriplegic since her diving accident at the age of seventeen, often shares candidly about her struggles. In a recent interview, Joni was heralded as a hero of faith. Many feel they couldn't respond to life in a wheelchair with her grace—her faith. Her answer? "But they could . . ." she said. "I've had to learn to lean hard on God. And anybody can do that." She views her accident as a salvation. She was, she recounts, ready to purchase some birth-control pills, go off to college, and live life her way.

The severe mercy of God's plan splintered her plans for a season of rebellion. God has since used her mightily, in ways she never planned, perhaps on a grander scale than would ever have been possible otherwise. Despite everything, she loves and trusts God with her entire being.

Yours might not be a paralysis of the body, but rather one of the heart. Job wished he'd never been born. Moses explained to God that he wasn't the man for the job. Paul pleaded for a thorn in the flesh to be removed. Perhaps you, too, have about decided that you're not going to participate in life anymore. You'll just be a spectator.

Oh, what we might be missing when we doubt that a God who is big enough to be God, is more than big enough to handle our tough problems!

GRACE FOR TODAY:

When we suffer, God desires to carry us when we cannot walk ourselves.

ALWAYS WITH YOU

Now faith is the substance of things hoped for,
the evidence of things not seen.

HEBREWS 11:1 KJV

T he Japanese prison camps of World War II were infamous for their shocking brutality and wretched living conditions, something young British captain Ernest Gordon discovered firsthand. Many men simply gave up hope and died, but Gordon survived due to the kindness of two fellow prisoners, both Christians. Their selflessness inspired him to reinvestigate the Scriptures, where he and others found strength to love even the prison guards and to survive their ordeal. Gordon's account endures in his book, *To End All Wars*.

Depending on where you teach, school can feel like a war zone. You may work in an urban district where street violence and crime are everyday factors, but even if you work in a suburban area or at an independent school where the battles occur on more intellectual planes, the most important question remains the same: Are you making a difference?

If you review the list of men and women recounted in Hebrews 11—sometimes called the "Hall of Faith"—you will see some critical common characteristics. First, these were ordinary people. What was extraordinary about them came from their encounters with God. Also, God gave them an uncommon vision that enabled them to look beyond their circumstances and trust what He asked them to do. Their faith made the difference.

Do you believe that you are where you are for a reason? That's faith. Do you believe that despite unfavorable circumstances, hardheaded students, unsupportive administrators, a godless educational system, and your own doubts, God will still accomplish His will in you and through you? That is faith. May your sovereign and heavenly Father strengthen you today to trust Him and His good and perfect will.

GRACE FOR TODAY:

God equips ordinary people to do extraordinary
things for Him.

THE MISSING INGREDIENT

Rachel was proud of the quiche she'd made for the teachers' brunch. She cooked very little and was eager for her colleagues to try it. Just imagine her embarrassment when Rachel observed several people tasting what she had made, only to see them set their plates aside. Rachel headed for the buffet table, and tasting it herself, she instinctively understood their reaction.

"What have I done?" Rachel murmured. It wasn't until she got home and saw the beaten eggs still in the bowl that she realized her mistake—quiche isn't quiche without the eggs.

Like most recipes, if you leave out a key ingredient, you won't get the results you're hoping for. So it is in your walk with the Lord. What have you been praying for—a spouse, a baby, a home, a raise? In recipes, the ingredients work in close relationship to produce the end product.

You can mess up proportions, but as long as you have all the ingredients, you'll have a reasonable facsimile of what you set out to create. But leave out key ingredients such as baking powder, soda, flour, or vanilla, and you'll have a cook's nightmare.

Similarly, a key ingredient in your relationship with God is faith. If you have some ingredients—Bible reading, prayer, church—but don't have faith, you won't get the results you're hoping for.

God's Word promises each believer a measure of faith, and even if that measure is as small as a grain of mustard seed, it will produce results. It may not be today or even tomorrow, but Scripture says that God isn't a man that He can lie. If He promised it, your faith can take it to the bank, because you'll eventually possess what He's promised.

> **GRACE FOR TODAY:**
>
> God asks us to keep on believing, including the important ingredient of faith in our prayers.

The righteous live by their faith.

HABAKKUK 2:4 NRSV

TO BE NEAR HIM

By John MacArthur Jr.

Jesus was talking to His disciples and asked, "Who do men say that I am?"

They answered, "Oh, some people think You are Jeremiah; some people think You are Elijah; some people think You are one of the prophets."

He said, "Who do you think I am?"

Peter responded, "Thou art the Christ, the Son of the living God" (Matthew 16:16 KJV). Then, I feel sure, he wondered, *Where did that come from?*

Jesus said, "Flesh and blood did not reveal this to you, but My Father who is in heaven" (v. 17 NASB).

Peter probably said, "I thought so. I surely didn't know that." You see, when Peter was near Jesus, he not only did the miraculous, he said the miraculous. Is it any wonder he wanted to be near Him?

When he was near Christ, Peter had miraculous courage. He was in the Garden of Gethsemane when a whole band of soldiers—as many as five hundred—came to arrest Jesus. They came marching in with all their regalia. In front of them came the chief priests, and before the chief priests came the servants of the priests. Peter was standing with the Lord. Maybe his thoughts went something like this: *They think they are going to take Jesus away? No, they won't!*

Because Peter did not ever want to be removed from the presence of Jesus, he took out a sword. He started with the first guy in line, who happened to be Malchus, the servant of the high priest. The Bible says that Peter cut off Malchus' ear, but if I know Peter, he was going for his head. Peter was ready to take on the whole Roman army. You see, when he was with Jesus, he had miraculous courage.[17]

—◇—

FATHER GOD, WITHOUT YOU, I CAN'T DO ANYTHING SIGNIFICANT. BUT WITH YOU, THROUGH YOUR GRACE, I CAN BE PART OF THE MIRACULOUS. WORK THROUGH ME TODAY. AMEN.

By you I can crush a troop, and by my God I can leap over a wall.

PSALM 18:29 NRSV

COMING UNSTUCK

This poor man cried, and the Lord heard him,
and saved him out of all his troubles.

PSALM 34:6 KJV

One author of adventure novels never sits down at the keyboard without his trusty pith helmet at the ready. His two sons, worried at the amount of time he spent staring at a blank computer screen, pooled their resources and bought him the pith helmet for Father's Day.

"Dad, whenever you get stuck," they said, "put on your jungle thinking cap and away you'll go!" The author claims the helmet works, and with it on his head the plot really takes off. It's a tool that has "unstuck" him on more than one occasion.

What has you stuck? A student who won't participate? A parent with unrealistic expectations? A car with a dead battery and one wheel in the grave? Keep your "tools" handy for getting beyond your troubles. Prayer, praise, and Scripture are power tools that have unlocked prison doors, healed physical infirmities, and redeemed men's souls. Is anything too great for God?

One of the apostle Paul's most effective tools was to boast in the Lord. To the Romans, he claimed Jeremiah the prophet's word from God, commanding the wise man to boast that he understands and knows the Lord "who exercises kindness, justice, and righteousness on earth." To know and have access to such a One is to get "unstuck" from the daily difficulties that afflict us and our work.

Toilets flood, noses bleed, math equations defy solution, but God never fails. Lean on Him, watch Him work, give Him glory, and just like ice on bubblegum, you will surely come unstuck.

GRACE FOR TODAY:

When we're stuck and need support, God comes to the rescue.

THAT WHICH IS PRECIOUS

There is no one holy like the LORD.

1 SAMUEL 2:2 NIV

For what would you trade your soul? A trinket? A life? A bargain in which it felt like you got the better end of the deal? It would have to be something you considered precious, no doubt.

The word precious took on a whole new meaning after the release of the *Lord of the Rings* trilogy. Before viewing the series, most of us used the word *precious* in sweet, but rather innocuous ways:

About a newborn baby—"Isn't she precious?"

About a MasterCard moment—"What a priceless [precious] experience!"

About a once-in-a-lifetime memory—"Oh, how precious!"

For Smeagol, the former Hobbit who turned into a hideously evil creature after being captured by the power of the ring, precious became an obsession. The ring itself was precious. Not because of appropriately held sentimental value, as we might value an heirloom or a wedding ring, but because he craved its power.

"Preeeecious!" the crazed Smeagol would howl, evil contorting his features. His obsession cost him his appearance, his reputation, his personality, and ultimately, his life.

> GRACE FOR TODAY:
>
> Because we were precious to Jesus, He sacrificed His life for us, so that we could devote our lives to others.

Scripture uses the word much differently. Peter says that God has given us "his very great and precious promises" (2 Peter 1:4 NIV); He calls us to be holy because we have been redeemed with "the precious blood of Christ" (1 Peter 1:19 NIV). He also reminds us that we are precious to Him. What a thought!

Nothing else must become more precious to us than Christ. He is the reason for all we do, including the extraordinary, precious task of teaching. Of molding and shaping lives. Of placing our finger on the pulse point of the future. Because He is precious to us and we to Him, holiness must become our one magnificent obsession. Nothing else is worth the cost.

THE HIGHEST STANDARD

Strive for the greater gifts. And I will show you a still
more excellent way.

1 CORINTHIANS 12:31 NRSV

Their scores weren't going to affect their chances to attend college, or even their current school standing, but two eighth graders still read ahead in their standardized test booklets, copied the questions, and returned with the next day's answers. When their cheating was discovered, the question fell hard: Why?

A survey of the community revealed the pressures at hand. Administrators, teachers, and parents had emphasized the importance of the tests for months as standards of comparison between schools and communities. Older siblings' diplomas hung in the balance of such scores. Real estate agents pitched the scores to prospective buyers. And the children absorbed it all.

Naturally, cheating is unacceptable, but if you've ever dealt with it, you know there's more at hand, and more at stake, than the act itself. When tests become the sole standard of excellence, the burden crushes everyone involved—students, teachers, and entire schools alike. The reality, nevertheless, is that such tests will be given. What, then, is the true standard of excellence?

God.

You knew that, but how does that knowledge play out at school? Despite all your hard work and preparation, sometimes you don't get the desired results. God, however, doesn't let your imperfection permanently separate you from Him. He alone is truly excellent, truly above all others, and He has wonderful designs in mind for your life. God alone prevents your failures from being final and allows your excellence to reflect His character.

When you regularly strive for moral excellence, and when you recognize and reward it in your students, they'll believe you when you tell them that their very best effort is both expected and all that anyone can ask of them.

GRACE FOR TODAY:

God prevents your failures from being final and
allows your excellence to reflect His character.

The Praise Potential

Now [they] exhorted and strengthened the brethren with many words.

Acts 15:32 NKJV

Mrs. Wright was a veteran teacher, five years from retirement, so when new teachers started at Memorial High, she kept an eye on them. This was Melissa's third year of teaching and her third school assignment, which caused Mrs. Wright some concern.

Throughout the fall semester, Melissa struggled and created quite a quagmire for herself. She was habitually late, frequently at odds with other teachers, and often had a bad attitude toward the principal. Mrs. Wright recognized that Melissa's career as a teacher might be short-lived if the young woman didn't change.

During Christmas break, Mrs. Wright began praying that God would use her to help Melissa, knowing it would be a challenge. The next semester, Mrs. Wright spent more time with Melissa, having lunch with her or sitting by her at teachers' meetings. Slowly, Melissa warmed up to the more experienced teacher.

One afternoon at a faculty meeting, the principal asked for new ideas. Melissa offered one that met with negative reactions and teachers rolling their eyes. Mrs. Wright instinctively discerned Melissa's hurt, and spontaneously replied, "Well, I think it's a good idea!" Melissa's face lit up.

In the days to follow, Mrs. Wright looked for every opportunity to praise Melissa. Some days she had to look hard, but as she affirmed the young teacher, Melissa began to change—first, in small ways, but after several months, in more noticeable ones. By the end of the year, Melissa's hardness seemed to dissipate, and the other teachers were beginning to accept her as a valued friend.

God's Word encourages us that there's power in praise—and praise directed toward people can soften even the hardest heart. Those who choose to bring out the good in others touch the very heart of God.

Grace for Today:

God's praise can bring out the best in us.

A PLACE TO THRIVE

Astronomers talk about a planet's suitability to sustain life based on its location in relation to the star around which it orbits. Too far from its star, and the planet may be too cold and barren to sustain life. Too close to its star, and the planet may be too hot and arid for life to gain a hold.

But if, like Earth, that distance from the star (sun) is just right for life—neither too hot nor too cold—it is said to be located in "the Goldilocks Zone."

Think of your classroom existing in the Goldilocks Zone. All your efforts have gone into creating a visually stimulating environment. It is a warm, inviting place. Your students have the freedom to explore and to discover who they are as individuals. You maintain the right degree of professional detachment, yet it is clear that you care deeply for them and the knowledge you want them to acquire. Children thrive in the Goldilocks Zone because the balance between love,

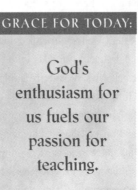

GRACE FOR TODAY:

God's enthusiasm for us fuels our passion for teaching.

acceptance, respect, and independence is carefully maintained.

Jesus strove in the relatively short span of His ministry to show His disciples how to grow a church of such life-giving vitality that even though He ascended into Heaven, it would survive and thrive with the power of the Holy Spirit until His second coming. The book of Acts tells us that such a church from early on was full of prayer and wondrous evidences of God. Every day they met together, ate together, and looked after one another.

In important ways, your classroom is not unlike that church. You pray for your students. You teach them the wonders of the world and how uniquely gifted they are to take their places in that world. You show them how to live in community and to care for their neighbors. Thank God for your Goldilocks Zone where hearts and minds can flourish.

In him was life, and that life was the light of men.

JOHN 1:4 NIV

CREATIVE THINKING

By John C. Maxwell

Everyone faces problems. The ability to creatively find solutions will determine the success or failure of each difficulty.

The Chinese symbol for crisis means danger. It also means opportunity. The key is to use a crisis as an opportunity for change. You'll never succeed if you throw up your hands and surrender. The Greek poet Homer understood the value of a crisis. He wrote, "Adversity has the effect of eliciting talents which in prosperous circumstances would have lain dormant."

Remember the story of the chicken farmer whose land was flooded virtually every spring? Even though the floods caused him horrendous problems, he refused to move. When the waters would back up onto his land and flood his chicken coops, he would race to move his chickens to higher ground. Some years, hundreds of them drowned because he couldn't move them out in time.

One year after suffering heavy losses from a particularly bad flood, he came into the farmhouse and in a voice filled with despair, told his wife, "I've had it! I can't afford to buy another place. I can't sell this one. I don't know what to do!"

His wife calmly replied, "Buy ducks."

Creativity is a trait not always admired by those who don't have it. They interpret creativity and inventiveness as stupidity and impracticality. If they see the creative person as salvageable, they will try to pull him back into the mainstream of thought. He will be told to stay busy, follow the rules, be practical, and not make a fool of himself. Traditional thinkers don't realize that creative thinkers are the geniuses of the world. Had it not been for someone's inventiveness, they might not have jobs![18]

―⚍―

DEAR GOD, YOU ALWAYS HAVE THE ANSWERS TO LIFE'S PROBLEMS. HELP ME TO SEE FROM YOUR PERSPECTIVE THE SITUATION I AM IN, AND GIVE ME CREATIVE SOLUTIONS BY YOUR GRACE. AMEN.

[Jesus said,] "I want you to be smart . . . for what is right—using every adversity to stimulate you to creative survival."

LUKE 16:9 MSG

CHANGE FOR WHAT?

Jesus Christ is the same yesterday and today and for ever.

HEBREWS 13:8 RSV

The only person who likes change is a wet baby. Change is like Heaven; everyone likes the concept, but nobody wants to start the process. We roll our collective eyes, or we giggle, but outside of a few adventurous types, most of us can relate.

And here's what gets us—life is all about change. We are expelled from warm buoyant comfort into a world of bright lights and loud noises. We learn to crawl, and then discontent seeps into tiny fists and knees, so we pull ourselves up and walk, declaring our independence with each wobbly step. Soon after, we run. We enter into formal education, we drive, we graduate, we marry, we procreate, we pursue, we work, we dream, we sleep, we move, and we change. It's inevitable. Still, we stubbornly cling to life as we would have it.

Perhaps we're not too different from two sisters who once discussed how they made Sunday pot roast. Each of them cut up onions, potatoes, and carrots and carefully seasoned the roast, and then both sisters whacked off the ends of the roast, put it all in a covered dish, and placed it in the oven. One day, they asked each other, "Why do you think Mom always cut the ends off the roast?" They called up their mother. Through her laughter she explained, "Because it wouldn't fit in my only pan any other way!"

GRACE FOR TODAY:

God wants us to embrace His changes for our lives.

You've heard it in faculty meetings: Because we've always done it this way. Don't question this. Don't buck the system. Or you have a new principal, fresh out of graduate school, who urges you to come up with three new creative projects every semester. Sigh.

Be the one who's ready and willing to initiate, suggest, and try new things. God just might mold you into the person you've longed to become.

HAVING FUN WITH YOUR MIND

When you eat the labor of your hands, you shall be happy,
and it shall be well with you.

PSALM 128:2 NKJV

Professor Basil L. Gildersleeve of Johns Hopkins University, honored internationally by several organizations and societies as the finest Greek scholar of his time, was once interviewed for *The Saturday Evening Post*. When asked what he considered the highest recognition he had ever received, Professor Gildersleeve replied, "I believe it was when one of my students said, 'Professor, you have so much fun with your own mind!'"

Behavioral scientists have found that people who enjoy their work and consider it meaningful are more productive, more concerned about the quality of their work, and more interested in improving their craft. As they increase their productivity and the quality of their work, greater opportunities for promotion and increased income arise, which often means they enjoy their work even more.

GRACE FOR TODAY:

God wants us to have fun as we teach.

Whether or not your ambitions include rising through the ranks to administration or the ongoing work of becoming the best teacher you can be, you should be having fun. What's better than doing enjoyable work that you feel really matters? The Bible makes it clear that joy is a key component of your relationship with God, and that many blessings come as a result of "the labor of your hands."

Teaching is full of rigors that challenge your enjoyment of the job. Endless meetings, constant grading, peculiar parents, and unsupportive administrators can make your work joyless. Unless you remember that hard times and trials are a way for you to share in Christ's suffering, you may forget that you will also share in His reward.

God had a purpose in making you the way you are, giving you the talents you have, and working through your experiences to shape you. Think of the aspects of teaching that you really enjoy, whatever they are—working with the kids, researching topics of interest, collegiality with other professionals—and go for it!

SILLY WORKS

Truth . . . [is] more than words. Learn how to apply them.
You'll need them throughout your life.

EPHESIANS 6:14, 17 MSG

Every morning before school, Marcie met Suzanne—the school counselor and friend who had led her to the Lord—for prayer. Today as Marcie walked up the steps, Suzanne noticed her friend had been crying.

"What's the matter?" Suzanne asked gently.

"I can't do anything right," Marcie sobbed. "I overslept, didn't have time to feed the kids, and forgot to iron Matt's shirt. We got into a fight and ended up screaming at each other. I'm a horrible person!"

"Sweetie, it's not that bad," Suzanne encouraged. "Coming out of an abusive childhood, you're conditioned to keep doing things the same old way, expecting a different result. In counseling, that's called insanity. Telling yourself the truth is the answer. Do you remember as a little girl in school learning different things by singing, rhyming or playing games?"

Marcie nodded her head.

"Well, silly ways of learning can still work for adults," Suzanne continued. "Believers in Christ are changed as they reprogram themselves with God's Word. He can give you grace for every situation, but He wants you to see life through the filter of His love.

"So I want you to go home and do something silly. Get a coffee filter and write on it scriptures about how God sees and loves you. Color it if you want. Then carry that coffee filter with you to remind yourself to filter everything through God's love. Hold it, wrap it around your cell phone, or clip it on your purse. Just use it to tell yourself the truth."

As a teacher, you often employ fun, creative methods to get through to your students. So if you're struggling, find some fun way to overcome it. Silly works, especially when God anoints it.

GRACE FOR TODAY:

So that we might discover truth, God sometimes employs unexpected methods.

ABCs

God's words are pure words, pure silver words refined seven times in
the fires of His word—kiln, pure on earth as well as in heaven.

PSALM 12:6 MSG

Say amen to the alphabet. Ponder the marvel of just twenty-six little letters that
when combined and recombined reveal the world of wisdom in all its glory.
Form them one way and tears begin to flow. Re-form them another way and laughter
rockets the room. If you love the language, your students will too. If they love the language, there's little they can't do.

Jesus was the Word. By no other name under Heaven can we be saved. No
greater words have been spoken than, "I am the way, the truth, and the life" (John 14:6
NKJV).

In the beginning, God spoke worlds into being. In the end, the Son of God gets
the last word. He who was seated upon the throne told John the Revelator to "Write
this down, for these words are trustworthy, and true." He then pronounced himself the
Alpha and Omega, the first letter and the last, the Beginning and the End.

Say amen to the alphabet. It is your highway into the hearts and heads of your students. Sing, shout, and season your speech with the overflow of your own heart.
Flavor your conversation with grace, and your classroom will raise a fine crop of
words pollinated by spelling bees. Eager wordsmiths are more apt to weed their language gardens of empty words that produce no fruit.

Jesus loved to explain and illustrate the loftier concepts of righteousness and faith
with word pictures and puzzles designed to make people think. Do the same with your
students. Make them reach to understand, stretch for the answers, delight in the sights
and sounds of words.

Say amen to the alphabet!

GRACE FOR TODAY:

God gave us language to communicate
His everlasting love.

THE CHOSEN

Somewhere in the hazy files of childhood memory (or from a more recent TV Land file), you might have stored this scene from an early situation comedy. A young black boy is caught taking something from a store. "My mom's gonna pay you for it, Mister, honest!" Skeptical, the shop owner says, "Yeah, and who's your mother?" Desperate, but plucky, the little boy turns around, points at fair-skinned Marlo Thomas and blurts out, "That girl!" That girl paid for the items. What an unlikely savior!

That story sounds familiar, doesn't it? We were the ones living on borrowed time without any appreciation for our Creator. We were the ones caught red-handed, stealing from the God who owns the cattle on a thousand hills. We were the lost ones, convicting ourselves by our own sins, unable to save ourselves. But then God sent an unlikely Savior.

Instead of choosing to send Jesus in a cloud of glory, riding in on the waves of the accolades, power, and praise He surely deserved, God chose to start Him out just as we began. As a baby. Helpless. Dependent. Fragile. God chose Jesus for the job of rescuing an ungrateful world because He had already chosen you.

When God created Adam and Eve, placing them in the sinless, perfect Garden of Eden, He already knew that things wouldn't stay that way. He loved us anyway. Remember where Scripture first records that Jesus was on the way to save us? It's way back in Genesis! The moment Satan successfully tempted Eve, God emphatically told him that this victory was empty. Hollow. Temporary.

Before the foundation of the world, God chose you. Hold that knowledge close to your heart as you choose to allow Him to complete the good work He began in you. Remember Him while you let Him work through you in your classroom.

> **GRACE FOR TODAY:**
> God chose us as His own dear children before the creation of time.

You are not like that, for you have been chosen by God himself.

1 PETER 2:9 TLB

PAY NOW OR PAY LATER

By John C. Maxwell

The value of a vision is that it encourages you to give up at any moment all that you are in order to receive all that you can become. You will be willing to let go of whatever might keep you from actually realizing that vision. You can probably think of times in your life when this happened to you. Do you remember when you first fell in love with the person you married? All of a sudden, other members of the opposite sex were not that interesting to you anymore. You were willing to trade in the pool for the one.

I have found that you do one of two things in life. You either pay the price now and enjoy later, or you enjoy now and pay the price later. But you will always pay the price. I'm constantly amazed at the shortsightedness of people who are not willing to pay the price now. Some people are shortsighted about their bodies. They're not willing to give up those pleasurable things that are destroying their bodies now in order to gain a few good years later. Some people are shortsighted about their finances. They can't give up any of today's luxuries in exchange for tomorrow's financial security.

Some people are shortsighted spiritually. They are so caught up in the pleasures of today that they can't see the pain of tomorrow: They're not willing to totally sell out for God. They're trying to avoid the price, but the price will always be there. You can either pay it today and enjoy life tomorrow, or you can enjoy life today and pay the price, plus interest, tomorrow. You cannot avoid the price.[19]

—◊—

FATHER, I WANT TO BE WISE AND PAY THE PRICE NOW FOR THE VISION YOU HAVE FOR ME. AT THOSE TIMES WHEN I'M TEMPTED TO TAKE THE EASY ROAD, GIVE ME YOUR GRACE TO HELP ME MAKE GOOD CHOICES. AMEN.

Don't be misled. . . . You will always reap what you sow!

GALATIANS 6:7 NLT

DRAW THEM IN

A cheerful look brings joy to the heart.

PROVERBS 15:30 NIV

Lena Caldwell stood in front of the class. "Children, I know some of you have never loved math, but I'm here to tell you those days are over. I love math. What's more, I guarantee that you will too." Her smile met with looks that told her she was mentally unstable, but she pressed on. "You think I'm nuts, but wait. Who likes to play games?" Hands shot up around the room. Lena then taught them a game—about math, unbeknownst to her students—and they had a blast. Hands shot up again when she asked who had enjoyed it. "Guess what? You just learned about factors."

GRACE FOR TODAY:

God gave us enthusiasm to share His creation with our students.

Enthusiasm is contagious, and it needn't be false. When you are passionate about your subject, when your students see that you find it interesting and that it matters to you, you'll draw them in.

You don't have to "sell" anything; simply share your eagerness, your zeal. If those seem to be lacking, start with a smile. This simple motivational tool accomplishes wonders. And when you can find the humor in your topic, and in everyday situations, you'll magnetize your students' interest like nothing else can.

As a Christian, your passion for life should be evident in all you say and do. After all, you belong to the Lord of the universe, and He has intimate and wonderful plans for your life. The God who created sunflowers and stars loves you as His own child. It's all right to get excited about that!

Teaching is sharing about God's glorious creation, about the history of the dust He made into men. When you feel the power of that in your daily living, through prayer, through His Word, through His Spirit, others will sense something different about you. They may even ask what it is.

ON THE WINGS OF WORSHIP

Your worship must engage your spirit in the pursuit of truth.
That's the kind . . . the Father [looks for]: those who are simply
. . . themselves before him in their worship.

JOHN 4:23 MSG

Want a surefire way to make it through those days when you wake up on the wrong side of the bed? Everyone has them—you oversleep, the kids won't cooperate, you scorch your best slacks, you forget you have carpool. Well, learn to wing it with worship.

The Word exhorts us that God inhabits the praises of His people. That's right—when you worship God, it brings His presence to the forefront of your real-time reality. You don't have to be in church. Worship is an attitude, not an effort, which you're probably more familiar with than you think.

You've seen a couple who is falling in love. They can't get enough of each other. They talk on the phone with nothing to say, just to hear each other's voice or to declare, "I love you." That's what worship is like and the kind of relationship God longs to have with you. He doesn't want you to feel obligated. He wants to share life with you on every level, and like any lover, God wants you to initiate the first move.

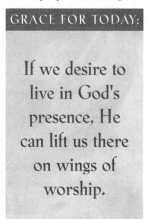

GRACE FOR TODAY:

If we desire to live in God's presence, He can lift us there on wings of worship.

So the next time your day seems to start off wrong, instead of taking it out on your dog and heading to school miserable and defeated, spend some time worshiping God. Whether you sing to Him in the shower for five minutes, listen to a teaching tape while getting dressed, or stick a praise CD in your car stereo on the way to class, the essential thing is to delight in Him and let worship defeat the enemy of your morning. Worship carries you into God's presence where you can rest in the assurance of His love.

A FRAGRANT CLASSROOM

Through us, he brings knowledge of Christ. Everywhere we go, people
breathe in the exquisite fragrance.

2 CORINTHIANS 2:14 MSG

D oes your classroom smell good? The dusty tang of chalk. The inky aroma of
new textbooks. The pungent heat of rubber erasers righting mistakes. Sweaty
children after late spring recess. The giant lilies you brought in as a declaration that
winter's over and new resurrected life has begun.

The happy, industrious classroom has a distinct aroma and flavor all its own. You
have a lot to do with that in the atmosphere you create, the security and cheer that your
room breathes to every student who enters there. Reassurance, anticipation, and bright
prospects smell especially fine to those who arrive hesitant, wounded, frightened, or
dejected. Make your classroom one place where they can inhale certainty, reassurance,
and the anticipation of the good to come. Learning can flourish when the air is sweet
with promise.

When Mary poured expensive perfume on the feet of Jesus, Scripture tells us that
the house was filled with fragrance. That is a lovely picture of what happens when you
enter your classroom in His name and dedicate the day in service to Christ. It is your
sacrifice to the Lord, and when you give your students your best, that gift rises up to
Heaven and becomes a sweet aroma in the nostrils of God.

Let your presence make a child's day. Let it telegraph faith, hope, and love. Let it
saturate the beautiful space you share with your students and surround them with life
and the vision of a better day.

Christ is our Rose of Sharon. That highland region in the Holy Land is sweetly
scented with spring flowers, and Christ is the sweet scent of eternal life in us. Allow
Him to bloom within your heart today and permeate your classroom with the sweet
smell of grace.

GRACE FOR TODAY:

We can bring the fragrance of God's presence into our
classroom and bless our students' lives.

WHAT'S THE POINT?

God gives those who please him wisdom, knowledge, and joy.

ECCLESIASTES 2:26 TLB

A low rumble begins at the back of the classroom; it's the distant thunder of collective student discontent. It is today's echo of that notorious song popularized by Pink Floyd in the 1980s that shouted to leave those kids alone because they didn't "need no education."

"Why do we have to know this stuff?"

"Come on! When will I ever actually use this?"

"This is boring!"

"This stuff happened too long ago. Who cares?"

"What's the point?"

Maybe you've asked the same questions yourself: I'm going to teach English literature. How's learning to play tennis in a required P.E. class going to help me with that? I'm a kindergarten teacher, for Pete's sake. Why do I need physics? Maybe you got the standard answer: "We want all our graduates to have a well-rounded education." *I'm getting well-rounded just from eating at the university cafeteria,* you thought wryly.

But if we belong to the Master Teacher, the instigator of physics, the One who gifted us with the ability to craft words into literary works, we learn for a higher purpose. We glorify our Creator when we delight in all that He left for us to discover. Such enthusiasm for learning can ignite an equal passion in our students.

But to effectively communicate to students that what they are learning is significant, you must first show them that they themselves are significant. Care about them, not just about a set of objectives. Show interest in their hobbies, their relationships, their fears, and their funny bones! Be available. Be authentic. Be awed. You get to teach creations of the Creator!

GRACE FOR TODAY:

Our Creator delights in us as we eagerly learn about His creation.

BEING THERE

Perpetua and Felicity stood before the throng in Rome awaiting their destiny. Under Emperor Septimus Severus' persecution, they had joined the growing number of Christians facing execution for their beliefs. Technically, Felicity was Perpetua's slave, but they had experienced the joys of young motherhood together, and with the indissoluble bond of their sisterhood, they had strengthened and encouraged one another. With a final kiss, together they met the end of their earthly lives at the hands of gladiators. Many in the crowd were converted, neither the first nor the last to be so inspired by the fearless joy exhibited by the two friends.

In few other professions are you so in the crux of people's changing lives as when you are a teacher. In the educational arena, young people experience the quest for hard-earned knowledge, the effects of security or vulnerability in their families, and the joy and sorrow of friendships won and lost. It's not a challenge for the dispassionate or the faint of heart.

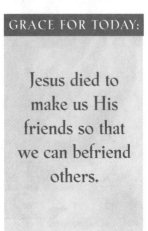

GRACE FOR TODAY:

Jesus died to make us His friends so that we can befriend others.

You can see the value of having a reliable friend with whom to share this calling. Because you're a product of your own education, upbringing, and relationships, you need at least one person who lifts your spirits just by being there, who is honest with you when no one else can or will be.

All true friendships involve an element of sacrifice and the desire to see the other person better off. Ruth left her people to support Naomi. Jonathan saved David's life at the cost of his own throne. Jesus endured the Cross to bridge the gap between you and God. The Bible says if you want a friend like that, you must first be a friend like that. Ask God to be let you be that person for someone and to provide such a friend for you.

Friends come and friends go, but a true friend sticks by you like family.

PROVERBS 18:24 MSG

NOTHING TO LOSE

By John C. Maxwell

I love the story about the old farmer who sat on the steps of his tumble-down shack, chewing on a stem of grass. A passerby stopped and asked if he might have a drink of water. Wishing to be sociable, the stranger engaged the farmer in some conversation. "How is your cotton crop this year?"

"Ain't got none," replied the farmer.

"Didn't you plant any cotton?" asked the passerby.

"Nope," said the farmer, " 'fraid of boll weevils."

"Well," asked the newcomer, "how's your corn doing?"

"Didn't plant none," replied the farmer, " 'fraid there wasn't going to be enough rain."

"Well," asked the inquisitive stranger, "what did you plant?"

"Nothing," said the farmer, "I just played it safe."

A lot of well-intentioned people live by the philosophy of this farmer and never risk upsetting the apple cart. They would prefer to "play it safe." These people will never know the thrill of vic-tory, because to win a victory one must risk a failure.

C. T. Studd made a great statement about risk-taking: "[Why] are gamblers for gold so many and gamblers for God so few?" This is the same missionary who, when cautioned against returning to Africa because of the possibility of his martyrdom, replied, "Praise God, I've just been looking for a chance to die for Jesus!" How can a guy like that fail? He has everything to win and nothing to lose.[20]

—⁂—

HEAVENLY FATHER, I KNOW YOU HAVE GOOD PLANS FOR ME, BUT SOME-TIMES I'M AFRAID OF TRYING NEW THINGS, TAKING RISKS. SOMETIMES THIS SPILLS OVER TO THE CLASSROOM, STI-FLING MY CREATIVITY. YOUR PROMISE TO ALWAYS BE WITH ME GIVES ME COURAGE. GRANT ME YOUR GRACE AND FILL ME WITH YOUR PEACE AS I WALK THROUGH THE DOORS OF OPPOR-TUNITY THAT YOU OPEN FOR ME. AMEN.

[The Lord says,] "Do not fear, for I am with you; do not anxiously look about you, for I am your God. I will strengthen you, surely I will help you, Surely I will uphold you with My righteous right hand."

ISAIAH 41:10 NASB

GOSSIP'S STING

He who covers a transgression seeks love,
but he who repeats a matter separates friends.

PROVERBS 17:9 NKJV

Megan arrived at school early to have time for coffee. In the teachers' lounge, a group of friends was engrossed in conversation.

"Megan, we just heard Nicole is expecting, and Andrea said that Mr. Bishop, the physics teacher, is the father," Carrie said, coaxing her to join them.

Megan, disinterested, continued fixing her coffee.

Andrea approached Megan. "Didn't you hear us? I didn't even know Nicole was dating."

Megan just smiled and left the lounge. "See you guys later. I need to get ready for class."

Andrea followed her down the hall. "Megan, wait up! Why is it every time we discuss another teacher you always take off?"

"Well, to be honest," Megan said, "I wouldn't call it discussing; I'd call it gossip."

"So what's wrong with a little gossip?" Andrea asked. "It's probably true."

"I learned a valuable lesson a few years ago when I went through a divorce," Megan replied. "My ex-husband didn't want to look bad at church so he shared bogus information as a 'prayer request' with a friend. As a result, on my daughter's twelfth birthday, not one of her friends showed up for her party. By then, the gossip had spread throughout the church. After my children and I suffered because of needless gossip, I made a decision that day I'd never be a party to it again."

Gossip is probably commonplace in most schools, but Christians have a choice whether or not to join in. Your fellow teachers were created by God, just like you, and He cares deeply about them and their needs. You may be the only light shining in a dark place, so shine bright and squelch the fires of gossip.

GRACE FOR TODAY:

God calls us to be peacemakers to silence the clamor of gossip.

THE LINES ARE OPEN

Look to the LORD and his strength; seek his face always.

PSALM 105:4 NIV

Singer Joshua Williams in his beautiful song titled "Sail into Heaven" reminds us that whenever we call out to the Lord from the earth, a divine response is set in motion above. His imagery includes angels coming down to hear even as the soul of the prayer "soars on the wings of time." He urges each of us in the course of a day to seek out a quiet place to pray, and by so doing, to keep those boundless lines of communication open.

King David ached for God continually. He used passionate terminology to express his longing for the Father. He spoke of how "my soul thirsts for you" and "how earnestly I seek you." But like ours, his thoughts strayed, his eyes strayed, his heart strayed. Too long without praying and he soon plotted the demise of an innocent man. Don't allow the stuff of life to block communication and keep you from God. This is especially important during the day when distractions run rampant.

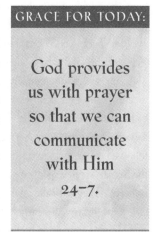

GRACE FOR TODAY:

God provides us with prayer so that we can communicate with Him 24-7.

Just as you note the emergency exits on an airplane before takeoff, scout out a quiet refuge or two at school before the year gets underway. It might be a location as mundane as the back stairs landing or even in your car. Not very glamorous—until you remember that you are having a few supernatural moments with the Lord of the universe!

Not practical, you say. You're fortunate to snag ten minutes to visit the restroom. God understands. In solitude at the bathroom sink, thank Him for His faithfulness, ask His blessing on the student who came to school in tears, or praise Him for the field trip that still needs chaperones. Jesus prayed everywhere, be it in a boat or in agony on the Cross. Don't be caught with your communication lines down.

THE CARE AND FEEDING OF LAUGHTER

Then was our mouth filled with laughter.

PSALM 126:2 KJV

L aughter is a great equalizer, stress reducer, ice breaker, and health aid. It allows us to accept fortune and misfortune with equal grace. Laughter tones the abdomen, releases seratonin in the brain, and has been known to reduce pain. Not bad for a free commodity, huh?

The trick is remembering to use it, cultivating opportunities to laugh, and feeding it with plenty of humor and good grace. Watch some old reruns of *I Love Lucy* or *Welcome Back, Kotter*. Get a flip deck with a guaranteed laugh for each day. Pray for it! Yep, ask the God who made the hyena's laugh to grant you some of your own.

James Dobson, founder of Focus on the Family, tells the story of his accidental first meeting with President Reagan, after Dobson and a friend received invitations to one of Reagan's inaugural balls. Having collected their coats early to avoid the rush, they saw eight to ten Secret Service men running toward the stairwell. On impulse, they followed, came face-to-face with the President, and trailed him to the podium! When the Secret Service agents discovered the security breach, they warned them to "Get out of here!" They took the advice with humility and great humor!

One first-year teacher determined that her classroom would operate perfectly. She allowed no rule to be broken and followed protocol to the letter. So on the day of the first unplanned tornado drill, she efficiently confused the fire and tornado drills, moved her students to the hallway, lined them up in rows, and smugly folded her arms. That lasted until the fire chief asked her how she planned to explain to the parents why only her students were toasted heaps in Upper A Hall! She learned to tell the story herself and laughed good-naturedly as others told it about her.

As a teacher, learn to laugh at yourself!

GRACE FOR TODAY:

When we need to reduce our stress, God gives us laughter.

WHO HOLDS THE FUTURE

I pray that your hearts will be flooded with light so that you can understand the wonderful future he has promised to those he called.

EPHESIANS 1:18 NLT

Corrie ten Boom placed her future in the hands of God, and her faith thrived in the horrid environs of Nazi-controlled Ravensbruck. Jim Elliot knew his hope couldn't be lost even as his life ebbed through the wounds inflicted on him by the Auca Indians he had come to evangelize. While in chains, Paul spoke to the church at Philippi of his "earnest expectation and hope" that everything he had endured would be used to glorify Christ. For these and many others, it was enough to know that God held the future.

One of teaching's greatest and most rewarding challenges is helping students find the balance between ensuring happiness to make life enjoyable and developing the character to make life meaningful. At every age and with every child, boundaries and responsibilities change, but their most basic needs don't. They need from you the same things that you require from God: faith, hope, and love.

A critical feature of being a Christian is having definite beliefs about the future. God knows the end from the beginning, and He has established a plan that includes you and everyone else. It's a sure thing that He has included your work with children in His plan, and He will help you accomplish what needs to be done, no matter how difficult it is for you to see what might happen next.

Your investment in the lives of young people is a vision for the future. Because of your efforts and prayers for them, seeds have been planted that will bear fruit if watered. Because of their interactions with you, you have been blessed by and prepared for God's continuing work in your life. How wonderful, how secure, it is to know that God is in control!

GRACE FOR TODAY:

God knows the end from the beginning, and He has established a plan for all of us.

FEELING DEFEATED?

John stuck his head around the door of Ms. Walker's office. "Just thought I'd say hey." Seeing her furiously stuffing her briefcase, he asked, "What's the matter?"

"Nothing a new career wouldn't solve," Ms. Walker said. "I just came from the dean's office, and another student transferred out, complaining—you know—I'm too hard; the workload's too demanding. A student I've been helping since the beginning of the semester!"

Ring any bells for you? Have you ever had days when you wondered why you were teaching? Ever poured your heart into your students and questioned whether it was worth it?

As a teacher, you're only human. Because you invest so much time in your students, it can be personally defeating when students complain, don't respond, or constantly have an attitude. It's times like these when you need to hook up to the modem of God's grace. Without Him, you'll be susceptible to continual defeat—feeling unqualified, feeling like you've failed, feeling like you've missed your calling.

The reality is that you're only a vessel—a vessel for God to use as He wills. Your job is to follow the direction of the Holy Spirit. It's His responsibility to deal with people's hearts—not yours. Paul encourages us in Scripture that some may plant and some may water, but the results are always up to God.

Today, breathe a prayer of release: "God, I turn my students over to You. Whatever happens to them is Your responsibility. I commit to do my best and leave the results up to You."

From now on, when those troublesome students get to you, trust God instead of thinking that you've failed.

> **GRACE FOR TODAY:**
>
> ## God's presence defeats our feelings of failure.

Even though . . . you . . . endure many trials for a while, these trials . . .
only . . . test your faith, to show that it is strong and pure.

1 PETER 1:6–7 NLT

EXACTLY LIKE HIM

By John MacArthur Jr.

When Peter was filled with the Holy Spirit, he had the same power as when he was standing next to Jesus Christ himself! Now here's something exciting! Do you know what the Spirit-filled life is? It is living every moment as though you are standing in the presence of Jesus! Not too complicated, is it? Someone might think I am confusing the issue because the Holy Spirit and Christ are different. But by what name does Paul call the Holy Spirit? "The Spirit of Christ" (Romans 8:9 NIV). Jesus said that when He went away, He would send allos "another" Comforter (John 14:16 NIV). There are two words in the Greek for the English word another: heteros and allos. Heteros means "another of a different kind," and allos means "another of exactly the same kind"!

Here is my Bible. If I said to you, "Give me allos biblos," you would have to give me another Bible exactly like mine, with all of my markings, cuts, and cracks. This is allos. When Jesus said, "I am going to send you another Comforter," He said allos, another "exactly like Me." The Spirit-filled life is nothing more than living in the conscious presence of the indwelling Christ.[21]

—⁂—

HEAVENLY FATHER, THERE IS NO GREATER PRIVILEGE THAN FOR ME TO BE LIKE CHRIST—IN MY PERSONAL LIFE AND AS A TEACHER. NOT ONLY DOES THAT GLORIFY YOU, IT MAKES MY LIFE AND PROFESSION A GRAND ADVENTURE, WITH YOU AT THE CENTER. FILL ME WITH YOUR SPIRIT SO THAT I MAY BE "EXACTLY" AS JESUS WAS WHEN HE WALKED THE EARTH. THINK THROUGH MY MIND, SEE THROUGH MY EYES, SPEAK THROUGH MY LIPS, HEAL THROUGH MY HANDS. WHEN OTHERS—INCLUDING MY STUDENTS AND OTHER FACULTY MEMBERS—SEE ME, LET THEM SEE YOU. AMEN.

Be filled with the Spirit. Speak to one another with psalms, hymns and spiritual songs. Sing and make music in your heart to the Lord.

EPHESIANS 5:18-19 NIV

A SATISFYING BALANCE

A devout life does bring wealth, but it's the rich simplicity of being yourself before God.

1 TIMOTHY 6:6 MSG

Contentment is an odd animal. It is desirable because it makes you comfortable in your own skin, pleased with the accomplishments that you and others have achieved, and grateful to God for the many blessings that led to your contentment in the first place.

On the other hand, lack of contentment, dissatisfaction with the status quo, has resulted in some of the greatest explorations, discoveries, and inventions of all time. It has changed laws for the better, voted scoundrels out of office, and brought criminals to justice. If there's a rock in your shoe, you're going to do something about it.

Finding the critical balance in education between the joy of teaching and the need for educational reform is no easy task. Stopping the schoolyard bully from punching his smaller classmate is the right thing to do. But what about delaying the start of school because your pay and benefits don't measure up?

When the apostle Paul said for the believer to be content in all circumstances, he was not suggesting that you not lobby for change where change is needed. In a shipwreck, as he would well know, you don't go down with the ship if you have the strength to swim to shore. Yes, you're grateful for the sea and the life it provides, grateful for the ship and the safe passage that it once gave. But if the two are now conspiring to drown you, think how much more grateful you'll be when you kiss the beach. Swim like there's no tomorrow!

Study Christ's example of how a devoted world-changer prays and acts. Seek Him for wisdom. Champion your students. Encourage your colleagues. And above all else, thank God for the teacher's calling.

GRACE FOR TODAY:

God teaches us to be content in all circumstances.

TRUE LOVE

Greater love hath no man than this,
that a man lay down his life for his friends.

JOHN 15:13 KJV

I f you've ever been in love, then you remember that breathless, giddy, head–over–heels, stomach–clenching, dry–mouthed feeling. It's exhilarating! It's exhausting. It fades.

We place great premium on the emotional side of love. The lyrics to popular love songs of every era bear this out. But no matter how ridiculous the words, we still hum along in our heads. Why? Because no other emotion makes us feel so wonderful, yet has the potential to hurt and wound in proportion.

Despite the power of human love, it will never surpass God's love for us. The desire, indeed the desperation, for that kind of love is what drives people to seek it in the most unlikely places. You see it in faculty members who are living together. You observe it in students wrapped around each other in the halls. Eventually the holy awareness that something we crave is glaringly lacking is what drives us to God. It makes us long for the Father. It leads us back Home.

Remember the prodigal son? He once knew that kind of love, yet threw it all away to squander his early "inheritance" on riotous living. (See Luke 15.) It sounds adventurous, kind of fun even, doesn't it? Ah, until we recall that it tells about the son dining with pigs and longing for home. But the kind of love that would send a Son to a Cross wooed him home, and a party like no other began. Oh, how Jesus loves you! How can you know? Because one day, He threw a party for you.

GRACE FOR TODAY:

When we choose to love God, He and all of Heaven rejoice.

BECAUSE IT MATTERS

Show yourself in all respects a model of good works,
and in your teaching show integrity.

TITUS 2:7 NRSV

The tension grew as the championship soccer game neared its conclusion. The teams had battled for nearly eighty goalless minutes when one of Westside's defenders appeared to handle the ball in the penalty box. The referee hesitated to give the call, but the action stopped as Clarkston's players demanded a penalty kick and Westside's players protested their innocence.

Jim Ashcraft watched the tumult from the sidelines, then saw his team's captain push his Westside teammates back and approach the referee. A moment later, the ref awarded the kick, which Clarkston converted to win the game. The captain caught Jim's eye and tapped his own wrist. He had illegally touched the ball. Afterwards, Jim hugged him. "It's all right, son. You did what you had to do, and I'm proud of you." A small smile broke through the boy's pained expression. "Thanks, Dad."

Everything you do matters. How could it be otherwise? You serve the God who created the universe with precision and forethought, who knows the number of your days, who is able and willing to make everything work out for the best because He loves you. Whether in the spotlight or out, you know that God expects you to do what's right, and that He will help you do it.

As a teacher, you have an amazing opportunity to display your integrity with maximum impact. Only their parents could have a greater effect on the kids you work with every day. When you respond to adversity with faith, to people you don't like with the love of Christ, it matters. When your students see the signs of your character, your consistency and honesty, your compassion and fairness, they'll see that there is a right way to do things.

GRACE FOR TODAY:

When God is the reason for everything you do, He
will uphold your integrity in front of others.

THE GOD WHO SEES

[Paul said,] "Am I now seeking human approval, or God's approval?
Or am I trying to please people? If I were still pleasing people,
I would not be a servant of Christ."

GALATIANS 1:10 NRSV

Have you thought how the glory of God leaves its mark on the world? It's all around you—the great cathedrals of Europe, towering monuments, graceful sculptures. But think for a moment. Do you know who sculpted Mount Rushmore, who designed the Empire State Building, who built the U.S. Capitol? Today the names of Borglum, Shreve, and Bulfinch mean little to most Americans. However, each of them spent endless amounts of time on details that they're credited little for today.

Take for instance, the Empire State Building. Constructed at the height of the Depression, its towering presence still glows across the New York skyline. This great feat was designed by R. H. Shreve and completed in only fourteen months. Today, however, you can't find a biography of his life or even Shreve's first name on the Internet.

So why is this trivia important to a teacher? Like teachers, these men made donations that continue to bless our country, although little is remembered about them. Teachers are one of the largest groups contributing to society, who make tremendous sacrifices of time and energy for little credit.

Like Gutzon Borglum, who spent fourteen years of his life sculpting Mount Rushmore, you need to recognize today that God is Jehovah Roi, the God who sees! God sees you today, as you give your heart and soul to teach and nurture His precious children, and it gives Him pleasure!

So if there are areas in which you are struggling or places where you're not seeing results, reflect on the beautiful things in this world that glorify Him, and know you're on that list. You are leaving a mark! What you are contributing might not be remembered by the world, but it counts significantly with the God who sees!

GRACE FOR TODAY:

God approves of who you are, not just what you do.

A CATCHY EXPRESSION

A major state university produced an advertising campaign featuring thirty-second radio spots. The effectiveness of the message was not in the slick production, an offer of deep discounts, or grand promises that would require a genie to fulfill. No, the power of these ads was that they centered on two of the most powerful words in the English language: thank you.

The speaker in one of the ads was a senior studying chemistry and oceanography. He was an assistant to a team of scientists conducting research into the effects of oxygen content on marine life in a dying body of water once rich in ocean life. You can sense the student's excitement in both his tone and choice of words. "This is my passion . . . ," he said, "and I'd like to express my gratitude to the people (of the state)." He was thanking them for supporting the univer-

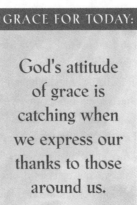

GRACE FOR TODAY:

God's attitude of grace is catching when we express our thanks to those around us.

sity and making the research possible.

A sincere "thank you" can be a scarcity in the world of high-pressure, performance-centered education. Certainly, you should make "please" and "thank you" central to good manners and respect in the classroom, but how often do your students hear you express your gratitude to the administration, the custodial staff, or the front-office personnel? For students to put gratitude into action with each other, they need to see and hear it in action among their adult role models.

It's truly catching. The more you honor your colleagues with your thankfulness, the more thankfulness they will express—and the more likely you will be to express praise and thanks to God above. Start your own positive "ad campaign" of thanks, and watch just how boundless "grace expressed" really is.

Gracious speech is like clover honey—good taste to the soul,
quick energy for the body.

PROVERBS 16:24 MSG

STUDENT OF THE WORD

By John MacArthur Jr.

Let me share how I study the Bible, and how the Bible has come alive to me. I began in 1 John. One day I sat down and read all five chapters straight through. It took me twenty minutes. The next day, I sat down and read 1 John straight through again. I did this for thirty days. Do you know what happened at the end of thirty days? I knew what was in 1 John.

Next, I went to the gospel of John. I read the first seven chapters for thirty days, the next seven for the next thirty days, and the last seven for thirty days. In ninety days, I had read the entire gospel of John thirty times. Where does it talk about the Good Shepherd? Chapter 1, right-hand column, starts in the middle.

Where does it talk about the vine and the branches? Chapter 15. Where does it talk about Jesus' friends? Chapter 15, over in the next column and a little farther down. Where does it talk about Jesus' arrest in the garden? John 18. The restoration of Peter? John 21. The woman at the well? John 4. The Bread of Life? John 6. Nicodemus? John 3. The wedding at Cana? John 2.

You might say, "My, are you smart!" No, I am not smart. I read it thirty times. Even I can get it then! Isaiah said to learn "precept upon precept, line upon line, . . . here a little, and there a little" (see Isaiah 28:10–13). Then you have hidden it in your heart. After a while you are no longer a concordance cripple![22]

―――

FATHER, YOU WERE SO GRACIOUS TO HAVE GIVEN US YOUR WRITTEN WORD. I WANT IT TO BE A PART OF ME. AS I AM FAITHFUL TO HIDE IT IN MY HEART, I PRAY THAT IT WILL TRANSFORM ME AND MAKE ME A FRUITFUL DISCIPLE. AMEN.

Study to shew thyself approved unto God, a workman that needeth not to be ashamed, rightly dividing the word of truth.

2 TIMOTHY 2:15 KJV

THE RESTLESS HEART

I have learned the secret of contentment in every situation.

PHILIPPIANS 4:12 TLB

At one time or another, we all have a restless heart. We don't necessarily want one, and sometimes we go so far as to promise ourselves we won't allow it anymore. We are contented with what we have—until we compare it to someone else's job, money, position, awards, planning period, or course selection.

We revel in what we have until that glossy new magazine arrives in the mail, featuring better cars and newer homes with custom features, fabulous landscaping, and a home theater. We count our blessings until someone else seems to have more of them. What's worse is that occasionally someone who does not follow Christ seems blessed more than we are. Unfair!

Conveniently, we forget that Scripture tells us that the rain falls on the just and the unjust; we don't like to remember that we live in a fallen world and sometimes things aren't equitable. We cry out to God and follow up with a litany of the many ways we have served Him. So, how do we tame this restless heart? With the lasso of contentment. How do we wield this lasso? Through the hard work of surrender.

> **GRACE FOR TODAY:**
>
> When we remember God's blessings, He makes us content.

The apostle Paul reminds us that contentment is something for which he had to work. He learned it. Most of us, including our students, simply don't learn tough lessons the first time they're presented. Thus learning implies an ongoing, continuous-tense verb. But thanks to a gracious Heavenly Father, we are allowed to ask.

Keep your eyes on your own list of blessings, but keep your heart turned outward toward the ever-present needs of others. Most of all, lift your life upward, seeking His will, His guidance, and the assurance that we can relax contented in His good, pleasing, and perfect plans for us.

FIRST THINGS FIRST

Steep your life in God-reality, God-initiative, God-provisions.
Don't worry about missing out. You'll find all your everyday
human concerns will be met.

MATTHEW 6:33 MSG

Tracy hustled through her busy morning, cooking breakfast, pulling the kids' previously packed sack lunches out of the fridge, putting stamps on the mail, setting aside a plastic bag of used kitty litter to toss in the dumpster, and stuffing some gym clothes in another grocery bag for an afternoon workout. She almost forgot her satchel filled with last night's graded essays but managed to get out the door and into her classroom with five minutes to spare.

After a busy school day, Tracy looked forward to a stress-relieving spin class. She plopped down on a locker-room bench and opened the grocery bag, only to be greeted by a mound of ripe Kitty Fresh. She sighed, hoping the garbage man hadn't picked up the trash with her sweatpants yet.

GRACE FOR TODAY:

God wants time spent with Him to be our first priority.

Busyness is a virtue in today's world. People who always seem to be able to take on one more task are admired. If you've ever multitasked on a superhuman level, it's a gratifying feeling that you're the only one who can get it done, that people are depending on your reliability.

So what's wrong with being busy? In and of itself, nothing. Being active and contributing capably add enjoyment to life. But there are downsides. Consider what often gets scrapped in favor of the next stress-adding task: eating well, getting enough sleep, and exercising. Your physical health is compromised.

More importantly, what about your spiritual well-being? Isn't your time with God in prayer or reading the Bible the first thing to get axed when you're busy? Does the sense of validation you get from overachieving replace the sense of your inherent value as God's beloved child? Take time to reevaluate your priorities. Make sure all of the things you're saying yes to aren't causing you to say no to God.

CUTTING IN LINE

[Share] the word; be instant in season [and] out of season.

2 TIMOTHY 4:2 KJV

Tiffany volunteered to get donuts for the teachers' in-service meeting when the secretary realized she'd forgotten to buy them. Since the meeting started in thirty minutes, Tiffany rushed to the market so she could return to school quickly. At the store, she quickly grabbed several boxes of donuts and rushed to check out, only to find just two cashiers open and long lines at each. Just as Tiffany approached the back of the line, a lady cut in front of her.

Aggravated, Tiffany shifted from one foot to another as the line moved at a snail's pace. To pass the time, people started chatting. Tiffany overheard "Connie Cut-in-Line," the woman who had behaved so rudely moments earlier, asking the couple in front of her if they were involved in a church. Noticing their little girl, she began telling them all about her church's children's program and about their couples' care group. After they checked out, "Connie Cut-in-Line" made arrangements to meet them in her church's parking lot the following Sunday.

Unbelievable! She cuts in front of me and then starts talking about God, Tiffany thought. Then God nudged her, *But you weren't going to talk to them about Me.*

Lord, You're right! Tiffany answered. I come in contact with so many people every day and never even think to start a conversation about You. You had to send someone You could trust to plant a seed, and having her cut in front of me was just part of Your plan!

So often as a teacher, you're rushed and focused because you have so many responsibilities. But God desires for you to always be walking in His peace so that if He chooses to speak through you, you'll feel His prompting and be available.

GRACE FOR TODAY:

If we make ourselves available, God can touch the people in our lives with His love.

PUT THE "RIGHT" IN RIGHTEOUS

*True instruction was in his mouth and unrighteousness
was not found on his lips.*

MALACHI 2:6 NASB

A children's author wanted to write a book about a little girl who lost her first four teeth. In order to make the book as accurate as possible, the author first consulted a dentist who coached her in the exact location of those teeth and the sequence in which they were likely to fall out.

In the story, the girl named the lost teeth after the things she bit into that had caused each of them to fall out. The fourth tooth was to be the victim of an animal shaped like an alligator from a box of Barnum's Animal Crackers. This gave the careful author pause. The alligator was shown on the box, but could she recall ever actually seeing an alligator cookie on the inside?

The one box she had at home contained no alligators. So the author bought all the boxes of animal crackers her local supermarket carried and dumped them out. No alligators. She called Nabisco, Inc., manufacturers of the crackers, and although the head office was certain there were alligators in the box, the director of public relations double-checked and learned that because the alligators were prone to breakage on the assembly line, they had, in fact, been discontinued.

How careful are you to get it right? To what lengths will you go to verify what you teach or to pin down a rumor that, unchecked, could slander a colleague or give a false picture of a student's family? How much time and effort do you devote to your relationship with God so that your teaching and all of the rest of your life ring true?

It's never too late to get the facts right, or to restore your connection with the Lord. First things first. A righteous reputation makes you strong; the stronger you are, the more your classroom is blessed.

GRACE FOR TODAY:

When we mirror the grace of God, He will give us credibility with our students.

THE COMPETITION

Perhaps something was left out of our collective college educations: a course on human relationships and the taming of our pride. It might have been called "How to Get Along with Others 101." Oh, we learned about it in kindergarten, but then as we matured, we promptly forgot. Occasionally, even teachers need a review.

The six most important words: "I admit I made a mistake."

The five most important words: "You did a good job."

The four most important words: "What is your opinion?"

The three most important words: "If you please."

The two most important words: "Thank you."

The one most important word: "We."

The least important word: "I."

What about you? How often are you using those phrases? Remembering your manners? Extending simple courtesies? Going all out for someone else? Knocking yourself out on a project without caring who gets the credit? Or do pride and self-interest keep rearing their ugly heads in your life?

Challenge yourself today. Keep tally marks of every time you say or think the word I. Add to those tallies a line for every time you are tempted (or give in) to interject a story of your own into conversation. Write still another for every time you participate in a conversation jump-rope style—you know, where you wait for an opening in the conversation so you can hop in!

Challenge your students to do the same as they work in small groups, pass to different classes, or talk with their friends.

Then end the exercise by writing one or two thank-you notes to others, particularly to those people who are responsible for having shaped your talents, encouraged your dreams, and cheered you toward your goals. You'll thank God, of course, and you just might find that one note will be written to a teacher.

> **GRACE FOR TODAY:**
>
> When we acknowledge everything comes from God, He can put our pride in its place.

By pride comes nothing but strife, but with the well-advised is wisdom.

PROVERBS 13:10 NKJV

THE HAPPIEST PEOPLE IN THE WORLD

By John C. Maxwell

Who are the happiest people in the world? Those who are living out their dreams. In giving themselves to something bigger than they are, they're giving themselves the impetus to rise above their problems. If you want to know real happiness, dream a dream that is bigger than you are; find something you can lose your life in.

When I counsel people, I find that their number–one problem is usually that they've lost their dreams, their goals, their purpose. When you lose a dream or your purpose in your marriage, you lose your marriage. When you lose your purpose for your health, you die.

Think of the great people who continued to pursue their dreams into old age. Think of Moses, who at eighty years of age led 3.5 million people out of captivity. Or Caleb, who at eighty–five years of age said, "Give me that mountain." Or Colonel Sanders, who at seventy years of age discovered "finger–lickin' good" chicken. Or Ray Kroc, who after seventy introduced a Big Mac to the world. Then there's Casey Stengel, who at seventy–five became the manager of the Yankees baseball team. And George Washington Carver, who at eighty–one became head of the Agriculture Department. There's Thomas Edison, who at eighty–five invented the mimeograph machine; and John Wesley, who was still traveling on horseback and preaching at age eighty–eight.

It's the dream that keeps us young; it's the vision that keeps us going.[23]

—◊—

FATHER, I WANT TO BE ONE OF THOSE HAPPY PEOPLE LIVING THEIR DREAM. FORGIVE ME FOR THE TIMES I'VE LOST SIGHT OF WHY I BECAME A TEACHER. REKINDLE THE VISION YOU PUT IN MY HEART SO LONG AGO, AND FILL ME WITH YOUR GRACE TO BE THE TEACHER THAT YOU KNOW I CAN BE. AMEN.

Do not cast away your confidence, which has great reward. For you have need of endurance, so that after you have done the will of God, you may receive the promise.

HEBREWS 10:35–36 NKJV

SOWING SEEDS OF CHANGE

Anxiety weighs down the human heart, but a good word cheers it up.

PROVERBS 12:25 NRSV

Tony took Emma by the hand and helped her up, mindful of the bright red abrasion etched into her knee. "Wow, that's quite a scrape you've got there," he murmured. The small girl pushed her bangs out of her face and nodded, a tear slowly rolling down one cheek. Tony knelt in front of her. "I'll bet Mark didn't mean to bump you like that. I don't think he saw you." Emma's lip quivered.

Tony leaned in and whispered behind his hand, "Sometimes boys are like that—they run around like headless chickens." He pumped his arms like wings a few times and made a silly, quiet chicken noise. Emma's smile started in her eyes and then slowly spread to the corners of her mouth. "Let's go get that cut cleaned up," Tony said, "and then we'll see if we can help Mark find his chicken head before recess ends."

> **GRACE FOR TODAY:**
>
> God extended His kindness toward us by sending Jesus to earth.

Kindness doesn't result from being better than everyone else but from the understanding that God, who had no reason to do so other than His love for you, extended kindness to you by sending Jesus to earth. Seeking to cheer up others is the natural response to the blessings God has given you, so that if you somehow manage to lift their burden a little they might ask you why you bothered.

Look for opportunities to show some form of kindness today. In fact, think of yourself as God's ambassador at your school. It's the little things that have the largest impact, the kind word spoken at the right time, the reassuring smile during moments of anxiety, the open-door policy that might only be used a few times a year. Sincere kindness goes against the grain, sowing seeds of change and reaping a new outlook on life.

A Schedule for Disaster

Come to Me, all you who . . . are . . . overburdened,
and I will . . . refresh your souls.

Matthew 11:28 AMP

As a busy teacher, do you ever operate out of the Martha syndrome? Scripture says that Mary couldn't pull herself away from Jesus, hanging on His every word. In contrast, Martha scurried about making preparations for the big feast. Mary sat at Jesus' feet until Martha collided with disaster and finally whined, "Lord, don't You care that Mary has left me to do all the work myself? Tell her to help!"

Jesus replied, "One thing is needed. Mary has chosen what is better, and it won't be taken away from her" (Luke 10:42 NIV).

Looking at the example of Mary and Martha can provide you with an important key to living a grace-filled life. How often, like Martha, do you let everyday stress and responsibilities crowd in until you think you can't take any more, the if-I-have-one-more-thing-to-do-today-I'm-going-to-scream scenario? For instance, you might have a 7:00 A.M. dental appointment, then school, soccer practice—and, oh yeah, your spouse can't pick up little Susie at ballet as scheduled so you have to swing by there after soccer. Then there's dinner, homework, and on and on until you drop into bed and start all over the next day.

Such days can lead to the mistake that Martha made; she thought she had to do it all. The Lord never meant for you to shoulder such a burden. In fact, He knows you can't do it all on your own and is just waiting for you to figure that out.

Mary's highest priority was putting Jesus first. She could have cared less about dinner as long as she could be with Him. Allow Jesus' words to Martha challenge your lifestyle.

> **GRACE FOR TODAY:**
>
> When we fit our schedules around God, He will refresh our souls.

LIGHT THE WAY

They looked to Him and were radiant.

PSALM 34:5 NASB

Estée Lauder was an amazing woman who built a cosmetics empire on the strength of a philosophy of beauty that was second to none. Raised in the era of white gloves and walking canes, she believed the pursuit of God-given beauty was as admirable as it was honorable. She urged a woman to enter a crowded room and imagine herself the person everyone is waiting to see.

Such a concept is not a bad pattern for teaching. You are beautifully made in the image of God. You have gifts and talents unique to you, and you enter the classroom every day armed with beautiful truth. All eyes in that crowded room turn to you. Hungry for the truth, eager for affirmation, desirous of acceptance, your students lap up your love and take pride in having you for their teacher.

Jesus recognized the neediness of those who sought time with Him. They yearned to understand His uncommon teachings. They traveled long distances to be in His presence. His very touch was life itself. He smiled upon them, bore with them, patiently repeated himself, and ultimately died that they and we might experience the pinnacle of faith and life without end.

What you offer your students is the sacrifice of your time, your wisdom, your empathy, your ability to imagine what they can become. How you run the classroom, the rules you establish, the atmosphere you strike, the respect you command become the gold standard for your class.

Do not settle for a lesser role than that of the person your students are waiting to see. Look to Jesus who bore His "popularity" as not something to be grasped or paraded, but rather as a catalyst for bringing the Light into human lives. You are a light bearer. Let it shine!

GRACE FOR TODAY:

God made us light bearers to shine forth His beauty
into the lives of others.

DO YOU TRUST HIM?

God's a safe-house for the battered, a sanctuary during bad times.

PSALM 9:9 MSG

In many youth groups and even gym classes, there is a ubiquitous activity known as the trust fall. It's done in the name of team building. Small groups of students form a line or a tight curve behind one lone student. The solitary person turns his back to the group, closes his eyes, and falls backward into space, trusting that his teammates will be directly behind him, ready, willing, and capable of catching him.

And you're right. Sometimes they fail to catch an unsuspecting participant. They get distracted. Or they're giggling and the timing's off. Worse, they think it would be so funny if the person just, well, fell!

In stunning contrast, we are asked on a daily basis to trust in a God we can't see, can't feel, and according to Scripture, can't meet personally, or His purity and holiness would obliterate us—unless we approach Him through Jesus. Unless we're smart enough to use prayer as the first resort, not a last desperate measure. Unless we're quiet enough to hear His still small voice and perceptive enough to let Him speak through the power of His unchanging written Word.

So the bottom line is, do you? Do you trust Him? Can you say and believe with your whole heart that God is who He says He is and will do what He promised? If you feel like you're free-falling today, your parachute is broken, the safety net is gone, and the trust line behind you has more gaps than a Halloween jack-o-lantern, will you reach out for His hand? It's the only way to live more dangerously and more safely than you ever have. So, do you? And if you don't, will you? It might be the most important answer you give.

GRACE FOR TODAY:

When we can't see God working in our lives, He asks us to trust Him anyway.

PRESSING ON

Aleksander found himself in a curious situation. Here he was, a new believer in the post-Communist Ukraine, with a whole nation waiting to hear about Jesus. On the other hand, the post-regime government was being extremely cautious about allowing the spread of religion. Aleksander's heart burned with the desire to share his faith, and when the government allowed him a two-month permit to show a film about Jesus, he determined to make the most of it. He hauled the movie across the country for eight weeks, showing it in theaters and public places to more than 80,000 people, each time leading a discussion afterwards about faith in Christ.

Aleksander set a goal and achieved it. While most people do not underestimate the value of setting goals, many don't consider the temporal nature of their mission. There are a number of useful tools to help you learn to set goals, to break them down into attainable sec-tions, to focus on performance rather than outcome-based results, and to write your plan down. What matters most, though, is that your goals are consistent with eternal values.

As you set goals for your students and for yourself for the school year, you consider what skills will be required to meet them and what level of challenge will stimulate without constant frustration. But you also remember the ultimate end of these efforts. Is it simply for them to become better spellers or for you to become more technology-competent?

When Paul wrote to the church at Philippi about running the race of life, he said the ultimate goal wasn't simply to win, but at the end to attain Christ himself. Jesus is the goal. Everything you do and strive for in learning and teaching should set that standard for success, that you and others might know Jesus better as a result of your efforts.

> GRACE FOR TODAY:
>
> ## Jesus Christ stands as our ultimate goal.

I've got my eye on the goal, where God is beckoning us onward—to Jesus.

PHILIPPIANS 3:13 MSG

DREAM COME TRUE

By John C. Maxwell

When you receive a vision that could change your life, or you're grabbed by a dream that could really help you become what you want to be, there's a natural sequence that happens. First there's the "I thought it" stage. That's when a dream just flashes by. Could it be? Maybe this is for me. Next is the "I caught it" stage. After we think about the visions that God gives us, we begin to talk about that dream and see ourselves in it.

I think everyone goes through these first two stages. But stage three makes the difference between the person who will be successful. It's what I call the "I bought it" stage. After we catch that dream, there's a time when we have to make an investment in it. We have to buy that dream.

But just as the successful person buys it, the unsuccessful person fights it. They begin to rationalize; they begin to think about why it wouldn't work, why it's not possible. People who are not going to reach their dreams stop at this third stage and never become what they could become for God.

The fourth stage is the "I sought it" stage. This is where desire comes in: We begin to want it so much that it possesses every part of us. Finally comes the "I got it" stage. This is where I say, "It's mine; I'm glad I paid the price; I'm glad I dreamed the dream."[24]

—∿—

GOD, THANK YOU FOR THE DREAM YOU'VE PUT INTO MY HEART. I DO WANT IT TO BE FULFILLED, AND I AM COMMITTED TO DO WHAT IT TAKES. AT THOSE TIMES WHEN I BEGIN TO WAVER OR DOUBT, FILL ME WITH YOUR GRACE TO HOLD ON TILL THE END. THANK YOU IN ADVANCE FOR THE GLORIOUS THINGS TO COME. AMEN.

Do you not know that those who run in a race all run, but one receives the prize? Run in such a way that you may obtain it.

1 CORINTHIANS 9:24 NKJV

TRAIN YOURSELF TO LISTEN

[His] sheep hear his voice.

JOHN 10:3 KJV

A s they were leaving school after a long day, Jason Sanders leaned against the coach's car and asked, "Tell me something—I'm ready for a couple of beers after teaching all day, and you look as calm as a fishing pond. Don't the kids get to you?"

"Oh, they could, but I don't let them!" Coach replied.

"Okay, so what's your secret?" Sanders asked.

"No secret—I just listen to God and sail through the day."

"Listen to God," Sanders said skeptically. "You're telling me God talks to you?"

"He sure does, son, but you have to listen for Him," Coach said.

"How do you listen to Someone who's invisible? I don't get it."

"You have to learn to listen," Coach said. "Tell me, what do you hear right now?"

> **GRACE FOR TODAY:**
>
> God is always speaking to us, but we need to listen.

"Nothing, except you in my face!"

Leaning against a tree, Coach challenged the searching teacher. "Listen with me."

"You're losin' it, man," Sanders said. "I don't hear anything."

"Just listen," Coach urged. "Hear the crow? Okay, the leaves rustling, the plane overhead, the squirrel? Oh, someone just whacked a softball over there. Kids playing. Teachers talking. Hear that? A police siren. The backfire of a truck. A coach's whistle. That's a lot of things you didn't hear a minute ago."

"I think I'm getting the picture!" Sanders said.

Just like Sanders, there's always room for teachers to learn new things. God wants all of His children to hear His voice. When you need to hear God, want to hear Him, and train yourself to be still enough to get to know Him, you will hear His voice. It's a promise! He loves communicating with His children.

A FUNNY THING HAPPENED

He will yet fill your mouth with laughter,
and your lips with shouts of joy.

JOB 8:21 NRSV

How much fun are you to be with? Is your classroom a pleasant, inviting place where your students can feel the pressures lift? Are there touches of whimsy, amusing pictures, and silly objects around just for the sheer joy of it?

Author Robert Louis Stevenson urged others to "sit loosely in the saddle of life." He was proof positive that to do so frees the imagination and lets the heart take wing. Although it was written in 1881, his best-loved *Treasure Island* is still jolly good fun and continues to sell well throughout the world.

By all means, spice up the place with a joke of the day, a goofy spring-loaded clown, or a couple of rubber chickens. But it is your heart of gladness, your radiant smile, and your good humor that most bring on the grins. There's healing in laughter that provides sweet relief to heavy souls. It teaches us to embrace life, and oh, is it ever contagious! It demonstrates, loud and clear, that you know who holds the ultimate victory over the things that wear and tear us down.

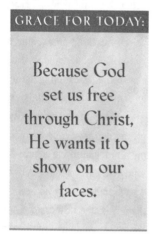

GRACE FOR TODAY:

Because God set us free through Christ, He wants it to show on our faces.

The Jews experienced that when they were released from bondage. The Psalmist commemorates their return from Babylonian captivity with a wonderful song (Psalm 126) of exuberant, boundless joy. You can just hear his laughter between the lines. In Christ, we are set free at last. That ought to show on our faces, and our students ought to be able to read it there, a countenance of happiness and mirth for what God has done for and in us.

Laugh a lot. It will make your students wonder what you're up to!

FINISH WHAT YOU STARTED

He who began a good work in you will perfect it
until the day of Christ Jesus.

PHILIPPIANS 1:6 NASB

Most of us begin each year, each week, each day, with a series of mini-resolutions. We plan to do better. We try to do better. We even determine to do better. Reading *War and Peace* from beginning to end. Reading the entire Bible through in a year, every year. Completing that deck in the backyard. Writing the great American novel. Learning an exciting new hobby. Keeping that resolution to drop those pounds and get in better shape. Keeping that resolution to never lose your temper in your classroom. A daunting list with one common feature—it's hard to follow through. Hard to complete. Hard to finish what you started.

More often than not, we continue making the same promises over and over simply because we can't do them on our own. Maybe that's the point! We won't accomplish much until we acknowledge that God is the source of our strength. He is the One who will carry us through. He remains faithful even when we are faithless.

Canvasses do not generally speak up about what they'd like to have painted on them. Garden flowers don't wave frantically, "Pick me! Pick me!" Clay does not scold the potter or demand to be created into a specific shape or as a particular vessel.

How often we forget that we, too, are clay. Created to worship. Created for His pleasure. But oh, how big His plans are for us! He has eternity in mind. He doesn't fail, and He made a huge promise: If you let Me begin a work within you, I will see you through to the end of this world. Don't you want to see Him finish the work He began?

GRACE FOR TODAY:

God will complete the work He started in us.

PRACTICING HIS PRESENCE

You will seek me and find me when you seek me with all your heart.

JEREMIAH 29:13 NIV

Brother Lawrence told the story of a monk who found himself led to the church doorsteps, where an inner voice had told him to wait for the spiritual director for whom he had prayed the past seven years. When the monk arrived, he found a barefooted beggar and wished him a good day.

"Thank you for your kind greeting," said the beggar. "I shall indeed have a good day. My only bad days come when I do not use them to honor God by submission and gratitude."

The monk realized that, despite the poverty he saw before him, here was his spiritual director. He said, "Where have you found God?"

The beggar replied, "When I forsook everyone but Him, I found Him in my inmost heart. Silent before men, I am always able to converse with God and find perfect peace."

Being aware of God's presence takes practice. It's not some magical ability that only really holy-looking people have. Like the beggar, God's presence is often found in the unlikeliest of places and persons, which is why you have to be in the habit of looking for it.

As you go through your day at school, what stands out and amazes you? Is it the balanced precision of geometric proofs, the sheer awe inspired by the Grand Canyon, the beauty of Monet's palette? Is it the teachable moment or the split-second flash when the child finally gets it?

In all these instances and so many others, you can see God's hand at work. Are you looking for Him? If you are, He won't be hard to find.

GRACE FOR TODAY:

God uses the silence of our ready hearts
to reveal himself.

A LESSON FROM *LES MISERABLES*

As a teacher, God desires to pour grace upon grace into your life so that you then can distribute grace abundantly to your students. Possibly, you may be the only source of edification for some children.

Words are a powerful source of grace; you know that because you've experienced the power of God's Word. You've also probably witnessed a poignant vignette on the power of words if you've ever read the book, seen the film, or experienced the musical *Les Miserables.*

In one scene, the ill–fated prostitute Fantine is dreadfully ill when Monsieur Madeleine comes to her defense and promises to reunite her with the child she's forfeited. Her hope of seeing her child again is the driving force that keeps her alive. Looking to arrest Monsieur Madeleine, the cruel Inspector Javert bursts into her chambers, and Fantine believes he's come for her.

In near delirium, Fantine pleads for her child. Then, with the growling sounds of a demonic despot, Javert sends venom straight to her heart, clamoring about the miserable state of a "whore" being treated like a countess and that he's there to put an end to it. The impact of this scene graphically illustrates Javert's words dealing the death blow to Fantine as she convulsively fumbles upon her bed, falling back dead on her pillow—a striking remembrance forever of the power of words!

Think about how good you feel when someone tells you, "You made a great presentation," or says, "That's awesome!" Or consider the hope you experience when you blow a situation and a fellow teacher encourages you with, "Ah, mistakes happen—no big deal."

As Fantine demonstrates, the human spirit is frail and requires nurturing to thrive and flourish, and it can best be bolstered by caring words. Receive them into your heart and then speak them to others.

> **GRACE FOR TODAY:**
> God's grace–filled words give us confidence to speak them to others.

Death and life are in the power of the tongue.

PROVERBS 18:21 KJV

PLANNED NEGLECT

By John MacArthur Jr.

The more you study the Word of God, the more it saturates your mind and life. Someone is reported to have asked a concert violinist in New York's Carnegie Hall how she became so skilled. She said that it was by "planned neglect." She planned to neglect everything that was not related to her goal.

Some less important things in your life could stand some planned neglect so that you might give yourself to studying the Word of God. Do you know what would happen? The more you would study the Word of God, the more your mind would be saturated with it. It would be no problem then for you to think of Christ. You wouldn't be able to stop thinking of Him.

To be Spirit-filled is to live a Christ-conscious life, and there is no shortcut to that. You can't go and get yourself super-dedicated to live a Christ-conscious life. The only way you can be saturated with the thoughts of Christ is to saturate yourself with the Book that is all about Him. And this is God's will, that you not only be saved but that you also be Spirit-filled.[25]

―∞―

FATHER GOD, I WANT TO EXCEED YOUR EXPECTATIONS AS A TEACHER AND BE A SHINING EXAMPLE OF JESUS IN THE EARTH. THE ONLY WAY I CAN DO THAT IS TO SATURATE MYSELF WITH YOUR WORD AND HAVE THE MIND OF CHRIST. I REALIZE THIS MEANS THAT I MUST GIVE YOUR WORD FIRST PLACE IN MY LIFE AND "NEGLECT" THE THINGS THAT PREVENT ME FROM GIVING MYSELF WHOLLY TO YOUR PRECEPTS. I NEED YOUR GRACE TO BE DISCIPLINED IN HOW I MANAGE MY TIME. LEAD ME AS I STUDY AND MEDITATE ON YOUR WORD, SO THAT I CAN THINK AND ACT LIKE JESUS TODAY. AMEN.

In your lives you must think and act like Christ Jesus.

PHILIPPIANS 2:5 NCV

DAY ONE

[And] He put a new song in my mouth, a song of praise to our God.

PSALM 40:3 NASB

What is it about the first day of school? No matter how long you've been a teacher, it never loses its luster.

All the pencils are sharp.

All the notebooks are new.

All their faces are washed.

It is a day when laughs ring pure like bells in dreams.

You've been waiting for this moment. They've been waiting for this moment. God has lifted every heart for this moment. The first day.

A new beginning. A fresh start. A diamond day.

First days are days when no one has a record, good or bad. Everyone's even. And it seems like you could teach anything to anyone.

The first day is a day when you feel just a tremor of what God must have felt that first day when He said, "'Let there be light,' and there was light." You can fathom just a little of what must have run through His unfathomable mind when He saw that the light was good and He used it to distinguish day from night, and morning and evening were born.

> GRACE FOR TODAY:
>
> **If we talk to God first thing in the morning, He makes every day extraordinary.**

Ask your students on this morning of mornings, "How can we keep the best of this day? How do we capture this joy to save for days of winter gloom and springtime mud? How do we honor the first day first and keep for all days its shimmer and shine?"

Good questions. New world questions. Genesis questions. Don't let the day go by without answering them, for soon it will be the seventieth day and you will want to remember.

Thank God for the first day. Savor it. Revel in it. Treasure what is special about it and unwrap ways to keep the spirit of the first day alive for the entire year.

Hands Up!

Stoop down and reach out to those who are oppressed. Share their burdens, and so complete Christ's law.

GALATIANS 6:2 MSG

Maybe it's a cultural thing, maybe an American thing, maybe just a pride thing. We don't want to ask for help. It begins when we're toddlers: "I do it myself!" Deep within us is buried the arrogant notion that we can pull ourselves up by our own bootstraps. Try it sometime in the literal sense—just know in advance where you'll land.

It's not possible to accomplish everything on our own, and it may not even be desirable.

When Moses served as sole arbitrator for the Israelites after their release from Egypt, he was exhausted. Moses' father-in-law gave him some sound advice: "What you are doing is not good. You and these people . . . will only wear yourselves out. The work is too heavy for you, you cannot handle it alone." He then suggests that Moses should suggest some capable men to share the load. (See Exodus 18:15–23.)

GRACE FOR TODAY:

God wants us to share the burdens of others.

On another occasion, the Israelites and Amalekites were in heated battle. Joshua was leading, but the Israelites were winning only so long as Moses held up his hands. The end of the story is as priceless as it is precious: "When Moses' hands grew tired, they took a stone and put it under him and he sat on it. Aaron and Hur held his hands up—one on one side, one on the other—so that his hands remained steady till sunset" (Exodus 17:12 NIV). By the way, the Israelites won big time. What a picture of the role that friends play during periods of discouragement!

Where are you today? Are you in need of someone to hold up your hands? Or can you look around the faculty lounge, the hallways, the playground, the bus runs, the janitorial closets, and see someone whose hands need assistance? Whether you put your hands out or your hands up, seek to help ease the burden of discouragement.

NO GREATER LOVE

For You, Lord, are good, and ready to forgive, And abundant in mercy to all those who call upon You.

PSALM 86:5 NKJV

B en Byrne's shoes clicked on the cold concrete floor of Death Row, his thoughts turned toward the man in the last cell. George DeVille, convicted of murder, considered the meanest man on the block, was sentenced to die at midnight. As chaplain, Ben knew he couldn't save men's lives, that he could only hope to lead them to the Savior of their souls. Some had accepted his presentation of the gospel, while others, including DeVille, continued to reject Christ.

This is it, George, Ben thought. *Now or never.* Then he heard sounds coming from George's cell. Ben squinted. George was singing "Amazing Grace"! The night of his execution, George DeVille received Jesus as Lord and Savior and was baptized before a dozen inmates and guards.

Aren't you glad that God is merciful? Your mistakes aren't final, and neither are the mistakes of your students. Forgiveness is the currency of understanding in relationships. It's important to teach children to forgive each other, to put the pardon for wrongdoing in the hands of the injured party, but what an impact when you're the one asking them for their pardon! That's when they truly see the power of forgiveness, the strength it requires to forgive and to be forgiven. That's when both you and your students receive a glimpse of God.

You're in daily contact with a segment, large or small, of the next generation. You know what kind of world they're growing up in, and you know, as a Christian, the internal struggles they face along the way. You've seen them make good choices and bad ones, and sometimes the good choices are paid back with evil and the bad ones are rewarded. God's forgiveness is the rope you toss them to keep them from drowning in the imperfection of it all.

GRACE FOR TODAY:

God's forgiveness is the rope that keeps us from drowning.

REMEMBER WHEN?

Patient persistence pierces through indifference;
gentle speech breaks down rigid defenses.

PROVERBS 25:15 MSG

D o you ever get frustrated with students who seem not to pay attention when maybe it's just that they hate to admit they don't understand? Have you ever explained something several times and still had confused students raising their hands? Ever found yourself thinking: *Why can't you get this? I've explained it three different times!* Well, these are the times when you need an injection of God's special grace to help you remember your own days as a student.

Remember when—you couldn't formulate a thesis for an English comp paper; couldn't get both sides of an algebraic equation to balance; couldn't comprehend the economic implications of the GNP; dropped organic chemistry (or some other challenging course), and changed your major because you just couldn't hack it? Often teachers can quickly forget how hard it was to tackle each new course. However, thinking back on those days when you couldn't grasp a math concept or dissect a frog without getting queasy will give you sympathy and patience for those struggling students in your classroom.

Today as you recall such personal and frustrating occasions, take a second look at your students who just don't get it and determine to see things from their limited understanding. Ask the Holy Spirit to assist you. As you develop more patience for the slow ones and greater tolerance for the stubborn ones, your teaching skills will become more effective, and you will find your sense of fulfillment in being a teacher multiplied exponentially.

GRACE FOR TODAY:

When we need patience, God has an abundant supply.

TEACHING THE TEACHER

What will you learn from your students today? Teachers with the longest careers are often those who anticipate the lessons their students will teach them:

How many dandelions can be stuffed up a child's nose.

How many different spellings there are of Tallahassee.

How much sadness and brokenness one child can bear.

How much power a single youthful smile has to evaporate dark clouds of frustration, weaken hurricanes of doubt, and calm the seas of discontent.

Learned teachers are those who heave a sigh of relief at the end of a trying day, but not an hour later wish that the classroom still rang with the vibrant life that "my kids" bring.

Why? Jesus said we have much to learn from children. Giant lessons of faith, forgiveness, obedience, and love.

Unless we become like the children, He said we will never enter the kingdom of heaven.

What does "like them" mean? In part, it means being trusting, generous, wholehearted, and open to change.

There's a simplicity and transparency about children that adults learn to mask. We need to guard against suppressing what God desires in us. The psalmist says that he learned the value of a still, quiet soul. Where did he learn it? From observing a weaned child and his mother. A weaned child has learned to stop fussing for his mother's breast and to take nourishment from other sources. A weaned child has achieved a place of calm acceptance and security.

Enjoy the teachings of your students. They are meant for your own growth and maturity.

> **GRACE FOR TODAY:**
>
> Unless we become like little children, God said we will never enter the kingdom of Heaven.

Therefore whoever humbles himself as this little child is the greatest in the kingdom of heaven.

MATTHEW 18:4 NKJV

CHANGED BY GOD'S WORD

By Evelyn Christenson

Should I let God change me through devotional reading or Bible study? That is not a fair question, because both are essential for a well-rounded, transformed life. Devotional reading is never a substitute for deep, systematic Bible study—but it is a complement to it. And the Lord does change me when I study His Word.

Paul gave Timothy excellent advice when he said, "Study to shew thyself approved unto God" (2 Timothy 2:15 KJV). He also counseled him to "remember that from early childhood you have been familiar with the sacred writings which have power to make you wise and lead you to salvation through faith in Christ Jesus. Every inspired Scripture has its use for *teaching the truth* and *refuting error,* or for *reformation of manners and discipline in right living,* so that the man who belongs to God may be efficient and equipped for good work of every kind" (2 Timothy 3:16–17, NEB, italics mine).

Digging into the Bible always produces joy and an excitement that changes me into a different person. My spiritual barometer, 1 John 1:4 NIV, applies here: "These things [are written] . . . that your joy [may] be full." Even if I'm willing to be changed by what God is teaching me, the end result is always joy. Deep Bible study also produces spiritual maturity—Christ-likeness—in me.[26]

—⁓—

HEAVENLY FATHER, THANK YOU FOR GIVING ME YOUR HOLY WRITTEN WORD. AS I STUDY AND MEDITATE ON IT, TRANSFORM ME BY YOUR GRACE SO THAT I CAN BECOME MORE AND MORE LIKE JESUS. AS FOR MY TEACHING, GIVE ME INSIGHTS AND CREATIVE WAYS TO TEACH MY STUDENTS SO THAT WHATEVER THE SUBJECT, THEY WILL BE CHANGED BECAUSE THEY ARE GROWING IN KNOWLEDGE. AMEN.

Do not be conformed to this world, but be transformed by the renewing of your mind, that you may prove what is that good and acceptable and perfect will of God.

ROMANS 12:2 NKJV

THE SUITCASE

Sin is no longer your master, for you are no longer subject to the law,
which enslaves you to sin. Instead, you are free by God's grace.

ROMANS 6:14 NLT

I magine that a wealthy friend invites you on a trip. He wires you the airline tickets and tells you not to worry about anything. Just bring a small carry-on bag with
the essentials. Maybe a good book to read. Camera? Got it. Clothes? Nope. He's purchased you a new wardrobe just for this trip. Shoes? No. He's even provided a new
suitcase, empty and ready for your souvenirs. Meals are included, too!

You're excited and on the edge of disbelief about this phenomenal gift. You begin
packing immediately. Your carry-on bag holds a tooth-
brush and various toiletries in travel-sized containers.
You throw in a good book and add your old camera just
in case. Despite your instructions, you lug an enor-
mous suitcase down from the closet and begin filling it
with a variety of clothes, suited for any occasion.

GRACE FOR TODAY:

**God's grace
bought us
free tickets to
Heaven.**

Then you start to worry about everything that
might happen—things that you might miss out on while
you're away. You won't be able to take out the trash, so
you put it all in a bag and stuff it into your suitcase, as
well. The pile of junk on the entry table goes in, as does
the accumulated pile of stuff from the corner of your
desk. Might get some grading in. You throw in some outdated textbooks too; you never
know what you might need.

Sounds crazy, doesn't it? But incredibly, this is exactly what we do with God's
offer of a free trip to Heaven, purchased by grace. He chooses not to remember our
sins, but we parade them in front of Him.

We lug our forgiven pasts around with us like month-old garbage, examining the
pieces and wondering if grace is real. Why not check your old bags at the gate and pick
up the new one He has waiting for you? You might find that the trip is heavenly.

THE WORLD IS CROWDED WITH HIM

It's in Christ that we find out who we are and what we are living for.

EPHESIANS 1:11 MSG

C. S. Lewis married Joy Davidman late in his life, well after his famous con-version from atheism to Christianity. They both knew she was dying of cancer at the time, but both had lived for a time a life devoid of any hint of God and so cherished their precious, fleeting moments together. After Joy's death in 1960, Lewis quite naturally found himself angry with God, wondering like Job if his pain was worth the life he'd lived to gain it. Ultimately, he realized that God was not experimenting on his faith or love. God already knew their quality; He wanted to see if Lewis did.

In order to find God's purpose for your life, you often have to look beyond your circumstances, beyond today's victory or defeat. Through the situation at hand, you can find a glimpse of what God is doing, through your life and in it, sometimes blessing, other times teaching or even correcting you. You know He loves you to be involved in such ways.

Your purpose, however, is more than those moments. When school is overwhelming, when grades are due, when children are rude, when parents and colleagues are spiteful, God calls you to remember why you're here at all. You're His. You belong to God, and He wants you to know Him, to love Him with everything you've got, even if it doesn't seem like much.

> **GRACE FOR TODAY:**
>
> To find God's purpose for our lives, He wants us to look beyond today's circumstances.

As a teacher, relish the opportunity you've been given to shape young lives. Though you can't always see Him, trust God that He will make your time with them meaningful and lasting, that in the greater pursuit of walking with God, you will impact one another for life.

PAY IT FORWARD

Ask yourself what you want people to do for you;
then grab the initiative and do it for them!

LUKE 6:31 MSG

Initiative—a momentum-moving tool for teachers—is something teachers may wane in but should never be without! Initiative always involves beginning, a new start, and it's up to God to determine the end result.

Thought much about initiative in your class lately? Young seventh-grader Trevor McKinney does in the popular film *Pay It Forward,* released in 2000. Trevor is assigned a social studies project: "Think of something to change the world, and put it into action." Trevor comes up with the idea: instead of payback, pay forward. He takes the initiative to do three good deeds for three people (something they can't do for themselves), conceiving that if they will then "pay it forward" by doing the same for three people, and so on, then like a domino-effect, the whole world would be changed.

Trevor is truly concerned about making things better, and as he makes his mark on the world, he eventually comes to the attention of the news media, but not without cost. In the movie, Trevor makes a new start with an unorthodox idea and takes the initiative to influence others. He has no concept of how far-reaching his plan can be, nor the innumerable lives he can influence.

Christ also took the initiative, committing himself to you on the cross, desiring that you would take the initiative to respond in kind to others with His love. Taking the initiative to invest yourself in your students, you also have no idea the lives you may be influencing for all of eternity. Your initiative today contributes in determining the culture of our society and the world that your students, children, and grandchildren will inherit tomorrow.

So pay it forward. Engage the Holy Spirit and be bold in employing your own creative initiative to impact, instruct, and make a difference in your students' lives.

GRACE FOR TODAY:

God took the initiative to invest himself in us so that
we could "pay it forward."

SWITCH GEARS

[The Lord] leads me beside still waters; he restores my soul.

PSALM 23:2-3 NRSV

G o fishing. Sometimes there's just no cure for the teaching blues except to wet a line. You might take long walks and explore the neighborhood. Some join a gospel choir. You might try glass art.

The important thing is to give yourself permission to take a sabbatical, be it for ten weeks or ten minutes. A seasonal change of scene is necessary for the health of a Canadian goose. Are you not worth more than a goose?

Get as far from lesson preparation and student evaluations as you can. A short-term missions trip to South America or a vacation in Hawaii staring down the throat of an active volcano will not only give you perspective, but some incredible object lessons when you return to the classroom. Teaching must never be all theory and secondhand knowledge. The benefits of living what you teach are immeasurable.

Jesus urged a lot of people to "switch gears" to aid their learning process and renew their spirits. The people He healed and the people who observed the healings were never the same again. Nor was the woman at the well ever the same again after her encounter with the Living Water. Christ made people think outside of the box. He gave them food for thought by simply drawing in the sand. Be they tax collectors, physicians, or centurions, they had a whole new take on life A.J.—After Jesus— because He preached change on the inside.

So go. Explore. Serve. Stretch. Reflect. Challenge your insides. Renew your spirit. Take time out and time away. Come back revived with something fresh to say. Hang out the "gone fishing" sign. A word of caution, though: If you do go fishing, you'll relax a lot more if you forget that fish travel in schools.

GRACE FOR TODAY:

God renews our spirits by showing us how to see life from His angle.

TO BE NOT WEARY

If we're honest, we'll admit that we had incredible dreams when we graduated from college. Dreams of bright airy classrooms full of every conceivable convenience, rows of books, stimulating décor, live plants, maybe even window seats, and a conversation corner or a tree house for the really ambitious!

Each morning we'd eagerly bound out of bed, anticipating another day full of laughter and learning. The students would sit in their seats, faces upturned, breathlessly awaiting the knowledge we had to share. The teachers would be like one big happy family. The principal would be a studied leader, pulling for excellence but always on your side. In our daydreams, some of us even threw in a parent volunteer so we would never, ever have to make our own copies. Budget cuts would be unheard of at our school, and the PTA would frequently remember to leave a supply of chocolates in our in-box.

> **GRACE FOR TODAY:**
>
> When we grow weary with teaching, God can give us renewed strength.

Most of our days don't exactly match up with our idyllic image. We get disillusioned. We get weary. The bounding out of bed gives way to something that looks more like crawling, and this after we've pressed the snooze button at least four times.

Rumors of budget cuts and layoffs float like bad exhaust about the copy machine in the lounge. You have a few students who don't seem eager to come to school at all, much less learn something. You glance at your paycheck stub, and after taxes and the stuff you're always buying for your classroom, the pay seems woefully inadequate for the hours you spend. It becomes so tempting, on such days, to just put in your time.

The blessing for us is that we serve Jesus Christ. He knew extreme weariness, irritation with crowds, slow learners, and a fast-paced schedule for seemingly little in return. Let Him under your wings and feel the weariness disappear.

He gives strength to the weary.

ISAIAH 40:29 NIV

UNLIMITED RESOURCES

By John C. Maxwell

A friend of mine was discussing the implications of Micah 6:8 NASB with his seven-year-old grandson: "What does the LORD require of you but to do justice, to love kindness, and to walk humbly with your God?" The little boy, who was memorizing this verse, said, "Grandpa, it's hard to be humble if you're really walking with God." That's great theology coming from a seven-year-old. When we begin to get a glimpse of the unlimited resources at our disposal—the power of God himself—then and only then will we sense the assurance that we are fully equipped to do whatever it is that God calls us to do.

We might feel like the little mouse who was crossing the bridge with an elephant friend. The bridge shook, and when they got to the other side, the mouse looked at his huge companion and said, "Boy, we really shook that bridge, didn't we?"

When we walk with God, that's often how we feel—like a mouse with the strength of an elephant. After crossing life's troubled waters, we can say with the mouse, "God, we really shook that bridge, didn't we?"

Hudson Taylor, the great missionary to China, said, "Many Christians estimate difficulty in the light of their own resources, and thus they attempt very little, and they always fail. All giants have been weak men who did great things for God because they reckoned on His power and His presence to be with them."

Like David, who said, "The battle is the LORD'S" (1 Samuel 17:47 KJV), we also need to understand that Jesus is our Source, and we can be directly connected to Him.[27]

—∿—

HEAVENLY FATHER, YOUR GRACE HAS PROVIDED ALL THE RESOURCES I NEED TO LIVE A SUCCESSFUL, GODLY LIFE. WALK WITH ME THROUGH THIS DAY, I PRAY, AND HELP ME REMEMBER TO RELY ON YOUR STRENGTH AND NOT MY OWN. TAKE MY WEAKNESSES AND MAKE THEM STRENGTHS FOR YOUR GLORY. AMEN.

I can do all things through Christ who strengthens me.

PHILIPPIANS 4:13 NKJV

BLUEPRINT FOR SUCCESS

When I think of the wisdom and scope of God's plan, I fall to my knees
and pray to the Father, the Creator of everything in heaven and on earth.

EPHESIANS 3:14-15 NLT

The two brothers watched the coin flip through the air, their aspirations turning with each rotation. Albrecht and Albert Durer shared the dream of pursuing their artistic talents at the Academy in Nuremberg, but because of their family's poverty, only one would be able to pursue it. The other would go to the mines to support his brother, in hopes that one day the favor could be returned and the situation reversed. Albrecht won the toss, went to school, and became an artistic and commercial success.

Despite his accomplishment, he could not return the favor, for Albert's hands had been devastated by the mines. Albrecht paid homage to his brother's sacrifice, painstakingly rendering his brother's mangled hands lifted up in prayer, a work entitled "Hands" that has been reproduced countless times to the comfort of millions over the past five hundred years.

> GRACE FOR TODAY:
>
> God's plans
> for our lives
> will always
> touch those
> around us.

Undoubtedly, you rejoice in the knowledge that God has a plan for your life. What comfort, to base the purpose and meaning of your life on the care, provision, and goodness of the Creator of the universe!

Why do you teach? Most likely it isn't the fortune to be made. Yet some of the benefits are ongoing, such as working with young people searching for their identity, the challenges each day brings to improve your craft, and the reward of seeing your students succeed in life. You can't put a price on these.

The deep, unfathomable beauty of God's plan is that it is all-encompassing. Each life you touch, each life that touches yours, is all part and parcel of God's grand-scale design for His favorite creation—people—and His vast blueprint to bring everyone into an intimate relationship with their loving Father.

NEED DIRECTION?

Call to Me, and I will answer you, and show you great and mighty
things, which you do not know.

JEREMIAH 33:3 NKJV

E veryone needs direction in life—especially teachers! However, maybe because
of their many responsibilities or maybe because they so often have the answers,
teachers (like anyone else) can forget to ask for direction from God.

This proved disastrous for Joshua when taking the people of Israel into the
Promised Land. The Gibeonites were a heathen nation in fear of Israel, and so they
planned a ruse. They loaded their donkeys with worn-out sacks, cracked wineskins,
and molded bread. Dressed in worn-out clothes and sandals, they went to Joshua,
telling him they'd come from a far land. Scripture says that the Israelites "sampled their
provisions but did not inquire of the Lord" (Joshua 9:14 NIV), and this disobedience kept
Israel from ever taking all of the Promised Land. The
Gibeonites were their next-door neighbors, and Israel
had sworn not to harm them.

By not inquiring of the Lord, Joshua was deceived
when he judged by appearances, false evidence, and
hearsay instead of getting and following God's word for
the situation. Like Joshua, every Christian is subject to
deception, hence the imperative to receive direction
from the Lord. An even bigger deception lies in pre-
suming to know God's response.

Where do you turn when you need direction? Do
you turn to a fellow teacher, your spouse, your pastor?
God wants you to go to Him—one, because He has
direction that will benefit you, and two, because He
longs for a relationship with you.

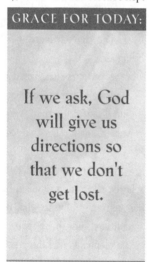

GRACE FOR TODAY:

If we ask, God
will give us
directions so
that we don't
get lost.

So the next time you're in a quandary—confused and needing direction—avoid
deciding your own course of action based on appearances, false evidence, and hearsay.
Stop by the throne room and have a chat with your heavenly Father. He'll gladly give
you the guidance you need and bless the outcome.

TURN THEM AROUND

Be easy on people; you'll find life a lot easier.

LUKE 6:37 MSG

If you have a bully in your classroom and nothing seems to work, take a lesson from the rubber plantation owners of India. Often, the plantations are located high in the hills on the edge of the forest territory where wild elephants roam. Large and unruly, used to having their own way, the lumbering beasts can damage the valuable rubber trees by stomping on them, knocking them over, or stripping limbs for food.

The remedy? Believe it or not, some resourceful owners, unsuccessfully having tried every other method to scare the elephants away, spread crispy crackers on the ground adjoining their plantations. When the elephants step on the crackers and their sensitive ears hear the snap and crunch, they are frightened at the sound and run away!

Inside many a human bully is an insecure child who has himself been bullied. Some have been mistreated by other children, some by parents or other adults in their lives. They have learned the tactics of intimidation all too well and are themselves ruled by anger.

So try the unexpected and take them by surprise. Enlist them as class helpers. Assign them extra-credit book reports on people like Mother Teresa who saw Jesus in "the least of these." Give them supervised responsibility for tasks of kindness, and reward them for service to others. Let them experience that compassion is its own reward.

Scripture teaches that anger is the province of fools, but that glory goes to the one who overlooks an offense, be it real or imagined. With patience and persistence, you can help the bully see that real strength lies with those who are thoughtful and well-intentioned, not those who throw their weight around. You might start with the story of the elephants and the crackers.

GRACE FOR TODAY:

God created a soft spot in the hard heart
of every bully.

THE RUT

God saw all that He had made, and behold, it was very good.

GENESIS 1:31 NASB

"**A**nd it was good." What a classically simple, understated, magnificent label. God's work was good. He ordained it. He knew it to be true. He is a never-ending source of creativity, ideas, and renewal. And His ideas are always good!

Meanwhile, you're fresh out of ideas for your students, and tomorrow you have to introduce:

How a bill becomes a law.

Fractions.

The Dewey Decimal System.

The Constitution.

The works of William Shakespeare.

Elements of dramatic theater.

The number line.

Solids and liquids (they'd like it done in kindergarten this year!).

Maybe you're introducing this unit or concept for the first time. Perhaps for the third or the seventeenth or the twenty-fifth time. Inwardly, you groan. You just can't think of a fresh spin. You're in a rut. Or maybe you've never done this unit before and you're nervous; they switched your grade levels over the summer. Or you're a first-year teacher. You've perused professional magazines and haunted the aisles at the teacher supply stores. Still stumped?

Try something new this year. Go straight to the source of everything. Why not ask the God who gave the hyena his laugh? Who made a kitten's paws infinitesimally soft. Who gives orders to the morning. Who enabled a deer to scale the heights and the eagles to soar with the clouds. The One who thought up puppies and can use water as snow, ice, rain, hail, and dew. The God who understands the Pythagorean Theorem. The Creator of gravity. The God of waterfalls, pounding surf, and majestic mountains.

GRACE FOR TODAY:

God's creativity elevates textbook learning into a voyage of discovery.

AMAZING LOVE

Jean finished packing the car and looked back at the giant tent covering her house. She and Carl were taking the kids on a short vacation while their home was being fumigated for termites, and all that was left was to find Marbles. With the fumigators ready to start, everyone began to hunt for the cat. After a few frantic moments failed to turn up the tabby, Jean thought, *Where would I hide if I were a cat?*

Knowing that Marbles' life was in danger, she began a systematic search, covering all of his usual hiding places one by one, until finally Marbles meowed from behind the dresser in their bedroom. Everyone sighed, and Jean pondered in a small way the mysterious, binding love that drove God to send His Son to earth in search of scared, hiding souls.

When you lose your way in life, as everyone does at one point or another, what draws you back to God? His faithfulness or His mercies are both compelling reasons. But really, these only show you the greater force at work—His love.

God loves you. That's not news, but when you're feeling lost, it looks like this: If God is all-powerful, He may do everything. If He is all-knowing, He will do the right thing. He is able to help you, but is He willing? Resoundingly, yes. God's unconditional love compelled Him to send His beloved Son to the cross. Doubt the whole world first before you ever doubt His love for you.

Teaching is much more than what you teach, or how. It's whom that matters most. And those kids, they mess up, don't they? They argue, complain, fail, and sometimes even threaten your mental health. But you go back, and you love them, even when they're unlovable. Sort of like God.

> ## GRACE FOR TODAY:
>
> God loves us like the Amazon River flows down to water one single daisy.

Nothing in all creation will ever be able to separate us from the love of God that is revealed in Christ Jesus our Lord.

ROMANS 8:39 NLT

We Will All Stand There

By Warren W. Wiersbe

The Judgment Seat of Christ is that future event when God's people will stand before their Savior as their works are judged and rewarded. (See Romans 14:8-10.) Because of the gracious work of Christ on the Cross, believers will not face their sins (Romans 8:1; John 5:24); but we will have to give an account of our works and service for the Lord.

The Judgment Seat of Christ will be a place of revelation; for the word appear means "be revealed." As we live and work here on Earth, it is relatively easy for us to hide things and pretend; but the true character of our works will be exposed before the searching eyes of the Savior. He will reveal whether our works have been good or bad ("worthless"). The character of our service will be revealed (1 Corinthians 3:13), as well as the motives that impelled us (1 Corinthians 4:5).

It will also be a place of reckoning as we give an account of our ministries (Romans 14:10-12). If we have been faithful, it will be a place of reward and recognition (1 Corinthians 3:10-15; 4:1-6). For those of us who have been faithful, it will be a time of rejoicing as we glorify the Lord by giving our rewards back to Him in worship and in praise.[28]

—⚬—

HEAVENLY FATHER, I THANK YOU THAT I WILL NOT BE JUDGED ON THE BASIS OF MY FAILINGS AND IMPERFECTIONS, BUT ONLY FOR THOSE THINGS THAT I HAVE DONE BY THE POWER OF YOUR GRACE. NOT ONLY DO I NEED YOUR GRACE IN MY PERSONAL LIFE, I ALSO NEED IT IN ABUNDANCE AS I TEACH MY STUDENTS. I LOOK FORWARD TO THE DAY WHEN I WILL STAND BEFORE YOU, CONFIDENT AND REJOICING. AMEN.

We will all stand before God's judgment seat. So then, each of us will give an account of himself to God.

ROMAN 14:10, 12 NIV

TAKE A STAND

It is true that I have given you power . . . to overcome all the enemy's power—there is nothing at all that can do you any harm.

LUKE 10:19 PHILLIPS

God's grace is not restricted; it covers all areas of life—both in the classroom and out. Recently at an area high school, vandals rammed a vehicle into the gate surrounding the athletic department and tried to break into the coach's van. Although they got through the gate, when they started for the van, security and policemen arrived, frightening the thieves away.

Three years before this incident, the athletic department had experienced numerous break-ins, resulting in stolen electronic equipment, computers, and a large-screen television—not to mention the graffiti spray painted on the building. It cost the school thousands of dollars, so the administration took measures to improve security by erecting a tall chain-link fence around the premises and installing an alarm system.

GRACE FOR TODAY:

God confers power on us, but we must operate it under His authority.

So what can be learned about God's grace for teachers from such a terrible event that happened outside the classroom? In the earlier break-ins, the thieves succeeded in getting inside the school and creating havoc. Some problems they caused took months to reconcile. However, since the school installed the alarm system and put up the fence, the thieves' attempts have been virtually thwarted.

Like a thief, Satan waits in the dark to spring upon his prey, attempting to steal, kill, and destroy, according to Scripture. But when you recognize his attacks, construct a solid perimeter with God's Word, install an alarm system through prayer, and post constant security by fellowshipping with other Christians, you interrupt the enemy's schemes. He may create some havoc in your school, but by establishing yourself in God's Word and His promises, you seal the enemy's fate, expose his impotence, and shut him out of your classroom.

NO QUICK FIX

Therefore the LORD longs to be gracious to you, and therefore He waits on high to have compassion on you.

ISAIAH 30:18 NASB

Two young students were overheard having the following conversation:

"Your grandparents sure do have a lot of fish in that one tank," said the first boy, "and now there's ten more babies in there."

"Yeah, it's too crowded," said the second boy in a tone both wise and a little frustrated. "It's because they won't get the fish fixed."

We wish that all our problems had such simple solutions. Sitcom conflicts resolve themselves in thirty minutes, but our real-life challenges can take days, weeks, months, or years to find closure. In especially tough situations, we may despair that change for the better will ever come.

The truth is, you won't win every battle in the classroom. Algebraic formulas or the finer points of writing a persuasive essay will remain a mystery to some kids. The chip on a student's shoulder was likely placed there long before you came along. No, despite your best efforts, not every troubled student will find the sun on your watch.

GRACE FOR TODAY:

God's blessings offer solutions, not quick fixes.

What is possible is for you to offer up your students to God by name. Ask Him to bless them as the Lord directed Aaron and his sons to bless the Israelites:

"The Lord bless you and keep you; the Lord make his face shine upon you and be gracious to you; the Lord turn his face toward you and give you peace" (Numbers 6:24–26 NIV). How wonderful that the acknowledgement of God among them not only extended spiritual blessing, but also day-to-day provisions of food, water, and health!

Your acknowledgement of God among your students will bless them in similar practical ways. Quick fixes are impractical expectations. Change takes time. Let God work.

THE NEED FOR PRAISE

God—you're breathtaking! Body and soul, I am marvelously made!

PSALM 139:14 MSG

All of us need it in healthy doses: praise. It's expressed poignantly and accurately in the little boy's words when he says, "Mama, let's play darts. I'll throw them and you say, 'Wonderful!'" Don't we all wish for cheerleaders in our lives who know the value of praise—those who are willing to sit high in the balcony seats, away from the spotlight, praying for us, applauding us, and encouraging us?

Think about the children in your classes this year. The ones on the playground. The boisterous ones in the lunchroom. The clumps of jostling students in the bus line. The ones who sit straggling in the cafeteria, waiting for parent pickup. Do any of them need a hug? An offer of tutoring before school? A short, sincere conversation expressing interest in them and what they do?

Think about the building engineers whose services we take for granted every day. My pencil sharpener didn't get emptied. I need more trash bags. Somebody threw up in the second row. Ugh! Yes, it's their job, but a warm thank you, a short note, an inexpensive candy bar, could convey such value.

Think about the first-year teacher down the hall who is wondering if this profession is survivable. What about a word of encouragement? An offer to grade papers together over coffee at a local Starbucks? And the elderly English teacher upstairs? Her husband is in failing health, and this is her last year of teaching before retirement. She's torn between elation and melancholy. She could use words of praise for her years of service.

Make a goal of writing a note of encouragement to someone every Monday. Leave it in their box. Tuck it in their backpack. Call a parent just to brag on their child. The power of praise, delivered in the right spirit, can leave a trail for seekers to find God.

GRACE FOR TODAY:

God wants our praise to leave a trail for seekers to find Him.

STRENGTH UNDER CONTROL

Show a gentle attitude toward everyone. The Lord is coming soon.

PHILIPPIANS 4:5 GNT

Kelly stood transfixed as the parent lashed out at her colleague Roberta, raving with complete misunderstanding about the student involved. But it wasn't the rant that astonished Kelly; it was her coworker's reaction. She watched Roberta's eyes flash momentarily—that seemed normal enough—and then they cleared, matching her calm expression. Roberta listened quietly until the verbal storm broke, and then she invited the parent into her room. Kelly peeked out the window of her own classroom door until she saw the parent leave, all smiles and handshakes.

"Bobbi!" Kelly said, bursting into the room. "How did you do that?"

Roberta shrugged. "I just listened. I've done this often enough to know it's not personal. Ultimately, we're all working for the good of the kids, right?"

This dedicated teacher proved that true gentleness is strength. Too often it's mistaken for being a pushover, for not having the fortitude to defend yourself. Consider Jesus. How many times could He have played the God card when even His closest friends were missing His point and being obnoxious? Picture James and John arguing over who would get to sit on which side of Jesus in the kingdom and Jesus saying, "Put a cork in it, guys. I'm God, and I don't have to put up with this nonsense."

Instead, Jesus chose a gentler path, one that led to the Cross. Not an easier path, but one paved with a greater love, a higher sense of purpose, that made His final response to His tormentors the only possible one: "Father, forgive them, for they know not what they do."

If you make a habit of responding like Jesus, God will give you what it takes to react with grace and dignity.

GRACE FOR TODAY:

God shows His strength by responding with gentleness.

A BEAUTIFUL MIND

Being an effective teacher requires a clear mind. God's grace bids you to live in the reality of the Cross—"old things are passed away; all things are become new." To really buy into that, you have to embrace the truth that you have the mind of Christ. Even teachers have baggage from their pasts, but God wants His daily grace to touch any unhealed parts of your mind so you can experience the reality of His promises.

Often, a big hindrance is listening to old tapes still playing in your mind. Everyone has them, though the script may vary—I can't do anything right; I'll never fit in; I'm never going to be what I really want to be; I'll never get married—you get the idea. These thoughts can sabotage God's plan for you if they control you instead of you silencing them. An excellent example of understanding this is illustrated by the life of John Nash Jr. in the film *A Beautiful Mind*. The schizophrenic Nash faces mental challenges that could have destroyed him, but he fights back and triumphs over his illness to receive the Nobel Prize. When being considered for nomination for the award, Nash was asked: "Do you still hear the voices?"

He replied, "I've gotten used to ignoring them, and I think, as a result, they've given up on me. I think that's what it's like with all nightmares; we've got to keep feeding them for them to stay alive."

What a powerful example to inspire you to receive more grace—grace to learn how to ignore your old thoughts and replace them with God's Word, empowering you to live your life in the reality of the new creature you are in Him.

GRACE FOR TODAY:

God's Word rejuvenates our thoughts.

[Cast] down imaginations . . . bringing into captivity every thought to the obedience of Christ.

2 CORINTHIANS 10:5 KJV

A WONDERFUL SECRET

By Luis Palau

When I became a believer, I learned about forgiveness and never really doubted that God had forgiven me. But I didn't understand much about how a Christian progressed in maturity and holiness. I longed to get past the continual struggles and find victory in my life.

I wasn't alone in my desire for greater victory. The other young men I spent time with wanted victory, too. And we needed it! We had many weaknesses. We made sarcastic remarks, despised certain denominations, and had our temptations with women—just to name a few. So whenever a big-name preacher came to our church for revival services, we would take him out for coffee and ask him how we could have victory in our lives. We never told him too much about our reason for wanting greater victory; we just hinted that we had some little weaknesses in our lives.

Over and over we were told to read the Bible, pray every day, and work for Christ. If we did those things, our advisers promised, we would be happy, holy Christians.

Not one of those great men of God ever said, "Listen, the secret is not reading, praying, and working. The secret is that Christ lives in you. All of the wisdom, power, and resources of Jesus Christ are available to you because He lives in you."

The secret of victory is not what *we do for Christ* but what *He does through us!* When we abide in Christ, and our relationship with Him is the most important part of our lives, He will bring us into authentic victory.[29]

―᚜―

FATHER, THANK YOU THAT CHRIST LIVES IN ME! BY THIS, YOU HAVE MADE ALL YOUR RESOURCES AVAILABLE TO ME, SO I CAN BE THE TEACHER MY STUDENTS NEED ME TO BE. I CHOOSE THIS DAY TO PULL ON YOUR POWER WITHIN ME. AMEN.

The mystery in a nutshell is just this: Christ is in you, therefore you can look forward to sharing in God's glory.

COLOSSIANS 1:27 MSG

YOU FIRST

Do you want to stand out? Then step down. Be a servant.

MATTHEW 23:11 MSG

W ould you put your faith in Winnie the Pooh? Ridiculous as that sounds, the children in your classroom come from homes where faith has been placed in everything from income and credit cards to fashion makeovers and fictitious beliefs. People have traded trust in the one true God for a modern muddle in which many are more apt to put their trust in the one true Pooh.

After all, Pooh Bear is cuddly and cute and harmless. He poses no threat, exacts no justice, and goes with the flow. Your students arrive in the classroom having been raised on a steady diet of material gain and spiritual neglect, their brains and hearts mushy from years of commercial overload and religious indifference.

> **GRACE FOR TODAY:**
>
> God wants us to model servanthood to show a more excellent way of living.

Part of your commission is to resurrect the virtues of faithfulness, honor, integrity, and respect. To teach them the beauty of learning as its own reward. To help them understand that they have a purpose in life and a unique position in the world. Not the arrogant, self-conceited, me-first-ism all too common in today's society, but the self-worth that comes from being made in the image of God.

Jesus saw this human struggle clearly demonstrated in His disciples when they vainly argued which of them would be the greatest. James and John were so drunk on themselves that they commanded Jesus when He entered His glory to let one of them sit on His right, the other on His left. With supreme self-control, the Master explained that even He came to serve, that self-exaltation was the road to ruin.

But sure as taxes, a me-first daily attitude will manifest itself in your students, from shoving matches in line to snickers during someone else's presentation in class. Recognize it for what it is, and with patience and compassion, show your students a more excellent way.

THE LIST

This is the love of God, that we keep His commandments; and His commandments are not burdensome.

1 JOHN 5:3 NASB

Most teachers like lists. Elementary teachers make beautifully written lists of spelling words in D'Nealian style. High-school teachers type and write lists of dates, vocabulary words, and formulas. Teachers make planning lists, lists of things to copy, and lists of goals. We read lists too. Lists of standards and documents that are due before evaluation time. Lists of core objectives that must be met on standardized tests. We read lists in professional magazines, and we come across some that are worthwhile while we are reading for pleasure, such as:

GRACE FOR TODAY:

> God can teach us everything we need to know to be a true disciple of Christ.

"Love God more than you fear hell.
Make major decisions in a cemetery.
When no one is watching, live as if someone is.
Succeed at home first.
Treat people like angels; you will meet some and
help make some.
Don't spend tomorrow's money today.
Listen twice as much as you speak.
Harbor a grudge only when God does.
Pray twice as much as you fret.
The book of life is lived in chapters, so know your page number.
Live your liturgy."
Not a bad list.

Consider one more list: "Love the Lord your God with all your heart and with all your soul and with all your mind and with all your strength. . . . Love your neighbor as yourself" (Mark 12:30-31 NIV).

That's an even better one. Trust God to sum up all we need to know about human relations with just a two-item list. Simple. Profound. It's the only list we'll ever truly need—the only one that includes complete surrender and complete obedience.

WORLD—CHANGING THOUGHTS

Let your speech always be gracious, seasoned with salt, so that you may know how you ought to answer everyone.

COLOSSIANS 4:6 NRSV

John Newton's wickedness consumed much of his early life. Motherless at seven, he sabotaged his ship-captain father's attempts to find him work. He deserted the British navy at the age of seventeen and finally took up the slave trade in Sierra Leone.

Years later, upon escaping Africa aboard a ship bound for home, a violent storm nearly sank him. Slowly, he began to turn toward God. Though he continued working as a slave trader for a while, gradually he forsook this occupation in favor of studying to become a minister. Years of faithful study yielded not only a pulpit from which he descried the evils of human trafficking, leading to reform in England, but also the humbled soul that penned the words to one of the best-loved hymns of all time, "Amazing Grace."

Grace, simply defined, is God's unmerited favor. Through Jesus, you get what you don't deserve. It's the central concept in your relationship with God, and so it suffuses every aspect of your life—not only what God has done for you, but also the way you see and treat everyone else.

Maybe your story as a believer is like John Newton's, or perhaps you've worked with students who, while troubled during their time with you, took root in God's truth and turned out to be fine, productive members of society. Either way, grace was the key, seeing beauty in the ordinary, making music from brokenness. God's thoughts toward you are gracious.

When your students exhibit all the ugliness of sin, when your friends and colleagues flaunt the stain of pride, when you yourself figure God made a mistake by setting you where you are, put on grace. Color your vision with it, for God has provided all of the grace you need to shine the love of Christ into the lives of those around you.

GRACE FOR TODAY:

Where the will of God leads us, His grace will keep us there.

Lord, Help!

Be pleased, O LORD, to deliver me: O LORD, make haste to help me.

PSALM 40:13 KJV

A s a teacher, have you ever felt that if one more thing is piled on your plate, you'll throw the whole thing at the ceiling? God sees what's on your plate, and He has a word for you today—don't panic!

God's Word is power. When He says, "Roll your work upon Me," (Proverbs 16:3), His intention is clear: Do it. But that requires surrender on your part.

The Hebrews represented Scripture with pictures. For this one, a weary traveler weighed down with a burdensome backpack comes upon a fellow sojourner who's willing to carry his load for a spell. Thus the traveler rolls the pack over onto the shoulders of the willing friend, one arm at a time, being careful the pack doesn't fall to the ground.

Whatever is weighing you down, make a decision to surrender it to Jesus. If the God of the universe is willing to shoulder your burden, why would you want to carry it? If you have thirty hours of work to do in twenty-four, give the problem to Him. If some of your work doesn't get done, it's God's burden to manage.

As you trust God with your life, He will cause your thoughts to line up with His will. A new routine for living will emerge. You will begin to roll your work as a teacher onto Him and hear Him direct you by saying, "This is the way today; walk in it."

Amazing results will follow when you surrender to God. Your plans will be established, they'll succeed, and God will be glorified through you.

GRACE FOR TODAY:

As we surrender our lives to God, He will cause our thoughts to line up with His will.

WHERE'D THE JOY GO?

You know that uneasy feeling that creeps up on you once in a great while? A kind of empty listlessness coupled with an overwhelming desire to run away and join the circus? Some describe it as that sneaking suspicion that you've given all that you have to give and it's just not enough. Called dissatisfaction, restlessness, or burnout, it can feel like swimming in molasses.

What does it mean, and how can you return to those happy days when you couldn't wait to get to school in the mornings?

Scripture is full of times of great joy. In his psalms, David often erupts in rapturous expressions of this celebratory state of being. Heart leaping, lips bursting with thanks, he writes of singing, shouting, and making a righteous racket, so swollen is he with the goodness of God. This despite enemies at every side and bushels of betrayal from within and without.

But in your hour of need, you have to ask if David ever faced down twenty-five or thirty wriggling, giggling, energy—pumping children ready to go in any direction.

God knows how shaky our ground can become. David's cup seemed to run dry as much as it ran over. But the apostle Paul liked the cup analogy. He helped the Corinthians drop their idol worship by urging them to partake in the "cup of thanksgiving," which he likened to the Communion cup and all that it symbolizes through the shed blood of Christ.

The Lord knows your pain and He desires to revive you and make your way new again. Acknowledge Him, give loud thanks, take a week off, and hold up your cup.

> **GRACE FOR TODAY:**
>
> **When our cup of joy runs dry, God will refill it.**

The Lord is near to the brokenhearted and saves those who are crushed in spirit.

PSALM 34:18 NASB

COMFORT FROM GOD

By Luis Palau

Several years ago, a submarine, with all its crew, sank off the Atlantic coast of North America. Once the vessel was located, frogmen went down to assess the damage and the possibility of salvaging the wreck.

As divers neared the hull of the vessel, they were surprised to hear a message being pounded in Morse code. Someone was actually still alive in the submarine! The divers listened carefully. The message was a frantic question that beat against the walls of the aquatic tomb: "Is there hope? Is there hope?"

You and I may pose the same question when a problem or tragedy strikes us. Who, after all, is totally free from the crushing pain of losing a loved one, the burden of ill health, the fear of financial difficulties, the anguish of a fragmented home, or any of a hundred other problems?

When such problems beset us, we may feel trapped and submerged by the weight of our circumstances. We wonder, *Is there any hope of overcoming this problem? Can anyone really comfort us in our pain?* We embark on a desperate search for comfort—but usually wind up unfulfilled.

The apostle Paul says God himself declares that He is the Father of compassion and the God of all comfort. In fact, Paul uses a derivative of the word *comfort* ten times in these verses. So when we face external pressures, we can be assured that we have a heavenly Father who is the Father of compassion and comfort.[30]

—⚏—

Lord, TOUCH ME WITH YOUR COMPASSIONATE HAND AND LIFT ME OUT OF MY PAIN AND SUFFERING. AS YOU COMFORT ME, GIVE ME OPPORTUNITIES TO COMFORT MY STUDENTS WHO ARE HURTING. I PLACE MY HOPE IN YOUR GOODNESS AND GRACE. AMEN.

Praise be to the God and Father of our Lord Jesus Christ, the Father of compassion and the God of all comfort, who comforts us in all our troubles, so that we can comfort those in any trouble with the comfort we ourselves have received from God.

2 CORINTHIANS 1:3-4 NIV

THE CALL OF THE SHOFAR

Samuel said, "Has the Lord as great delight in burnt offerings
and sacrifices, as in obedience to the voice of the Lord?
Surely, to obey is better than sacrifice."

1 SAMUEL 15:22 NRSV

"I need you to obey the first time," we tell our children. "Okay, put on your listening ears and zip your lips," we tell our students. When it's preceded by a sharp hand clap, they know we mean business.

And when we're not exhorting students to listen to us, they're learning to have their school lives governed by the buzz, clang, or peal of school bells. Bzzzz! The first bell of the day—time to get to class. One long continuous blast is the fire-alarm bell. Single file out onto the parking lot in an orderly manner. Three short bursts—tornado drill. Huddle against the wall in the crouch-and-cover position. Ding—tardy bell. Beep—time to switch classes. Brrrrng—lunch is over.

Our lives are arranged by signals. Red light: Stop. Green light: Go. Yellow light: Caution. The ping of the microwave: Coffee is heated, or popcorn is finished. The buzz of the kitchen timer: Dinner is ready. The song of the alarm clock: It's time to get up. The beep of the smoke alarms: Check the batteries or check for smoke.

The bells, horns, and signals all help get our attention.

God had a signal for the Israelites too—the shofar. It was a trumpet, usually fashioned from a ram's horn. It was used to alert the Israelites to danger, or call them into battle or to action. Jewish people still use it today as a call for accountability on the Day of Atonement.

For Christians, God's Word and His Holy Spirit are the "shofars," convicting us, urging us to act, prompting us to be people of obedience, and warning us of Satan's schemes. We would do well to add this most important of all "bells" to our daily schedules, indeed, our lives.

> GRACE FOR TODAY:
>
> God's Holy
> Spirit calls us to
> obedience.

ON THE RIGHT PATH

The LORD will guide you always; he will satisfy your needs in a sun-
scorched land and will strengthen your frame.

ISAIAH 58:11 NIV

Hector felt uncomfortable in the spotlight. He knew it was an honor to receive a regional award recognizing the success of his restaurant chain, and he was proud to represent his family and his community. He wondered how best to express his thoughts to the reporters on hand. But as he looked back to the poverty of his childhood years and his parents' prayerful faith, he knew what he had to say. Everyone in the audience knew what Hector had overcome to be there that day, but as he took the podium, waiting for the applause to subside, he pointed skyward.

"Without my parents' guidance, without their example of faith," he said, "I would never have put my trust in God, who has brought me here today."

God made you to lean on Him. That goes against so much contemporary wisdom, which exalts independence and says anything other than self-reliance is weakness. The truth is, people are weak. Some may seem to be safe from common weaknesses, such as caring what others say, but chances are, they're also invulnerable to intimacy, to genuine contact with another person.

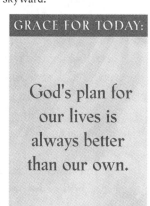

GRACE FOR TODAY:

God's plan for our lives is always better than our own.

God's plan is better. Throughout His Word, by His Holy Spirit, through the counsel of fellow believers, and in every circumstance, He guides you. You trust Him because you know He has a good plan for your life and He will carry it out.

God's principles of guidance work beautifully and effectively in your classroom. You set the tone for learning, establish standards, provide instruction and direction. Yet, because you're aware that it's all a part of God's plan, you encourage your students, listen to them, share your own imperfections and lessons learned. As you trust God's guidance, so others will trust Him through you.

NONNEGOTIABLE

God demonstrates His own love toward us, in that while we were still
sinners, Christ died for us.

ROMANS 5:8 NKJV

The daily-grace word for today is worth! And it is an important one to remember because your worth is priceless and nonnegotiable.

There will be days in your teaching career when parents will assert that little Johnny is not learning, implying that it's all your fault. Or if you teach at the college level, you may have students protest to the dean, trying to manipulate their way into an easier class after the add date. They may intentionally try to make you look bad, complaining that you're too hard or demanding.

In situations like these, your heart needs to be fixed on the truth—that you are of great worth. Once at an Association of Christian Teachers convention, one speaker stood before the crowd and made a lasting impression. He pulled a crumpled, muddy one-hundred-dollar bill out of his pocket and carefully held it by one corner as flakes of dried mud fell to the floor.

"I know this is a dilapidated bill covered in mud, but anybody want it?" he asked. Without hesitating, a young teacher bolted to the platform and grabbed it out of the speaker's hand.

"Do you know why this young man didn't hesitate?" the speaker asked the crowd. "Because no matter how worn-out or muddy this hundred-dollar bill is, it's still worth one hundred dollars at any bank you would take it to. It's value has not changed because of what's happened to it."

The same is true for you! Christ Jesus determined your worth on the day He died on the Cross. God said that day that your life was worth the death of His Son so that you might live with Him forever. Keep this in mind the next time someone's not pleased with you, and remember that Jesus paid a high price, settling your value forever.

GRACE FOR TODAY:

God determines our worth as priceless
and nonnegotiable.

BREATHLESS

God formed Man out of dirt from the ground and
blew into his nostrils the breath of life.

GENESIS 2:7 MSG

How's your breathing? It is said that most people don't really know how to breathe. Their breathing tends to be too shallow, which leaves them far more susceptible to the damaging effects of stress and anxiety.

The Christian mystics believed in saying the name of Jesus with every breath they took as a constant reminder that He is near us and as necessary as oxygen itself. For them, part of being still and knowing that He is God was this exercise entwining human respiration and divine inspiration.

You might take five minutes a day to simply breathe deeply. Slowly take in as much air as you can, then exhale every last cubic inch of that air. It will help if, with each breath you inhale, you count to yourself—1 . . . 2 . . . 3 . . . 4—and then exhale, counting again at the same tempo. Increase the number gradually, thinking of nothing but the counting while you allow your body to replenish itself with life-giving oxygen.

Scripture tells us plainly that our every breath is a gift from God. Job said that in God's hand is the life of every creature and the breath of all mankind. His friend Elihu concurred that "the breath of the Almighty gives me life." How wonderfully symbolic then is a brief, but regular, focus on our breathing as a statement of God's grace.

This is especially important whenever you find yourself breathless from responsibility, short of breath thinking about the next school levy, or facing the breathtaking prospect of an increased class load. Deep, steady breathing is a reassuring reminder that God is merciful.

It may also prove useful in counting to ten.

GRACE FOR TODAY:

Since all Scripture is God-breathed, God can help us
breathe easier by its study.

THE FLEDGLING

As a young single mother and teacher, Grace moved to a new town and accepted a teaching job, determined to make ends meet and to make a difference while she was at it.

During the first set of before—school meetings, she looked around at the other teachers. They hailed each other in fond greeting after having been apart all summer. They commented on vacation tans, different haircuts, and new clothes. They talked about students, rolled their eyes at the crackly old speaker system, and sat in tight, already accepted, already known groups.

Grace put on a brave smile, breathed a deep prayer, and joined a group around the table. She listened more than she talked and smiled often, trying to convey the radiance of God's joy. After a month of teaching, God planted an idea in her heart: The faculty of this school were to be her mission field. She wanted to encourage believers in the workplace and attract new recruits for God's kingdom.

> **GRACE FOR TODAY:**
>
> When we plant seeds of grace, God will guarantee the harvest.

She made up colorful flyers announcing a before–school Bible study every Thursday morning. She prayed. She made a pan of homemade cinnamon rolls for the first meeting, arrived at school early, and promptly tripped on the rug in the main entrance. The pan of rolls landed upside down. Carolyn, the librarian, looked around and seeing no one else in the hall, swept the rolls back in the pan single-handedly.

"We'll pray for them," she whispered.

Grace giggled. "The rolls or the teachers?"

"Both!"

Twelve teachers and staff members attended that first study. On other weeks, numbers climbed to twenty. Grace might never see the firsthand results of those planted seeds, but she doesn't need to. That part is God's business. She's just the teacher.

Could your school use a "Grace"?

[My word] will not return to me empty, but will accomplish what I desire and achieve the purpose for which I sent it.

ISAIAH 55:11 NIV

AMAZING GRACE

By Warren W. Wiersbe

What is grace? It is God's provision for our every need when we need it. It has well been said that God in His grace gives us what we do not deserve, and in His mercy He does not give us what we do deserve. Someone has made an acrostic of the word *grace*: God's Riches Available at Christ's Expense. "Of His [Christ's] fullness we have all received, and grace for grace" (John 1:16 NKJV).

There is never a shortage of grace. God is sufficient for our spiritual ministries (2 Corinthians 3:4-6) and our material needs (9:8), as well as our physical needs (12:9). If God's grace is sufficient to save us, surely it is sufficient to keep us and strengthen us in our times of suffering.

In the Christian life, we get many of our blessings through *transformation*, not *substitution*. When Paul prayed three times for the removal of his pain, he was asking God for a substitution: "Give me health instead of sickness, deliverance instead of pain and weakness." Sometimes God does meet the need by substitution; but other times He meets the need by transformation. He does not remove the affliction, but He gives us His grace so that the affliction works *for* us and not *against* us.

Paul claimed God's promise and drew upon the grace that was offered to him; this turned seeming tragedy into triumph. God did not change the situation by removing the affliction; He changed it by adding a new ingredient: grace. Our God is "the God of all grace" (1 Peter 5:10 NIV), and His throne is a "throne of grace" (Hebrews 4:16 NIV). The Word of God is "the word of His grace" (Acts 20:32 NIV), and the promise is that "He giveth more grace" (James 4:6 NIV). No matter how we look at it, God is adequate for every need that we have.[31]

—⁓—

FATHER, THANK YOU FOR YOUR AMAZING GRACE. TRANSFORM ME BY IT THAT I MAY TOTALLY FULFILL MY CALL TO TEACH. AMEN.

When I am weak, then I am strong.

2 CORINTHIANS 12:10 NIV

LEAD ON SOFTLY

I have taught thee in the way of wisdom; I have led thee in right paths.

PROVERBS 4:11 KJV

Vinnie was eighty-four, a World War II veteran, and currently the gardener at the First Street Mission. Pastor Steve wondered if Vinnie had survived Normandy only to fall victim to the street gangs that roamed the area. They had tormented Vinnie for months, even stealing his retirement watch, but Vinnie always dusted himself off and just continued gardening.

Steve marveled at both Vinnie's green thumb and his commitment, but years later, after Vinnie had died, it was his legacy that humbled Steve most of all. A young man answered the call for a new gardener, and Steve found out that he had been the gang leader.

> GRACE FOR TODAY:
>
> God wants us to lead by His example.

"I returned his watch later that year," the gang leader said, "because it was the only time my cruelty had been returned with love. Please let me give something else to honor him."

Leadership is vital for the health of any organization or group of people, and the best leadership of all features some mix of vision and flexibility. After all, you would run an activity for kindergarteners differently than you would head up a committee for curriculum review. The one aspect that works best under any circumstance is when you lead by example. Show folks the way you want things done, and then let them do their thing.

Schools often look for better methods, but God wants better people. Every time you take a little more than your share of the blame, or a little less than your share of the credit, you are becoming the leader God wants you to be.

You're one of the most important examples your students will ever see of what it takes to make a change in the world. Take care that those who walk in your footsteps step where you step . . . in God's footprints.

TAKE IT WHEREVER YOU GO

I am not ashamed of this Good News about Christ. It is the power of
God at work, saving everyone who believes.

ROMANS 1:16 NLT

It was a new school year, and Rachelle had a new outlook on teaching. She'd spent the summer on a mission trip and learned a valuable life lesson. The poverty and starvation in the mountains of Ecuador brought her face-to-face with children so hungry that they would pull leftover food from open trash fires. For the first time, Rachelle understood what it meant to see people truly hungry—both for food and for God's Word.

While Rachelle assisted in a medical clinic, a young girl named Shani came in, obviously in pain. The wait was long, so Rachelle tried to ease her pain by telling her about Jesus healing a man born blind. Afterward, Shani asked, "You know more stories?"

"Oh, it's not a story," Rachelle said. "It's true—it really happened!"

"Can be so?" Shani asked excitedly. "Who's dis Jesus?"

GRACE FOR TODAY:

When we share
God's love
with a stranger,
He produces a
friend.

Rachelle gladly shared God's love and explained how Shani could receive Christ as her Savior. Shani responded instantly, and Rachelle sensed with confidence that God was healing the girl. When she left the clinic, all her pain was gone. Stopping by the desk to tell Rachelle good-bye, Shani asked, "Rasell, you know 'bout dis Jesus all you life; why you not come tell Shani sooner?"

That summer changed Rachelle. She realized God had set the standard by sending His Son to communicate His love in a tangible way, and she knew He didn't want her to stop doing that just because she was back at school. This teacher learned that God still desires to spread His love to others through His obedient children, one person at a time.

Like Rachelle, you are God's hands of kindness, His arms of compassion, His voice of truth. Be open to how God may use you to spread the gospel of His grace around your school.

WINNING THEM OVER

Go easy on those who hesitate in the faith.

JUDE 1:23 MSG

How interesting that no two people think exactly alike. Magazine editors count on freelance writers to provide fresh perspectives on Christmas, for example, because every one of us has experienced that season in our own unique way. Good thing, or else the December issues of our favorite periodicals would quickly become stale and repetitive.

Mark Twain said, "It were not best that we should all think alike; it is difference of opinion that makes horse races." Much of the color, pizzazz, and interest of life comes from competing human thought. Presidential elections are won through debate and persuasive rhetoric. Get enough people to agree with you, and you can change your address to that of the White House.

There are many similarities in the teaching profession. You bring your own unique set of experiences and view of life with you into the classroom. Your success depends to a large extent on how persuasive you are with the facts and how effective and compelling you are at winning over the doubters, the wary, and the undecideds. There's no feeling quite like that of finally getting a classroom—or a country—moving together in the same direction.

Jesus certainly dealt with a large variety of competing agendas and personalities. Be they Roman rulers, Jewish authorities, squabbling disciples, needy multitudes, or those bent on betrayal, He taught them, healed them, convicted and confounded them, all the while pointing to the heavenly Father and His kingdom. Little wonder that one of the titles Jesus used for himself was Teacher.

Take joy in your very special calling. And the next time a student stubbornly digs in their heels and resists the truth, say a prayer of silent thanks that, as Jesus knew all too well, it takes all kinds.

GRACE FOR TODAY:

God made each one of us unique to spice up our classroom stew.

WHAT'S YOUR ANSWER?

Always be prepared to give an answer to everyone who asks you to give
the reason for the hope that you have.

1 PETER 3:15 NIV

It's true, you know. If you want to lead in the manner of current "leaders" in popular culture and sometimes even in politics and service positions, you can't stand
on principle. There can't be any absolute truth, and you must bend your convictions on
any position to suit whatever crowd you're addressing. If you want to lead like that,
being wishy-washy is okay.

But if you want to lead like Jesus led, your life should prompt others to ask why
you seem so different, and you'd better have solid knowledge of what you believe and
why. The only possible basis for that kind of leadership is becoming grounded in God's
unchanging Word.

Once a student walked into a high-school classroom before school and asked her
teacher what made her think that the God she talked about was the right one. The
teacher briefly shared her faith based on three points. First, evidence. She knew and
outlined the evidence for biblical truth and the life, death, and resurrection of Jesus.
Second, experience. She had already prepared a short testimony of how God had
proved true to her personally. Third, she mentioned the fact that there is no escaping
the critical element of faith. Any belief system takes a measure of faith. But this teacher
stated with conviction that her faith was based on solid ground.

Have you ever thought about what your answer would be if a colleague or student asked you the reasons for your faith? If not, this would be an excellent day to start.
We're called to be leaders, kingdom movers and shakers, and warriors of faith in this
spiritual battle.

But put on your full spiritual armor. (See Ephesians 6.) You never want to meet
the enemy clad only in spiritual underwear.

GRACE FOR TODAY:

God calls us to be leaders of faith in our schools.

ALL DUE HONOR

The wind howled in the night, driving the rain down the alley in skittering waves. The woman pulled her soaked shawl over her hair. She had heard they would bring him this way. Her every heartbeat was a prayer: Let this be the right place. Protect him, Lord. Establish Your Church in this godless land. Voices echoed off the walls, followed by flashlights and footsteps. A group of soldiers moved past, roughly escorting a young man in handcuffs. His eyes met hers, and he reached for her hand. Their fingers touched before a soldier slapped them apart.

"Enemy of the state," the soldier barked. "Move aside!" They moved the man along, but he looked over his shoulder and said, "Courage, Mother. Jesus will not forsake China!"

The young martyr's loyalty to Christ was a virtue engendered by God's love. As well, your commitment to be the best spouse, parent, friend, and teacher you can be all draw from this wellspring, the very source of which is God. Through good times and bad, you stick it out because you're committed to the welfare of those you love.

When someone is faithful to you, loyalty is a fair return on their investment. God invested His Son in you; offering your life back to Him is what Paul calls your "reasonable service." Your devotion to God plants fruitful seeds in everyone around you—seeds that bloom to change the world.

Impart to your students an allegiance to the truth. Earn their respect by being fair, honest, and consistent, and do all you can to make sure that their commitment to these qualities doesn't stop when they leave your room. When your kids see that you care about them as people and not just as students, they'll see that your values extend beyond the four walls of your classroom.

GRACE FOR TODAY:

God engenders loyalty in us to follow Christ and change our world.

Never let loyalty and kindness get away from you! Wear them like a necklace; write them deep within your heart.

PROVERBS 3:3 NLT

Buy a Hot Dog, Mister?

By John C. Maxwell

A man lived by the side of the road and sold hot dogs. He was hard of hearing, so he had no radio. He had trouble with his eyes, so he read no newspapers. But he sold good hot dogs.

This man put up signs on the highway advertising his wonderful hot dogs. He stood on the side of the road and cried, "Buy a hot dog, Mister?" And people bought his hot dogs. He increased his meat and bun orders, and he bought a bigger stove to take care of his trade. He made enough money to put his son through college.

Unfortunately, the son came home from college an educated pessimist. He said, "Father, haven't you been listening to the radio? Haven't you been reading the newspaper? There's a big recession going on. The European situation is terrible, and the domestic situation is worse."

Whereupon the father thought, *Well, my son's been to college. He reads the paper and he listens to the radio; he ought to know.* So the father cut down his meat and bun orders, took down his signs, and no longer bothered to stand out on the highway to sell his hot dogs.

Of course, his sales fell overnight. "You're right, son," the father said to the boy. "We certainly are in the middle of a big recession."

Confidence shakers see the negative side of everything. When they get you to buy into it, the very thing that was helping you be successful becomes your downfall. Our confidence has a great reward. If we keep it and build on it, we will be more than recompensed. Confidence in oneself is the cornerstone to success.[32]

―⚬―

DEAR FATHER, FORGIVE ME FOR ALLOWING CONFIDENCE SHAKERS TO ROB ME OF MY ASSURANCE THAT I'M BEING THE TEACHER YOU'VE CALLED ME TO BE. BY YOUR GRACE, RESTORE MY CONFIDENCE THAT I MIGHT FULFILL YOUR PERFECT WILL FOR MY LIFE. AMEN.

Do not throw away your confidence, which has a great reward.

HEBREWS 10:35 NASB

A GIFT FOR ALL

By grace you have been saved through faith, and this is not
your own doing; it is the gift of God—not the result of works,
so that no one may boast.

EPHESIANS 2:8-9 NRSV

Everyone has heard the story of Adam and Eve. It's the story about man's first sin—a story that many of us would rather avoid. Few people mess up and come right out and say, "I'm so sorry; I sinned!" For the most part, sin is not something people quickly jump to identify with.

> **GRACE FOR TODAY:**
>
> God gave
> His only Son
> to buy our
> salvation.

When Adam and Eve chose their own way instead of God's, they didn't instantly die physically, but they did instantly die spiritually, and that's why they ran and hid from God. They no longer had the nature of God. Instead they now had a "sin nature," one centered on self rather than on God. Consequently, everyone born into this world since then has inherited that sin nature and a predisposition for living life their own way.

That's why Jesus Christ came and died as the substitute for us to atone for man's sin. God didn't merely forgive sin—He paid the penalty for it with His Son's precious blood so we could go free.

What incredible value Christ's redemption places on your life as a human being and as a teacher. This is the ultimate in forgiveness, and it beckons you to make a decision to personally receive His saving grace into your life if you haven't done so already. God desires for you to discover the reason He uniquely created you and to experience the wonderful plan He has for your life.

BUCKLE UP

**Yet in all these things we are more than conquerors
through Him who loved us.**

ROMANS 8:37 NKJV

Every morning during his ministry to overcome the spiritual darkness of Ireland in the fifth century, Saint Patrick got dressed as he prayed a lengthy prayer for God's protection. Among the many things he prayed for as he buckled up for the day was Christ's protection "against poison, against burning, against drowning, against wounds . . ."

While you may not face the physical dangers Patrick faced, you must sometimes feel like all the forces of darkness are arrayed against you. The language students use, the television mentality they possess, and the deadly outside influences they find attractive are so potentially destructive that you just want to run and bar the door against those things.

The apostle Paul told the Philippians that it brought tears to his eyes to think of how many live as enemies of the Cross of Christ. They are those whose god is their stomach, whose minds dwell on earthly things. But not long after that, Paul told the believers to think about whatever is right and lovely, whatever is excellent and praiseworthy, as a way to combat the darkness.

And so you enlighten your students about the risk and adventure of the first manned flight, ocean exploration, modern medicine, and democracy. You urge them to read the great writers, study the champions of liberty, and delve into the wonders contained in a single raindrop. You let them peek into the mind of God so that the beauty and light of His creative majesty washes over them.

Demonstrate that which is good and glorious and Paul says that the God of peace will attend you. With Him in you and alongside you, you will get through, you will push back the corrosive effects of this world, you will overcome evil with good. Patrick did and an entire nation was lifted from pagan darkness.

> **GRACE FOR TODAY:**
> When we flood our students' minds with God's light, He makes sure the darkness has nowhere to hide.

THE BEAUTY OF BALANCE

Fix your attention on God. . . . God brings [out] the best . . .
[and] develops well-formed maturity in you.

ROMANS 12:2 MSG

G od uses many pictures in Scripture to simplify profound truths. One of those portraits is of the village potter, molding wet clay on his wheel.

As a teacher, you've probably seen art classes in which students work with clay to mold a vase or a jar. The wet clay is balanced upon the potter's wheel and spun around while the potter forms their masterpiece. Even if the clay tilts too much to the right or to the left, the artist can keep molding it as longs as it stays on the wheel and doesn't fly off. But if the clay is too wet, it won't hold a shape, and if the clay is too dry, it can't be molded.

Similar to the clay, God wants you to stay on His wheel so He can continue to mold you and bring symmetry and balance into your life. If you fly off the wheel, you stop the process and are of no value even to yourself. If you're too wet—have no structure, no boundaries, no self-esteem—you will not be able to hold the shape of the image of Christ in which you've been created. On the other hand, if you're too dry—have a hard heart, are stubborn, rigid, or inflexible—you can't be molded at all. Like the clay, you will need to be pounded, ground, and soaked until you're pliable enough to put back on the wheel.

As a teacher, it's sometimes hard to keep your life in balance and allow the Master Potter to mold and shape you. What comes first? Grading papers until midnight, or spending time with your family? Think about God as the potter today and stay centered on His wheel, so that He can mold you into a vessel of honor for His eternal purposes.

GRACE FOR TODAY:

If we stay pliable in God's hands, He will bring
balance to our lives.

BUILDING ON THE TRUTH

We will lovingly follow the truth at all times—speaking truly,
dealing truly, living truly—and so become more and more
in every way like Christ.

EPHESIANS 4:15 TLB

A king stopped his horse along the road to offer a beggar a ride to the next city. When they arrived, the king told him to dismount, but the beggar said, "You get off! In this city who's to say whether this horse is yours or mine?" The king fumed at his impudence but decided to let a judge decide the matter. They each made their case, but the beggar's deceptive story almost had the king convinced that he'd stolen his own horse! The judge told them to leave the horse with him overnight and come back the next day.

When they returned, the judge imprisoned the beggar and scolded him for his ingratitude. Astonished by the judge's wisdom, the king asked how he had known the truth.

"Simple, your majesty," the judge said. "I watched both you and the beggar pass the stable I'd put the horse in last night. When the beggar passed, the horse ignored him. But when you walked by, it lifted its nose toward you and whinnied softly, recognizing its beloved master."

Honesty is the cornerstone on which all other virtues are constructed. Without it, entire lives are built on ulterior motives, hypocrisy, and superficiality. Being honest with yourself is hard, but once accomplished, you open the door to God, and He builds His character and integrity into your heart.

If you've ever done a unit on honesty, you know your kids—even the good ones—aren't exactly paragons of virtue. Partial truths appear to be vital to just getting along in life, so it's up to you to draw a line in the sand.

The most effective way to do that is first to ensure that you're always honest with your students. Rather than enforcing your authority, share with them times when you struggle with doing the right thing too. Your honest actions will win the day.

GRACE FOR TODAY:

When we are honest with ourselves, God can build
His character and integrity into our hearts.

KILLING THE IMAGINATION

There's a list of phrases, preferably accompanied by sighs, eye rolling, and slumps of disapproval, that every teacher should learn if they want to squelch enthusiasm, squash imagination, and bring the exchange of new ideas to a screeching halt.

> Work is drudgery.
> Teaching is a duty.
> We've always done it this way.
> Talking about this is useless.
> We've never tried that.
> It takes too much time.
> Learning takes place best in the atmosphere of straight lines and complete silence.

You wouldn't want to be in that classroom, either, would you? Deploring the idea of accepting change or of being flexible and open to new ways smacks of arrogance, or at least laziness. And yet, it's so tempting for all of us to think, *This is what works. Let's not change it. I know best.* But that's not usually best for any of us.

Notice what the slight exchange of a few words and a new attitude can do to those phrases.

> Work is a privilege.
> Teaching is a calling.
> Why not try something new?
> Never met a topic that couldn't at least be talked about.
> Let's try it!
> What's a few more minutes?
> The best place to learn might be in a circle, outside under the shade of a tree or in a lively discussion.

Just for today, loosen up. Take your students outside. Teach them an old topic in a fresh way. Ask them to look at the world, at a question, at a problem upside down, as if they were hearing it for the first time or speaking a different language. Let them teach the other students and you for few minutes. Collaborate on a project. Explain how multiple subjects fit together. Stuff the arrogance of sameness deep into your supply closet and leave it there, at least for today.

GRACE FOR TODAY:

God wants us to use our imaginations and discover fresh ways to teach.

Be not wise in thine own eyes.

PROVERBS 3:7 KJV

DO IT WHILE YOU CAN

By John C. Maxwell

Too often people wait too long to forgive other people. Forgiveness should be given as quickly and as totally as possible. Do it now. Don't be in the position of the young man who needs and wants his parents' forgiveness, but because they are physically unable to communicate, he cannot be sure that they understand him. Every day he goes to the hospital and asks, but he gets no response. Because of his procrastination, he will never experience the joy of their forgiveness and reconciliation.

One of the most striking scenes in 1978 was Hubert Humphrey's funeral. Seated next to Hubert's beloved wife was former President Richard M. Nixon, a long-time political adversary of Humphrey's, and a man disgraced by Watergate. Humphrey himself had asked Nixon to have that place of honor.

Three days before Senator Humphrey died, Jesse Jackson visited him in the hospital. Humphrey told Jackson that he had just called Nixon. The Reverend Jackson, knowing their past relationship, asked Humphrey why. Here is what Hubert Humphrey had to say: "From this vantage point, with the sun setting in my life, all of the speeches, the political conventions, the crowds, and the great fights are behind me. At a time like this you are forced to deal with your irreducible essence, forced to grapple with that which is really important. And what I have concluded about life is that when all is said and done, we must forgive each other, redeem each other, and move on."

Do you know how to die victoriously? Quit keeping score of the injustices that have happened to you. If you are at odds with anyone, take the first step; confront the problem and ask for forgiveness.[33]

—⁂—

HEAVENLY FATHER, I CHOOSE TO FORGIVE AND BE FORGIVEN. HELP ME AS I MOVE FORWARD ON THIS PATH TO FORGIVENESS. AMEN.

Bear with one another and, if anyone has a complaint against another, forgive each other; just as the Lord has forgiven you, so you also must forgive.

COLOSSIANS 3:13 NRSV

HELP IN THE HERE AND NOW

Do you not know that you are the temple of God and that the Spirit of God dwells in you?

1 CORINTHIANS 3:16 NKJV

The Holy Spirit is definitely Someone you want in your corner. In Scripture, He's called the Comforter, the Counselor, and the Helper. He teaches you what you should say and when you should say it, and He will guide you into all truth and remind you of that truth regularly. (See John 14:26.)

Not a bad description for a teacher.

God the Spirit is God the Teacher, present with us and in us. The Lord says in Ezekiel that He will move us to follow His decrees and to be careful to keep His laws.

> **GRACE FOR TODAY:**
>
> God's strong hand leads, guides, protects, and empowers us to teach.

As our Comforter, the Spirit is our courage. Just as forte is the musical term for "strong," cum forte, "with strength," is the idea behind this title of "Comforter." It is not a soft comfort such as a child might receive from a favorite blanket. It is the reassuring comfort of a strong hand and muscular arm leading, guiding, protecting, and emboldening you.

He is our Counselor in the legal sense—someone who helps another in trouble with the law. The Spirit will always stand by and support Christ's people: our Defender. He will challenge and exhort us to live devoted lives of integrity and to walk out of the courtrooms and classrooms of life with our heads held high, our shoulders back, and a heart true to what matters most.

Peter tells us that the Spirit who resurrected Christ is the same Spirit who quickens us. Don't ever think you go to school alone to teach alone. You go to school with might and power and God in you and beside you. There are no multiplication tables big enough to compute a blessing so grand!

MAKING PLANS

Commit your works to the LORD and your plans will be established.

PROVERBS 16:3 NASB

In Ray Blackston's evocative second novel, *A Delirious Summer*, Allie, a poet–turned–missionary in South America, writes some poignant thoughts about our plans and efforts to understand God: "We spend vast amounts of time and energy crafting a thesis in our heads of how life should play out, then almighty God spends an incredibly brief amount of time blowing our thesis to bits."

At first reading that might sound harsh. Doesn't God want us to make plans? (As a teacher, a "plan–less" day is incomprehensible!) To succeed in this life? Well, no . . . and yes.

For those who undertake the additional education involved in obtaining a master's degree, it usually ends with the writing of a thesis. A thesis is to education and history majors what a hypothesis is to a scientist; we assert something, and then we try to prove it.

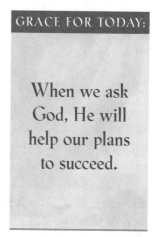

GRACE FOR TODAY:

When we ask God, He will help our plans to succeed.

For the Christian, however, that process is a bit backwards. We agree to accept something—God—whom we can't see. We agree to receive something—grace—that we can't fathom. And we do this through faith, which we can't prove. Is there evidence of God's existence, of Jesus, of the Resurrection? Absolutely! Does archaeology continue to support biblical assertions? A resounding yes! But all of that is just icing on the cake.

Instead of demanding that God fit in with our plans, we are asked that we plan according to His will. Yet we are assured that when we ask within that will, our plans will succeed. Clearly, God is a God of plans, second chances, and dreams. So go ahead, tell God your wildest dreams, your secret ambitions, your longings, your plans. Just know that what He has in store may surpass them all!

AN ETERNAL SPRING

Be of good courage, and he shall strengthen your heart,
all ye that hope in the LORD.

PSALM 31:24 KJV

December 1989 saw the end of both Ceaucescu's dictatorship in Romania and Cristian Soimaru's complacence. Cristian had decided to study law as a way to help build his nation anew, but a trip to a fast-food restaurant changed his life forever. A dozen street kids came up to him, begging for food, money, even just a moment's attention, and something clicked inside him. He saw the children's plight—their desperation—and he began to befriend them. In 1994 Cristian partnered with Angie Thomson to help build Orasul Sperantei—"City of Hope"—a home for orphaned boys and girls. "Giving hope is so close to God's heart," Cristian said. "Just to help one life makes a difference."

Cristian realized that hope is essential to any sense of satisfaction in your life. No matter how rough things are, you have to believe that they can get better, even if it takes a miracle. Because Jesus is risen, you have hope for a forgiven past, a fruitful present, and a glorious future.

When the things that break God's heart break your own, you see with greater clarity the power of the hope He offers you in Jesus. Even your own corner of the world is filled with sadness, loneliness, and despair. You can hope to make a small but significant difference, one person at a time, just by reaching out with God's love.

Your actions may not change the situation, but never underestimate what it means to offer hope that someday it might change. Each time you give up your lunchtime to help a kid with her math, or stay after school to listen to a student talk about problems with his friends, or take the time to call the parent of a struggling child about that day's modest success, you are sharing hope.

GRACE FOR TODAY:

Our actions may not change things, but God can use
us to offer hope that someday change will come.

THE GREAT I AM

[Jesus said,] "Surely I am with you always."

MATTHEW 28:20 NIV

When God told Moses to go to Pharaoh and command the Egyptian ruler to let His people go, Moses argued that Pharaoh wouldn't listen to him. But God told Moses to inform Pharaoh that: "I AM hath sent me unto you" (Exodus 3:14 KJV). What a revelation of our all-powerful God! The Hebrew meaning for the word I AM is interpreted as: "I'm in existence to be whatever you need me to be."

With God's help, Moses led the children of Israel out of bondage and into freedom. That same mighty power is still available to all who desire God's presence and want to have a relationship with Him.

God—omniscient, omnipotent, and omnipresent—wants you to experience Him in the fullness of who He is. To do that, it's necessary to live in the moment because that is where God makes himself available to you. He is in the past, but you are not, so you cannot connect with Him there. All your mistakes, failures, and regrets are only memories. God dwells in the future, but you do not, so all of your "what ifs"—your problems and fears—have no substance. God the Father chooses to live in this moment with you. He is I AM—not "I was," nor "I will be." He is God right now.

Meet Him in this moment and allow His peace to stop such nagging thoughts as:

Will I ever get married?

Will I ever get my doctorate in education?

I wish I hadn't yelled at that child.

If only I hadn't gotten that charge card.

God is here today. He is always waiting to be I AM for you—in the here and now. Today, tell Him you're ready to take hold of His grace and start living moment by moment.

GRACE FOR TODAY:

When we live in the moment with God, He makes life more enjoyable.

OVER THIS WAY

We are not born with maps. Maps are made and making them requires effort. Wise, but few, are those who "map out" their path, knowing that the more detailed and considered the route, the more the journey may be enjoyed and the more confident the traveler is of actually reaching the desired destination. Sketchy maps are dangerous and misleading at best.

The early explorers either had no maps for where they were going, or the maps they had contained huge gaps. Of course, we only ever hear about the explorers who survived despite their lack of details. The Marco Polos and Christopher Columbuses of the world are famous, in part, because they were among the fortunate few who lived to report what they found and to write, lecture, and excite others to the possibilities of "new worlds." They filled in the sketchy maps.

Your students count on you to provide them with detailed and accurate maps for navigating life. The more truth you give them with which to fill out their life maps, the wider and more realistic their worldview will be. You are literally giving them the tools and the information necessary to understand the reality they inhabit and to make informed decisions that will affect their future.

Jesus gave His disciples a great deal of information with which to navigate three worlds: the one in which they lived, the kingdom of God, and the world to come. Armed with that much truthful detail, they were able to "go and make disciples" and set a gospel fire that to this day blazes across the earth.

Talk to your students about the importance of charts by which to sail the seas of their existence. Maps are a wonderful analogy for finding the right directions to a life well lived.

> **GRACE FOR TODAY:**
>
> God provides a living map to eternal life in His Word.

May the Master take you by the hand and lead you along the path of God's love and Christ's endurance.

2 THESSALONIANS 3:5 MSG

THE DESIRES OF YOUR HEART

By Charles Stanley

When the time came for me to buy my daughter a car, I asked her what she wanted. She had been praying, and she knew the exact year, model, color, and interior of car she wanted. So we began looking. I had taught her to be specific in her prayers but I had no idea she would be so specific. Regardless of what kind of car we saw or how good the price was, she stuck by what she had originally asked God for. This went on for months.

Then one night my son was looking through the want ads and he found a car just like what Becky was looking for. It was the right make, color, model, and year. We went to look at it that night, and after talking with the owner for just a few minutes, we knew it was the right car. It didn't take much prayer to know if we were making the right decision; all the praying had been done.

God encourages us to pray specific prayers. Once we decide on something, we must stick with it in our prayers; otherwise we demonstrate a lack of faith. The psalmist does not say, "He shall give thee the *needs* of thine heart." But rather he writes, "He shall give thee the *desires* of thine heart" (Psalm 37:4 KJV). We must understand that what we are asking for is not really the issue. It is the attitude of our heart that matters. God wants to bless His children, but the relationship and method must be right.[34]

———

DEAR FATHER, THANK YOU FOR CARING ABOUT EVERY ASPECT OF WHO I AM, INCLUDING MY HOPES AND DESIRES. I OFFER THOSE DESIRES TO YOU. TRANSFORM THEM BY YOUR GRACE IN ACCORDANCE WITH YOUR PERFECT WILL FOR MY LIFE. AMEN.

In everything, by prayer and petition (definite requests), with thanksgiving, continue to make your wants known to God.

PHILIPPIANS 4:6 AMP

UNFORGETTABLE

The Son of Man did not come to be a slave master, but a slave who will
give his life to rescue many people.

MATTHEW 20:28 CEV

K en Blanchard, author of *The One Minute Manager,* talks about the fine attitude
of the frontline workers who are employed by the San Diego Padres baseball
club. From food-service workers to security guards, they believe themselves to be in
the memory-making business. It is in exceptional service that they take leadership in
ensuring that the fans enjoy the game and memories are made.

When one female fan went to a food-service window during a game and asked for
milk, she was politely told by a male employee that they
did not sell milk in the stadium. That might have been
it, except that the man had been taught to lead through
service. He asked her where she was seated and
informed her that he would find her the milk her baby
needed.

The worker left the stadium, found a grocery
store, purchased the milk, and delivered it to the
woman's seat. Now that's leadership! However her
team may have played that game, she had a wonderful
memory for all time, and her opinion of the Padres was
sky high.

You are the leader of your classroom. Every day
your students grant you the opportunity to demonstrate
your leadership. Every nose you wipe, every shoulder
you pat, every mind you stretch, and every heart you warm grows your leadership
skills. Not everyone is eager to plunge into the ocean of learning, but if you're the first
in and you show how great the water is, your students will cavort like seals.

Don't be afraid to do the unexpected. Not only will you get the point across, but
you might just make a memory!

GRACE FOR TODAY:

God wants us to
follow His lead
so that we can be
better leaders in
our classrooms.

HUMBLE WISDOM

Whoever exalts himself will be humbled,
and he who humbles himself will be exalted.

MATTHEW 23:12 NKJV

D uring his illustrious basketball career, David Robinson won it all—two NBA championships, Rookie of the Year, League MVP, and two Olympic gold medals. In the last years of his career, however, came perhaps his finest hour, as he groomed young All-Star prospect Tim Duncan to take his place as the San Antonio Spurs' "go-to guy."

Putting aside the ego that many professional athletes feel is their birthright, Robinson graciously passed the torch to his teammate. Drawing from the biblical David's experience with King Saul gave him perspective. "I'm blessed that God has given me the ability to just enjoy the victory," Robinson told *Sports Illustrated*. "So Tim killed the tens of thousands. That's great. I'm happy for him."

One of teaching's peculiarities is in how difficult it is to be humble in a profession where humility is required of you on a daily basis. It's surprisingly easy to get a big head when, for example, you help a student learn to avoid run-on sentences in her writing, and you are immediately besieged by ten others who think semicolons are for winking smiley-faces in their text messaging.

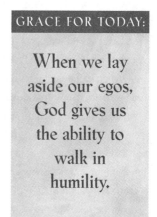

GRACE FOR TODAY:

When we lay aside our egos, God gives us the ability to walk in humility.

The simple beauty of knowing Christ is in seeing yourself for what you are, a fallen individual in need of God's grace, and yet living in that grace, knowing that you are God's beloved child, whom God humbled himself to save. Humility isn't humiliation; it's freedom from self-importance.

You've heard the old adage about taking your work seriously but not yourself. Let your students see you for who you are: an accomplished, capable, talented professional full of knowledge, wisdom, and compassion. But make sure they also know you see yourself as imperfect, capable of error, and yet not defined by either your successes or your failures.

ANSWERS ARE WAITING

Against all hope, Abraham in hope believed and so became the father of many nations, just as it had been said to him, "So shall your offspring be."

ROMANS 4:18 NIV

Thirty-year-old Jaynelyn had been a teacher at East Central for eight years. Even though her greatest desire was to be a mother, some days it seemed like her dream would never come true. For two years Jaynelyn had been dating Scott, and during that time, he had proposed twice and broken off their engagement both times. Scott always got cold feet when it came to setting a date for the wedding. Jaynelyn became so depressed, it was all she could do to drag herself to school.

One morning Mrs. Quarles found Jaynelyn crying alone in the teachers' lounge. She couldn't understand how any guy in his right mind could do such a thing to such a wonderful young woman, but she was quite sure that God had a plan for Jaynelyn. The young teacher just needed to hold on to God—not Scott—until His plans came to pass.

Offering Jaynelyn another tissue, Mrs. Quarles said, "Sweetie, I've walked this road of trust many times, and believe me—you'll get through this. Do you remember how God told Abraham to sacrifice his son Isaac? He had no inkling that God had a ram waiting at the top of the mountain to substitute for Isaac. That ram didn't appear out of thin air. It was moving toward the thicket at the same time Abraham was climbing that mountain with his son. Just wait and see, Jaynelyn. God's got a ram—a Scott—waiting for you at the top of your mountain too."

In the midst of life's struggles—like a single teacher wanting to marry or a math teacher with financial woes—never cease believing that God has a plan for you. Keep trusting Him as you trudge up your mountain. He has something waiting for you at the top!

GRACE FOR TODAY:

When we trust in God, He makes all things possible.

ALWAYS IN STYLE

There is one glory of the sun, another glory of the moon, and another
glory of the stars; for one star differs from another star in glory.

1 CORINTHIANS 15:41 NKJV

D o you possess a personal style? What fashions do you favor? Bright colors,
signature accessories, or sandals with socks? Each style reflects a personality, a mood, or even a philosophy of life. Informal or jazzy footwear, for instance, may
signal a playful, relaxed manner or spontaneous outlook. High gloss wingtips or a
skirt-and-heels look may reflect a more serious, let's-get-down-to-business
approach.

The people featured in the Bible certainly represent the range of personal styles.
David might strike us as a bold, athletic, and at times reckless, type-A personality,
whereas we might rate Moses as more accepting, decisive, and long-suffering, with a
CEO's sense of the "fine print" when it comes to how things ought to be done.

Your students cover the range of personal styles too—some happy and bubbly, a
few brainy and absorbed, still others brooding and cynical, perhaps going to great
lengths to perfect a cool detachment. This mix can be interesting, frustrating, and at
times downright unnerving or exhilarating—sometimes all of them at once. How well
you recognize and manage the mix is what marks your personal teaching style.

At times, your classroom will seem like the Corinthian believers with their bick-
ering factions and differing opinions on what was good and acceptable for the Church.
The congregation had its worldly ones, its babes in understanding, the jealous, the
quarrelsome, the arrogant, and the faithful. But despite their differing styles and right or
wrong thinking, Paul charged them all to be of one mind and to live at peace.

Not unlike what you do every day at school. Like Paul, you have the authority and
the privilege to build up your students and show them how it all fits together. Might
you do that in red high-topped sneakers or rainbow-colored canvas clogs?

GRACE FOR TODAY:

God gave us each our own particular style.

SOUL RAIN

The first day that needed rain hits the earth, it's usually welcomed—welcomed by a parade of students with bright umbrellas who engage in gleeful puddle stomping. As you drive to school, the glistening yellow school buses seem a cheerful harbinger of spring. The gentle slap of the windshield wipers tap out a soothing rhythm and thoughts turn to cozy things. Baking. Good books. A visit to the library. A visit with our parents, or perhaps with good friends.

But moody creatures that we are, a few days of rain, either on the earth or in the soul, can cause gloom to set in. Our students manifest it with noses pressed against water-streaked glass. With restless roaming. With endless questions and pent-up energy. We acknowledge it with glum reluctance. A gradual ripping of the facing of contentment; a corrosion of inner peace. We aren't any good at dealing with "the blues."

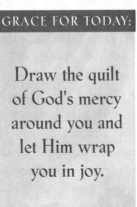

GRACE FOR TODAY:

Draw the quilt of God's mercy around you and let Him wrap you in joy.

At best, we mope and lay in with a supply of melancholy books and movies. We retreat. We isolate. At worst, soul rain causes self-pity. A feeling of being picked on. All normal, in short doses. As Barbara Johnson wrote, "Sometimes it seems as though it rains on the just and the unjust, but chiefly on the just because the unjust are always stealing the just's umbrella!" So we have a choice. Whine about the rain, or be thankful for the umbrella.

Non-clinical depression is generally caused by too much introspection, too much self-focus, or even too much selfishness. Look outward. There is always someone worse off than you. Look upward. There is never a problem too big for God, nor one so small that we can't carry it to Him. Surrender your struggles, your fears, your inadequacies to God. And then, a soul rain will become a soul reigned, instead, with God on the throne.

[God has said,] "Never will I leave you; never will I forsake you."

HEBREWS 13:5 NIV

PRE-STUDY PRAYER

By Evelyn Christenson

As I study God's Word, approximately one-third of my study time is spent in prayer. This prayer time is divided into four categories: before the study, while observing what the Scripture really says, while interpreting what it means, and when applying it to myself or those whom I'm teaching.

First, I pray about my personal preparation. Praying for *cleansing* before starting to study establishes a clear communication with God. Then expressing in prayer the hunger and thirst after righteousness that I feel in my heart assures me of "God's filling." (See Matthew 5:6.)

Next, it is important for me to pray, "Lord, *remove all preconceived ideas* about this portion of Scripture I am about to study." It is always possible that something I have heard or studied previously has not been correct. Praying for God to remove all preconceived ideas will enable Him to reveal fresh insights to me. I also pray that God will *take control* of the study time so that all observations, interpretations, and applications will be truth. I must acknowledge my dependence upon Him if I want accurate, powerful, life-changing lessons.

Then, I ask God *to be my Teacher,* inviting the Holy Spirit to be operative in me as I study. Paul prayed for the Christians at Ephesus that God would give them "the spirit of wisdom and revelation in the knowledge of Him, [that] the eyes of [their] understanding being enlightened; that [they] may know what is the hope of his calling" (Ephesians 1:17-18). The Bible is more than a textbook of poetry, history, psychology, law, and letters; it is a living, personal message from God's heart to our hearts! And studying it thoroughly, deeply, and systematically produces *changed* people.[35]

―᜶―

FATHER, THANK YOU FOR YOUR WONDERFUL WORD. LEAD ME IN MY STUDY OF IT TO LEARN WHAT YOU HAVE FOR ME TODAY. AMEN.

I have recited your laws, and rejoiced in them more than in riches. I will meditate upon them and give them my full respect.

PSALM 119:13-15 TLB

THE REAL THING

Let all who take refuge in you rejoice; let them sing joyful praises forever.
Protect them, so all who love your name may be filled with joy.

PSALM 5:11 NLT

Matt pushed the church door open, less surprised that it was unlocked at two A.M. than that he actually went in. Something more than his duty to investigate as a police officer compelled him forward. He hadn't been in a church since he was a child. He had watched his life's ambitions fulfilled with his promotion to sergeant and then dissolved in dissatisfaction and alcohol.

As he entered the sanctuary, Matt's flashlight revealed an open Bible. He read the Psalm and something sparked inside. He gave his life to Jesus that night, and the next morning, while trying to describe to his wife the cleansing he'd felt, discovered that she'd given her life to Christ in that very sanctuary two weeks earlier. They wept in each other's arms, overcome by joy.

Joy is not what you feel but what you know. If happiness in life were dependent only on your emotions, how miserable you would be. God loves you, sent His Son to die so you could live, and works even now to make you more like Him. Rejoice!

Joy encouraged Paul in prison, making the chains chafe less and the damp coldness bearable, inspiring the call to always, in every circumstance, rejoice in Christ's love. He endured because he knew God was with him.

Your daily interactions in the classroom are unique chances to demonstrate joy. Are you glad to be there? Are you excited about what you'll be studying today? Let them know. Kids see right through fake smiles and overexuberance, so let your bearing reflect your belief that each day, with all its trials and triumphs, has value because God is there with you. And He always will be.

> GRACE FOR TODAY:
>
> God gave us joy to endure every circumstance of life.

CRISIS MODE

We are troubled on every side, yet not distressed; we are perplexed, but
not in despair; persecuted, but not forsaken; cast down, but not
destroyed.

2 CORINTHIANS 4:8–9 KJV

H as your classroom ever spiraled out of control because something tragic or
unexpected happened to you or one of your students? Life happens to all of
us—car wrecks, illness, financial troubles, or even natural disasters like tornadoes or
hurricanes. And what's the first thing that usually comes to most people's minds at such
times? Why, God? Why me?

In 1 Kings 17, God offers encouragement to a desperate woman, the widow of Zarephath, whose life was
in crisis. There was a famine, and God sent the prophet
Elijah to her to be fed. Funny thing, though—God had-
n't told the widow about it. So when Elijah arrived and
asked her for bread, she told him that she was eating
her last meal and then was going to die. But, being obedient, she fed the prophet, and God supernaturally provided sustenance for them both.

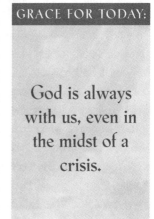

GRACE FOR TODAY:

God is always
with us, even in
the midst of a
crisis.

There's no word for crisis found anywhere in the
original languages of the Bible. The closest word to
crisis is anagke, which means "distress," and translates
as "necessity imposed by external conditions." So just
maybe, God never intended crisis to be viewed as it is today.

Most of us default to crisis mode when thrown into difficult situations, because
we don't look beyond the predicament to see what God has promised to provide in all
situations. "Why me?" always leads to a dead end. Asking God what He wants you to
do or learn from such situations is the key to unlocking His grace.

The next time you perceive a crisis, ask for the grace to see it as an opportunity
to minister comfort to a hurting child or offer a word of encouragement to another
teacher. Trust in God's goodness and see life through His eyes.

SEEING WHAT YOU MEAN

If I speak with human eloquence and angelic ecstasy but don't love,
I'm nothing but the creaking of a rusty gate.

1 CORINTHIANS 13:1 MSG

Have you ever prayed for a new way of seeing or hearing or touching another person? Saint Patrick, Mother Teresa, and Martin Luther King Jr. are people who prayed and sought God for new metaphors, new phraseology, new ways of working through the senses to help people perceive the truth.

And so God impressed it upon Patrick to use the three-leaf clover as analogous to the Trinity for a powerful object lesson to the nature-worshiping Druids. Mother Teresa dreamed of being turned away at the gates of heaven because, Peter told her, "There are no slums up here." Martin Luther King Jr.'s own "I have a dream" speech provides an image of hope and desire common to all people, one that sends a thrill of recognition through its listeners every time it is replayed.

Jonah learned many a lesson about humility and obedience by spending time in a fish. The thousands who saw one boy's loaves and fish turned into a bountiful catered lunch listened with a renewed awareness to every word Jesus spoke from that time forth. Not one of the downcast disciples who doubted Mary Magdalene's tale of a resurrected Christ could change what she had seen with her own eyes.

Your students crave new ways of perceiving. You can capture not just their minds, but their hearts, too, with your eloquence, but temper it with love. Ask the Lord for vivid examples, fresh expression, and impassioned conviction that will reach inside your students and scour away the plaque clogging their arteries of perception.

GRACE FOR TODAY:

Since God commands all language, He can help us to
be more eloquent teachers.

"I'M BORED!"

So . . . whatever you do, do all to the glory of God.

1 CORINTHIANS 10:31 RSV

It's been said that teachers hope to die during an in-service because the transition from life to death would be so unnoticeable. And after years of experience attending such gatherings, many of us would agree. There are those teachers who have perfected the art of napping, while angling their bodies in a position that looks receptive. Others furtively grade stacks of papers behind strategically placed books. Still others open a book under the protective auspices of their briefcases. Others just look bored.

In fact, *Lancet,* a British medical journal, gives this advice on how to sleep in public: "The head should rest on a tripod formed of the trunk and of the arms firmly placed on the table. . . . The fingers should . . . press the skin of the forehead upwards to wrinkle it. This gives an appearance of deep concentration."

Bored can mean weary, dull, and tiresome. Boredom refers to the state of being bored by a dull or tiresome person or thing. Our students whine about boredom in classrooms where we are expected to compete with the speed and stimulation of computer games, videos, and MTV. We moan about it when things don't go at our pace.

But do you ever wonder if such a complaint is offensive to God? He made a world full of vibrant color when He could have made it black and white. Scientists surmise that we use only between 30 and 50 percent of our brain's capacity, and yet look at what we've managed to create, invent, and master with the paltry part we do use! Perhaps when a bad case of boredom hits, a slower pace with eyes wide, mind open, and heart grateful could be just the remedy.

GRACE FOR TODAY:

When we moan in boredom, God asks us to count our blessings.

YOU BELONG TO HIM

Swimming alone in the lake, Karen's weekend quickly went from bad to worse. She and Jim had taken the kids for a family weekend, but in the undercurrent was Jim's newfound faith in Jesus, which she had considered a weakness and an imposition on their happiness. But she couldn't deny it— he was different. At peace. To top it all off, her spiritual crisis was now being compounded by a powerful stomachache, out in the middle of the lake. She couldn't swim, but as she felt herself start to sink, a strong hand wrapped around her chest and pulled her up.

"Don't worry, I've got you," Jim said. With each powerful stroke towards shore, Karen's anxiety faded in the security of her loving lifeguard's arms. *Does God love like this?* she wondered. That night, before the fireplace, Karen was ready to listen to her husband.

It's easy to put a stronger emphasis on job security than on your strong standing in Christ. Taking care of your immediate needs and planning for retirement are powerful concerns, but they mustn't consume you at the cost of your spiritual growth. Your security is your citizenship in Heaven, your adoption into God's family.

Once you are God's, nothing can separate you from Him. No matter how hard the situation may get, no matter how much you may resist God's work in your life, He will not let you drown. You are free in a way the world cannot know to live boldly, gratefully, and joyfully.

The way you run your classroom reflects that sense of security. You set rules and standards to create a safe, secure learning environment, but not so that complacency should set in. By promoting the freedom and growth that order and respect provide, you're pointing your kids toward Christ.

> **GRACE FOR TODAY:**
>
> God enables us to keep a firm grip on life when we set our hearts on Him.

You will be secure, because there is hope; you will look about you and take your rest in safety.

JOB 11:18 NIV

An Encouragement to Pray

By Charles Stanley

Some people question whether we should ask God for material things. The answer is simple. Wise parents do everything in their power to satisfy their children's needs. This goes for material needs as well as nutritional and spiritual needs. The material gifts we give our children are proof that God wants to give to us in the same way, but to a greater degree. Do we have a privilege that God has deprived himself of? No! In fact, there is no way we can out-give God, materially or in any other way.

Another hang-up people have is in regard to their unworthiness to have God answer their prayers. But the basis of all God's answered prayer is His love for us. Calvary settled the question of worth once and for all. According to His love, we are worthy of the greatest gift He had to give—His Son. After that, anything else we ask for is secondary.

Why do we have so much trouble believing God for the minor things in life? It is Satan who says, "Who do you think you are, to ask God for anything?"

To this question there is only one answer: "I am a child of the King. I am so worthy in the eyes of God, He sent His only begotten Son to die for me. If He died for me, certainly He will give me whatever I need."[36]

—⁂—

HOLY FATHER, BY YOUR GRACE, YOU HAVE GIVEN ME EVERY GOOD GIFT, ESPECIALLY THE GIFT OF YOUR SON. NOT ONLY HAVE YOU GIVEN TO ME, YOU HAVE ALSO MADE ME WORTHY TO RECEIVE YOUR GIFTS. WHAT A WONDERFUL FATHER YOU ARE! AMEN.

[Jesus said,] "Ask and it will be given to you; seek and you will find; knock and the door will be opened to you. For everyone who asks receives; he who seeks finds; and to him who knocks, the door will be opened."

MATTHEW 7:7–8 NIV

TURN THE TABLES

No more pretense. Tell your neighbor the truth. In Christ's body we're all connected to each other. . . . Don't give the Devil [a] foothold.

EPHESIANS 4:25–27 MSG

E laine stormed off for school after a major disagreement with her husband. Being an introvert, she lived by the old adage, "Grin and bear it."

Her husband followed her out to the garage and said, "C'mon, Elaine. Let's talk, or this will ruin our whole day."

"Just forget it!" Elaine said. "It doesn't matter!"

Sound familiar? If you've had an altercation with someone recently, is there any chance that you're the one refusing to talk about it?

Consider this—when we refuse to discuss a problem, it prevents all possibility of conflict resolution. Then the enemy of our souls divides and conquers, cutting us off from other people. Anger now rules our emotions, and the result is two or more parties with hurt feelings who are unable to resolve the situation.

> GRACE FOR TODAY:
>
> God can help us resolve our communication problems if we let Him.

But here's the greater dilemma: When we refuse to communicate and walk in love toward one another, the enemy succeeds in not only shutting down our life-stimulating relationships with those we love, but he also quenches communication between us and God.

Allowing this type of pattern to continue unchecked will leave a person wondering, *Where's God? Why isn't He doing something?* We can't live in disunity with others and experience intimacy with God at the same time. Relationships require give-and-take, and communication is the door by which we share ourselves with others.

Whether it's relating to another teacher, our spouses, family, or God, communication comes down to just being real. Sure, it requires vulnerability, love, and patience, but the alternative is loneliness and separation from those we love.

So take a leap of faith and talk to that person you've been avoiding. You might be surprised at the outcome and win back a friend.

SUFFICIENT MOISTURE

He shall be like a tree planted by the rivers of water, that brings forth
its fruit in its season, whose leaf also shall not wither;
and whatever he does shall prosper.

PSALM 1:3 NKJV

S wedish ivy houseplants require plentiful water in the milder seasons. Extra
humidity is required during warm summer months, and daily misting or setting
the pot on a tray of moistened pebbles is recommended. What happens if the plant is
allowed to dry out? Its lower leaves shrivel and fall off. Keep up the neglect and the
next level of leaves will fall and so on, until you have one barren and very dead ivy
plant.

Are you staying well-watered? Are you getting
the attention you need? Are you beginning to shrivel
inside from neglect? A teacher can easily droop from
all that giving out, from always having to have the
answers, from always being in demand. Eventually, you
dry up.

You need periodic misting, a little tray of moistened pebbles you can call your own. A day at the spa.
An hour of Bach. A Reuben sandwich with extra
sauerkraut. A college course, just for your own
enrichment. Treat yourself. One teacher went to the
circus—without children. How grand to laugh and clap
and cheer the performers and not have to share the
peanuts.

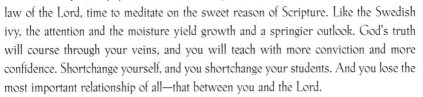

GRACE FOR TODAY:

When we take
time out to
spend with
God, He will
water us with
His presence.

Most importantly, you need time to delight in the
law of the Lord, time to meditate on the sweet reason of Scripture. Like the Swedish
ivy, the attention and the moisture yield growth and a springier outlook. God's truth
will course through your veins, and you will teach with more conviction and more
confidence. Shortchange yourself, and you shortchange your students. And you lose the
most important relationship of all—that between you and the Lord.

GOD'S GLORIOUS PROVISION

[Jesus said,] "Look at the birds of the air: they neither sow nor reap nor gather into barns, and yet your heavenly Father feeds them."

MATTHEW 6:26 RSV

If you've ever studied birds, then you know that vultures are interesting creatures. They feed mainly off the carcasses of animals—roadkill, if you will. They aren't particularly beautiful birds, except when they soar. And perhaps they can soar like that because they haven't a care in this world.

Because they spend much of their time feeding in a less than sanitary atmosphere of decay, their legs attract some undesirable germs. But God has provided something even for that—urine! When vultures urinate, they accomplish two things with one function. First, since their black color attracts heat, the urine cools them off in the heat of summer. Second, the urine sanitizes the germs on their legs. Bet you weren't thinking of that when you last saw vultures gathered on the center line of the highway. But God did. You see, He's interested in more than just survival; He's planned for our provision.

Some of the most beloved verses in the Sermon on the Mount are found in the section on worry. (See Matthew 6:25-34). We tend to think of older history as a simpler, easier time—surely not much to worry about. But it's simply not true. As soon as Adam and Eve were evicted from Eden's garden, they had to start being concerned about survival. Jesus tenderly addresses our tendency toward fretting. Don't worry, He says, about food or drink or clothing. Why? The answer is as simple as it is breathtaking: "Your heavenly Father knows that you need them." Did you catch it? He already knows!

What has you worried right now? Retirement? Layoffs? Your health? The strain of purchasing groceries when there's too much month left at the end of the money? Remember the lilies. Remember the vultures.

GRACE FOR TODAY:

God has already planned for our provision.

TAKING CARE OF HIS TEMPLE

Beloved, I pray that in all respects you may prosper and be in good
health, just as your soul prospers.

3 JOHN 1:2 NASB

S ue loved recess. She often joked that not only was it her favorite subject in
school, but also the reason she'd stayed a teacher for twenty-three years. Her
other worst-kept secret was that she'd played basketball in college, a subject she herself never brought up. Inevitably, though, the truth would come out in the first few
weeks of each school year as her fifth graders were left wide-eyed by her nothing-
but-net twenty-footers on the playground.

"Wow, Mrs. Hennessey," they'd exclaim. "They had basketball back when you
were in school?" Sue always laughed at that, and when they'd ask her why she was still
so good, she would always give the same answer. "Clean living and God's grace."

It's noteworthy that, when life gets really busy, the first two things you typically
drop from your routine are exercise and devotions—the cornerstones of your physical
and spiritual health. As Paul told the Corinthians, your body is indeed God's temple,
His earthly residence and place of business.

Your overall health is important to God's plan, not only for your life but for the
lives into which you'll share His grace and truth. It's easy to be so spiritually-minded
that you let your health slip, but then you're only hindering your ability to enjoy God's
blessings.

Take time to eat well, exercise, and develop healthy relationships in and out of
school. Nurture your relationship with Jesus, because a sound spirit energizes mind
and body. God's promise to equip you for every good work notwithstanding, take care
of the vessel He chooses to use—you.

GRACE FOR TODAY:

God expects us to take care of our bodies and
maintain our health.

FIGHTING DEPRESSION

Some teachers have a secret problem that no one would ever suspect—depression. Often teachers are only acknowledged when someone has a complaint or something's gone wrong—not for the hundreds of times they've helped a child or made a lasting difference. So teachers are susceptible to depression like anyone else.

Depression can overtake you like an invading army if you don't fight it off, and there's a consequence of not fighting: You forfeit the joy-filled victorious life God has promised you. That's why God says, "Fight!" Sometimes fighting means talking to a neutral third party in counseling. If it's a chronic problem—a chemical imbalance in the brain—it may mean taking medication. But if it's just the blues we all suffer occasionally, changing your routine or attitude might just be the remedy.

God gave the Israelites the Promised Land, but they had to fight for each city, and then God gave it into their hands. Life requires fighting the battle with faith every day. Expect troubles, but when they come, fight! Be aware of circumstances that trigger the blues and try to avoid them, but if you can't, fight by turning to the Scriptures for words of encouragement. Some people say they live in the Psalms because it helps them conquer depression. God wants you to be about "the Father's business," but living with depression makes it difficult or even impossible.

Clinical depression is like a thick black fog obscuring light and truth. It makes life a prison and feels as though you've been sentenced to hard labor. Victory over depression can come when you realize that you don't have to take on Christ's suffering. He has already paid the price.

Use the tools God has given this generation to fight depression, whether it be counseling, medication, or confronting a stressful situation. Fight for your freedom!

> **GRACE FOR TODAY:**
>
> If we use the tools God has provided, He will help us fight depression.

In my anguish I cried to the LORD, and he answered by setting me free.

PSALM 118:5 NIV

CHRIST LIVES WITHIN US

By Luis Palau

It's easy to forget that even though it is glorious to be a Christian and to have the great treasure of Christ living within us, we are not exempt from the troubles of life. But we can respond to these daily problems differently because Christ lives within us.

Sometimes we're perplexed and confused by life. Our friends may turn against us. We may be unable to resolve a problem at work, home, or church. Things may happen to us that we don't understand, but we are not driven to despair because Christ lives within us.

We may not face ongoing, physical persecution for the sake of Christ, but Christian students are gunned down for their faith, and churches are bombed for their witness. At some time or another, we all face social persecution. We may become good friends with our neighbors, but when we begin to share the Good News with them, they may not invite us to their parties anymore. But persecution isn't the end of the world. And dying for Christ is not the end of life—it is the glorious entrance into eternity with God. No matter who turns against us in life, we never will be forsaken by the indwelling Christ.

Finally, we will be struck down, but never destroyed. I like to watch boxing. It reminds me of spiritual warfare. When a guy takes a hard punch and reels to the floor, you may think he's been knocked out and the match is over. But then he gets up and starts throwing punches again. As Christians, we may be knocked down, but the indwelling Christ enables us to get up and go again.[37]

—⁓—

HEAVENLY FATHER, YOUR GRACE—CHRIST DWELLING WITHIN ME—IS MORE THAN ENOUGH TO TRANSFORM MY TREMBLING HEART INTO THE HEART OF A CHAMPION. AMEN.

We are often troubled, but not crushed; sometimes in doubt, but never in despair; there are many enemies, but we are never without a friend; and though badly hurt at times, we are not destroyed

2 CORINTHIANS 4:8–9 GNT

BLESS THE CHILDREN

The grace of the Lord Jesus Christ, the love of God, and the communion
of the Holy Spirit be with all of you.

2 CORINTHIANS 13:13 NRSV

When the pastor pronounces the benediction and thereby concludes the worship service, we are sent on our way with a blessing from God. One of the most common—and most beautiful—benedictions used is the timeless blessing with which Aaron and his priestly sons blessed the Israelites. Who can forget those awesome words of optimism: "The Lord bless thee, and keep thee: The Lord make his face shine upon thee, and be gracious unto thee: The Lord lift up his countenance upon thee, and give thee peace" (Numbers 6:24–26 KJV).

> GRACE FOR TODAY:
>
> God has placed
> us in our
> students' lives to
> bless them.

But every bit as awesome is God's benediction on the benediction: "And they shall put my name upon the children of Israel; and I will bless them," (Numbers 6:27 KJV). It was intended to be God's stamp of ownership on His people.

How do you end your school day when the final bell rings? Do you have a signature parting? A cursory "Away you go"? A slightly more substantial "See you around"? Perhaps a final admonition of "Don't forget your homework/permission slip/project notebook"?

What if you blessed them instead? Nothing fancy. Maybe just a "Safe journey!" or "Have a great evening!" "Until tomorrow" sounds promising, if oblique. What about a straight out "God bless you, kids"?

But they're not listening, you protest. They're only thinking about the friend they're hurrying to meet or the afternoon snack waiting at home. You're just fortunate that you don't get trampled in the rush for the door.

Don't be so sure. Leave them encouraged with a little something to ponder. Ask God to keep them and protect them. Make sure the last words your students hear really count.

FEARFULLY, WONDERFULLY MADE

God's blessing makes life rich; nothing we do can improve on God.

PROVERBS 10:22 MSG

T ime out! Stop and think of everything that you are doing right at this moment as you are reading this. You're breathing. Heart beating. Sitting upright. One foot propped up on your desk. Glancing toward the noise in the hallway. Perhaps gazing out the window at the day. Wondering if the copies you need for today's lesson are in the return box. Wondering about dinner tonight. Making a mental grocery or chore list.

Most of this, you don't even have to think about! You don't command yourself to breathe; it just happens. You don't demand that your heart beat; it just does. And all the while this goes on, your mind flits through dozens of thoughts, so closely on the heels of another that it seems effortless—simultaneous even.

Yet when's the last time you thought of this miracle—the last time you were wholly conscious that life is a gift? Emily's character in the play *Our Town* dies but is allowed to observe life here on earth. She recalls a list of things she enjoyed but took for granted during her life. Sunflowers, freshly ironed dresses, coffee. Then she asks the stage manager a poignant, telling question. "Do human beings ever realize life while they live it? Every, every minute?"

> **GRACE FOR TODAY:**
>
> **God's fingerprints can be seen in the details of His creation.**

Sadly, it's doubtful. Are you taking anything for granted today? Health? The stunning changing of the guard every season, as autumn leaves fall and usher in the winter snow? When snow melts and green shoots spring up from the earth? As the earth opens up for planting and the lush golds and greens of summer take over? A job you enjoy? A car to drive? A home full of everything you need and even some things you don't?

Take your lunch or your planning hour outdoors today if possible. Look around and be reminded that all creation is a gift from One who delights in giving.

ALWAYS TWO SIDES

Judge not according to the appearance, but judge righteous judgment.

JOHN 7:24 KJV

John Wesley, the famous eighteenth-century minister, told about a man for whom he had little respect because he thought him to be greedy and penny-pinching. Wesley publicly criticized the man one day when the fellow contributed only a small amount to a worthy charity. Afterward, the man had a private talk with Wesley, explaining to him that, before his conversion, he'd run up many foolish bills, but now he was inspired to skimp on himself and pay off his creditors one at a time.

"Christ has made me an honest man," he said. "I can give only a few gifts above my tithe. I must settle up with my fellowmen and show them what the grace of God can do in the heart of a man who was once dishonest." Wesley apologized, asking the man's forgiveness.

Only God, who knows all the facts, is able to judge people righteously. People are quick to jump on each other's faults and misjudgments, too seldom realizing that their own judgments are colored by their own flaws and experiences. By taking stock of your own heart, you'll better be able to discern what's going on in others' lives.

A common misconception is that Christians are not to judge anything at all, ever. It's the one time you can usually count on someone who doesn't know the Bible to quote scripture to you: "Judge not!" On the contrary, you're called on to show God's wisdom and discernment in all your ways.

Your good judgment is critical to running a secure classroom. Your students are looking to you for resolutions, for you to show them how to think and make decisions based on having as many facts as possible. God alone knows what's in a person's heart, but you can rely on Him to guide you to make the right call.

GRACE FOR TODAY:

If we rely on God to discern the truth,
He will grant us good judgment.

GOD'S VISION

We look not at the things which are seen, but at the things which are not
seen.

2 CORINTHIANS 4:18 KJV

Have you ever looked out over your classroom of students and wondered what makes each one tick? What a challenge! Yet if you ask, God can give you vision and insight to understand their characters, which are being influenced by you and those around them.

As teachers, the opportunity to influence your students is usually limited to one brief year. But even in that short time, God can enable you to channel their energies in the right direction because He has a great vision for each one of them. His vision for your students is "to prosper [them] and . . . to give [them] hope and a future" (Jeremiah 29:11 NIV). Teachers may be only a small part of the equation, but don't underestimate how God can work through you. God's vision is paramount.

So as you get to know those difficult and challenging students or those preppy or superficial ones, ask God for His vision. In Scripture, most people saw David only as a lowly shepherd boy, but God and the prophet Samuel saw David as a king!

You may have students who are daydreamers; God may have gifted them with creativity. Others may seem to lack self-confidence; God may have planted in them seeds of true humility. Still others may appear stubborn or headstrong; God might be in the process of developing persistence and resolute character in them because He's raising them up to be political or spiritual leaders.

How exciting it is when God shares the vision He has for each one! Do your part in helping them grow into men and women of godly character.

GRACE FOR TODAY:

God gives us vision and insight to
understand our students.

FLOWER POWER

When you're riding high and things are clicking and your students are getting it, it's time for flowers. When nothing works and the heat's not fixed and the brightest student has begun yawning by ten in the morning, it's time for flowers. When you're sick and you shouldn't be there and your head feels as heavy as an anvil, isn't it time for flowers?

Half a dozen golden daisies—sunny flower faces beaming like kids at a carnival—bring the sunshine inside. Petals orange as ripe pumpkins. Stems straight as Marines on parade. Six nurses in a vase.

Give your students flowers as awards for work well done. Celebrate birthdays with lavender–flavored cupcakes. Grow bulbs in the classroom and be on blossom watch as the flowering nears. Celebrate growth.

> **GRACE FOR TODAY:**
>
> God gives us plants and flowers as a metaphor for our growth.

The glory of Zion in Scripture is likened by the prophet Isaiah to a well-watered garden. A man of wisdom, says the psalmist, is like a tree planted by streams of water. Seedtime and harvest, pens the writer of Genesis, is a sure sign of the earth's endurance. God is all about growth.

When Paul wrote to the Colossians, he reveled in the fact that "all over the world" the gospel was producing fruit and growing. Flowers and growing things in your room are a promise of new life, of the flourishing of truth. Pot, plant, and pick these encouraging signs of progress, these living symbols of joy and comfort.

A room filled with plants and flowers is a room where growth is a given.

The Sovereign LORD will show his justice to the nations of the world. . . . His righteousness will be like a garden in early spring, filled with young plants springing up everywhere.

ISAIAH 61:11 NLT

AUTHENTICITY

By Luis Palau

During preparation for one of our evangelistic festivals in South America, a poor, shabbily dressed man attended our counselor–training course. Although the training is open to all spiritually mature Christians, generally the better-educated, socially established lay leaders of local churches attend these classes. But because this man was also illiterate, he brought his young nephew to read and write for him.

Although the man attended every class, we didn't expect him to do much counseling. Like many illiterate people, however, he had a fantastic memory and learned much through the counseling classes.

Following one of the evangelistic meetings, every available counselor was busy except the illiterate man. At just that time, a doctor walked in, requesting counsel. Before anyone could stop him, the shabbily dressed man took the doctor into a room for counseling.

When our counseling director learned of this, he was a bit concerned. He didn't know if the illiterate man would be able to communicate effectively with the sophisticated doctor. When

the doctor came out of the counseling room, our counseling director asked if he could help him in any way.

"No, thank you," the doctor replied. "This fellow has helped me very much."

The next day the doctor returned with two other doctors. Our counseling director wanted to talk to him, but the doctor refused, asking for counsel with the illiterate man. By the end of the festival, that illiterate man had led four doctors and their wives to Christ! He couldn't read or write, but he lived an authentic Christian life.

So often we look on the outside for signs of victorious Christian living. But the outward appearance doesn't count. Outward appearances reveal little of authentic Christian living. What really counts—what really makes a Christian's life vibrant and real—is the power of the living Christ within.[38]

—m—

FATHER, HELP ME TO LIVE AN AUTHENTIC CHRISTIAN LIFE TO WHICH MY STUDENTS AND COLLEAGUES CAN TRULY RELATE. LET THE LIGHT IN ME DRAW THEM TO YOU. AMEN.

Man looks at the outward appearance, but the LORD looks at the heart.

1 SAMUEL 16:7 NASB

TO LISTEN FOR A SONG

[Of Wisdom] "Good counsel and common sense are my characteristics; I
am both Insight and the Virtue to live it out."

PROVERBS 8:14 MSG

Simon Verity is a master stone carver who perfected his art while restoring thir-
teenth-century cathedrals in Great Britain. After each calculated blow of his
chisel, Verity had to pause and listen to the stone's song. A solid strike meant the stone
was safe. Solid. But a higher-pitched note might mean that a chunk of the rock was
ready to break off. He had to adjust the angle and force of his carvings and blows to the
sound of the stone. The sound indicated what the stone needed and what it could take.

As teachers we, too, need to listen carefully to the
song of our students. One student might need a daily
dose of encouragement. Another might be crying out
for a firmer hand in the discipline arena. Still another's
high-pitched whine might indicate a need for affection
and affirmation. Buried under a song of confidence
might lie a descant of hunger for praise. Yet another
student might need an extra dose of guidance, an extra
nudge toward competing in that speech contest, or a
heartfelt letter of recommendation on a college applica-
tion. To know the score and the tempo, we must tune both our ears and our hearts.

GRACE FOR TODAY:

God grants
wisdom to all
who ask it of
Him.

Over and over Scripture tells us that wisdom is priceless. That all we have to do
if we lack wisdom is to ask it of God. As we seek that wisdom for our classrooms,
let's ask if we may also be given the ability to hear the individual notes of a song and
the drive to make of them a symphony.

LIFELONG LEARNING

Let the wise listen and add to their learning.

PROVERBS 1:5 NIV

Haddon Robinson recounts the story of a Chinese boy who wanted to learn about jade. He went to study with a wise, experienced teacher. This fellow handed him a piece of the stone and told him to hold it tightly. He then spoke of many other things—philosophy, men and women, and the world around them. After an hour he took back the stone and sent the boy home. The process continued for weeks, and the boy became frustrated. When would he learn about jade? He was too polite, however, to interrupt his venerable teacher. Then one day when the old man put a stone into his hands, the boy cried out immediately, "That's not jade!" By handling the real thing, the boy knew immediately when he was being deceived.

Teachers understand better than anyone else that learning is a lifelong process—a way of life—and only by exposing your students to the truth will they recognize falsehood. Your greatest desire is that your students should love to learn, to learn to think, to think about life, and how best to live it. To do so is to help them live authentically, to steer them away from worldly values that emphasize temporal, material rewards.

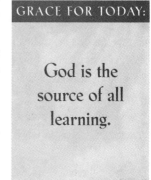

GRACE FOR TODAY:

God is the source of all learning.

As a Christian, you model a positive attitude about learning in a unique and wonderful way, simply because of your relationship with God. You know that God could show you a thousand new things about himself every day and you would still never learn all there is to know about Him. What an inspiration it is to learn even one new thing about His nature and character!

A CHILD OF THE KING

Therefore, if anyone is in Christ, he is a new creation; old things have
passed away; behold, all things have become new.

2 CORINTHIANS 5:17 NKJV

As a teacher, have you ever wondered how your students see you? Do they see the person God sees? Do you act like a new creation in Christ?

God brought His people out of Egypt, intending to establish their significance before the world, but of all those who came out of Egypt, only two—Joshua and Caleb—actually entered the Promised Land. They were the only ones who believed what God had said about them. After spying out the land, the other spies reported back that the people were as big as giants and that there was no way the Israelites could defeat them. (See Numbers 13:31–32.) They forfeited God's promises by esteeming their perception of themselves over the truth God had spoken to them. Faulty perception defeated them.

If you see yourself as weak, powerless, and rejected, that's how you will act. Your perceptions become reality. Instead, immerse yourself in Scripture to find out how God sees you—as a child of the King, a person of great worth. Because you are a child of the God of the universe, you have access to His throne room through the power of prayer.

God's Word also says you are the apple of His eye, precious in His sight, a new creation, righteous in Christ, forgiven, and extraordinarily valuable. You are significant.

Store these nuggets away in your heart and take them out in those times when you are alone with Him. Then start acting like a child of the living God.

GRACE FOR TODAY:

God says in His Word that we are significant to Him.

TAILOR-MADE

Wisdom is the principal thing; therefore get wisdom.
And in all your getting, get understanding.

PROVERBS 4:7 NKJV

"Twenty Steps to Losing Weight." "Eleven Keys to Staying Young." "Ten Secrets to Business Success."

The magazine racks are filled with tantalizing promises of improved lives if only you follow the tips and tricks contained within. Parenting magazines tell you how to get your child to eat her peas. Fishing magazines demonstrate how to land the big one. Sports magazines reveal inside information on how a star player trains for a crucial game. Even religious publications use enticing headlines to draw you in: "Thirteen Ways to Please God."

How often have you wished for a magic formula or list of surefire ways to get Johnny to read or Lori to smile or Jimmy to remember his lunch money? "Magic" solutions don't work for everyone, and one-size-fits-all teaching went out with decoder rings. Your students are individuals who require customized understanding.

In the eighteenth chapter of the gospel of John, it is recorded that Christ boldly declared to the mob that came to arrest Him that He was Jesus of Nazareth. What a counterpoint to the three times later in the same chapter when Peter denied Jesus! Even the sentence structure is identical. Jesus answered, "I am He." Peter rejected the label of "His disciple" and answered, "I am not (he)." When Jesus next saw Peter, after His resurrection, He neither berated him for his disloyalty nor wrote him off. He wanted Peter's discernment and pledge to stay the course. There is indication that He received the results He wanted by personalizing His response, by using words about future ministry that were at once gentle and supportive: "Do you love Me? Feed My sheep."

Study how differently Jesus dealt with each of those He loved. He saw them as unique individuals, just as you do your students. No blanket solutions. Teaching requires patience, love, persistence, and a sharp eye for detail. God is in the details.

GRACE FOR TODAY:

God sees our students as unique individuals.

AN APPLE FOR THE TEACHER

Each year's crop of students is not unlike the surprise box, offered on the insert pages of many mail-order catalogs. If you've ever ordered one, then you know they're unpredictable. One box might contain only ten or so items that are clearly on clearance for a reason— no one else wanted them, either! But every now and then you get a box with a treasure amidst a hodge-podge of ordinary, serviceable items.

There are more than 2,000 apple varieties grown in the United States. Apples that are tart and sweet. Apples that are good for pies, breads, scones, dipping with caramel or peanut butter, and apples for eating straight off the trees at an apple farm on a crisp autumn day. There are apples that make wonderful applesauce, cider, and chutney. Each has a different taste, texture, look, and use. Even bruised apples, if caught quickly, can become part of a flavorful tart.

> **GRACE FOR TODAY:**
>
> God made each of us, including our students, unique individuals.

Kind of sounds like people, huh? Tall, short, shy, outgoing. Blue-eyed, brown-eyed, green-eyed. Straight-haired, curly-haired. Verbal, kinesthetic, and auditory learners. Leaders and followers. Optimists and pessimists. Science says that only 1 percent of our DNA differs from that of other human beings. Sounds like our great Designer reserved that part for making us unique. As teachers, it's part of our job to find the best fit for each "apple."

Jesus often spoke of bearing fruit, being known by our fruit, and sowing seeds. He talked about laborers and the harvest. That's powerful stuff. Who knows how many apples may grow from the seeds you have helped plant in any given apple, in any given classroom, throughout any given year. May the orchards you've helped tend grow sturdy and strong!

A word fitly spoken is like apples of gold in a setting of silver.

PROVERBS 25:11 RSV

IN JESUS' NAME

By Charles Stanley

When most of us pray, we add the phrase "in Jesus' name" to the end of our prayers. For some it is a habit, for others it is considered a magic phrase that assures an answer. We read John 14:14 and mistakenly decide that the only qualification to having our prayers answered is to say "in Jesus' name." This is a mistake. For there is another qualification: We must abide.

Praying in Jesus' name is more than a phrase we add to a prayer; it is a character of the prayer itself. To pray in Jesus' name means that we are asking something because it is in character with what Jesus would ask if He were in our circumstances. It means that the prayer is in keeping with His nature and character as He lives His life through us. Since He indwells us, He not only desires to live through us, but to intercede through us, as well.

Many times we make what may appear to be mundane requests. But they are real needs to us, and God is willing to meet them. Whether they are for spiritual or material needs, it makes little difference to Him; He is our loving Father who delights in meeting all our needs. But before we add "in Jesus' name" on the end, we must make sure that everything in the prayer is in keeping with His character.[39]

—⁂—

HEAVENLY FATHER, I OFFER MY HEART TO YOU. FILL IT WITH YOUR DESIRES, YOUR CONCERNS, YOUR PRIORITIES. SHOW ME BY YOUR GRACE HOW TO PRAY IN KEEPING WITH YOUR NATURE AND ACCORDING TO YOUR WILL. IN JESUS' NAME. AMEN.

[Jesus said,] "If you abide in Me, and My words abide in you, ask whatever you wish, and it will be done for you."

JOHN 15:7 NASB

DOING THE RIGHT THING

The wise of heart is called perceptive, and pleasant speech
increases persuasiveness.

PROVERBS 16:21 NRSV

Charles Francis Adams, nineteenth-century politician and diplomat, kept a diary. One day he entered: "Went fishing with my son today—a day wasted." His son, Brook Adams, also kept a diary. On that same day, Brook wrote, "Went fishing with my father—the most wonderful day of my life!" What Charles saw as a waste of time, his eight-year-old son saw as an investment in their relationship.

Knowing the difference between wasting and investing boils down to knowing your purpose in life. If your bottom line rests solely on academic rigor and classroom structure, you'll judge accordingly. Likewise, if you can accomplish those goals while always remembering that your young charges are developing human beings in need of compassion, love, and respect, those attributes will guide your decisions.

You regularly question your effectiveness in the classroom. Even with immediate feedback and post-lesson debriefing, there is almost always a nagging doubt that leads you to ask, "Could I have done it better?" Rather than being a discouragement, that voice is your lamppost, constantly guiding you towards adjustment and improvement.

When Elijah was on the run from Jezebel, God led him to a cave on Mount Horeb. There God passed by him in the form of a great wind, then an earthquake, and then fire. God wasn't actually communicating with Elijah in any of these momentous occurrences, however, but in the still, small voice that spoke to him afterward.

Similarly, God speaks and moves in the stillness of your dependence on Him; His guidance is the source of your effectiveness. In trusting Him, your speech will address the right things, not just saying things correctly. Your actions will deal with the heart of the matter, not just the appearance.

BE A BLESSING

The one who blesses others is abundantly blessed;
those who help others are helped.

PROVERBS 11:25 MSG

Tryouts for the fall play *A Midsummer Night's Dream* were open to both upper— and lowerclassmen, and after a week of arduous auditions, the last candidate—a ninth grader—was the final student to take the stage. After quickly reading her lines, she ran offstage before Mrs. Rockey could even comment. As a recent college graduate, the drama coach could easily remember what it was like auditioning for a part and sympathized with the young student.

Leaving school a half-hour later, Mrs. Rockey stopped by the restroom and found the girl in tears. Although the teacher was running late, she took the opportunity to offer encouragement.

"I sat in and saw all the others try out," the girl sobbed. "I'm horrible compared to them! I don't stand a chance."

"Hey, you're being far harder on yourself than even I would be," Mrs. Rockey said. "True, you might not have the experience and confidence that some of the seniors have, but that doesn't mean you're not good. Give yourself some credit! Auditioning can be a scary experience. Did you know we had only three ninth graders try out at all? I'd suggest waiting until the jury's in and be proud of yourself for taking the risk!"

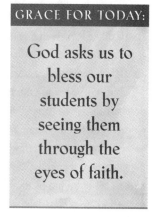

GRACE FOR TODAY:

God asks us to bless our students by seeing them through the eyes of faith.

Mrs. Rockey could have just gone on her way, but she'd learned a lesson that was destined to make her an influential teacher. By encouraging the tenderhearted student, Mrs. Rockey boosted the girl's confidence and ensured that she would try acting again.

It's easy to criticize. However, those special teachers who have learned the art of blessing their students will look at a situation and choose to see the positive. Look around today and find a student who needs to be blessed!

YES, YOU CAN

But Jesus looked at them and said to them, "With men this is impossible, but with God all things are possible."

MATTHEW 19:26 NKJV

Ever notice how the list of things your students like rarely contains academics? Sometimes it's pretty hard to come up with an anecdote for the faculty lunchroom about a kid who loves geometry or takes great pleasure in the study of shifting political allegiances in pre-Renaissance Europe. But not so difficult to find kids who like assemblies or fire drills.

We all get like that sometimes. Scripture is full of hard lessons, difficult concepts, and object teachings that strike awfully close to home. It can be uncomfortable. Prayer can be difficult, as well, to keep fresh and passionate. Church eats up time we could use to get ready for class Monday morning. There is much to learn, much perfecting yet to do, and often avoidance seems the best course of inaction.

But how do you convince your students to take the plunge if your own toe is nowhere near the water? How do you get Charlie to attempt that essay, do that research, or face his fears and volunteer to do his oral presentation first?

Of course, it was Jehovah himself who asked the mother of all questions: "Is anything too hard for the LORD?"(Genesis 18:14 NKJV). This was right after Sarah laughed at the idea of giving birth at her ripe old age, with or without God's promise. Sarah regretted her faithless laughter, and even tried to deny it. But God repeated that she had, in fact, laughed, and by doing so had rendered God's word too preposterous to believe.

Your students must know by your example that you have faith that they can do it. When they are shaky, fearful, unprepared, and reluctant, they need to see in you firm resolve that they can get it, they can prevail. Build your faith in God, and you will build confidence in your students.

GRACE FOR TODAY:

When we trust God, He can help us build confidence in our students.

THE SECRET

Gossips can't keep secrets, so never confide in blabbermouths.

PROVERBS 20:19 MSG

Y ou walked in this morning, eyes puffy and red-rimmed. You tried to shuffle to your in-box in a cloud of anonymity, but the social butterfly teacher from Upper B-hall noticed you and pulled you into the copy room.

She was sympathetic and promised her confidence. But by third period, it seemed that everyone knew about your horrible day. The fight with your spouse, the speeding ticket in the school zone, and the fact that you're not getting along with your student teacher.

Or perhaps, you were the one who noticed that someone else's morning obviously began not just on the wrong side of the bed, but perhaps from the floor! You hesitated and then decided to approach them and listen with genuine empathy.

Either situation provides an opportunity for either betrayal or confidence. Oh, may wisdom be our constant companion! When you need to share with someone, talk about it with God first. Make sure that prayer is your first action, not your last resort.

If you do choose to vent to a colleague, ask God for wisdom and a discerning heart. Sometimes the most approachable, accessible people are also the ones who like being in the loop and sharing some of the tape!

If someone shares a confidence with you, accept that responsibility with caution. Make your boundaries clear. If they share something that must be reported, either to school or law enforcement authorities, tell them in advance whom you are telling and why. Then make certain that it doesn't go anywhere else with you. Keep your word. Always.

Whether you need to tell someone a confidence, or someone approaches you with a burden to share, the quest should always be the same. Choose with wisdom. Guard your heart; guard your lips.

GRACE FOR TODAY:

God wants us to ask Him for wisdom and discernment before sharing a confidence.

YOU ASKED FOR IT

A proud young man approached Socrates. "O great Socrates, how can I attain wisdom?" The soldier-turned-philosopher led the man to the sea and chest deep into water. Then he asked, "What do you want?" The young man smiled smugly. "Wisdom, O sage philosopher." Socrates gripped the man's shoulders and pushed him under. Thirty seconds later Socrates let him up. "What do you want?" he asked again. "Wisdom," the young man sputtered, "O great and wise Socrates." Socrates plunged him under again. After forty seconds, Socrates let him up. "What do you want, young man?" The fellow gasped, "W-wisdom, O wise and wonderful . . ." Socrates jammed him under again, this time letting almost a full minute pass. "What do you want?" "Air!" the man spluttered. "I need air!" Socrates nodded. "When you want wisdom as much as you have just wanted air, then you will have wisdom."

Asking God for wisdom is much easier than asking a sage but surly Greek philosopher. There are, nonetheless, a couple of important requirements to asking God: First, ask with confidence and boldness, expecting God to give you wisdom.

Also, keep asking God each time you need wisdom to handle a certain situation. It's not like one of the genie-type deals, where one request for infinite beauty or wealth covers you for life. God wants you to go to Him when you need Him.

Kids today through various technologies have access to incredible stores of knowledge and information. If anything, your job as a teacher becomes that much more critical, because they can't get wisdom from the Internet or text messaging. Simply by being who you are in Christ, with instant messaging coming directly to you via the Holy Spirit, you can be a role model for true wisdom—the proper application of knowledge.

> **GRACE FOR TODAY:**
>
> If we continually ask, knock, and seek God, He will provide us with abundant wisdom.

If you need wisdom—if you want to know what God wants you to do—
ask him, and he will gladly tell you.

JAMES 1:5 NLT

CONTINUAL PRAYER

By Alexander Maclaren

What is prayer? Not the utterance of words. They are but the vehicle of prayer. Prayer is the attitude of a person's spirit, and the elements of prayer may be diffused throughout our daily lives.

Prayer can be a constant consciousness of God's presence and our contact with Him. In such communion, when God's Spirit and our spirit draw closer together, there is frequently no need for speech. Silently our hearts may be kept fragrant with God's felt presence and sunny with the light of His face.

There can be a continual presence of a desire after God. All our daily experiences of God's grace, combined with all our communion with Him that unveils His beauty to us, can stir longings within us for more of Him.

Our continual submission to God's will is also essential for all prayer. Many people have the notion that praying is urging our wishes on God, and answered prayer is God giving us what we desire. The deepest expression of true prayer is not, "Do this, because I desire it, O Lord." Rather, it is, "I do this because You desire it, O Lord."

So there should run all through our daily lives the music of continual prayer beneath our various occupations, like some prolonged, deep, bass note that bears up and dignifies the lighter melody rising, falling, and changing above it. Then our lives can be woven into a harmonious unity based upon a continual communion, a continual desire after God, and a continual submission to Him.

—m—

HEAVENLY FATHER, OH, HOW I LONG TO BE IN CONSTANT COMMUNION WITH YOU. AS I GO ABOUT MY DAY, HELP ME TO BE MINDFUL THAT YOU ARE EVER WITH ME SO I CAN GROW IN MY RELATIONSHIP WITH YOU. THEN, AS I INTERACT WITH MY STUDENTS AND COLLEAGUES, MAY THE SWEET AROMA OF YOUR PRESENCE DRAW THEM UNTO YOU. AMEN.

Continue in prayer, and watch in the same with thanksgiving.

COLOSSIANS 4:2 KJV

A SYMPHONY OF LIFE

Walk with me and . . . learn the unforced rhythms of grace. . . . Keep
company with me and you'll learn to live freely and lightly.

MATTHEW 11:29-30 MSG

As a teacher, have you ever considered the role of rhythm in your life? The dictionary expands the meaning of the word rhythm beyond music to encompass movement or variation that is characterized by the regular recurrence of different qualities or conditions. It's extracted from the Greek word *rhein*, meaning "to flow with." If you happen to be a music teacher, you can appreciate that without rhythm, music would cease to be music because the dissonance would be overpowering.

> **GRACE FOR TODAY:**
>
> **If we let Him,
> God will write a
> symphony with
> our lives.**

Similarly, there's a rhythm to God's grace—movements and variations for every circumstance of life—and likewise, without the Holy Spirit's rhythm, life can become overwhelming. God desires that His children get in the flow of His rhythm and learn to live there moment by moment, embracing the direction He takes them in life.

How do you live in the rhythm of God's grace? By practicing His presence every day. When you seek God out in Scripture or in your quiet time with Him, you learn to be attentive to His Spirit, who flows continuously like a symphonic masterpiece from the throne room of God. Listen to God's music, letting the Master Composer write the transitions to turn the discord in your life into harmony with those around you. Play in His orchestra, and you will bear spiritual fruit to feed your students.

So jump in the river and live in God's rhythm rather than in the dissonance that surrounds you every day in the classroom. Practice listening and connecting to God's Spirit, and you'll write a symphony with your life.

IS EVERYBODY HAPPY?

The Lord's servants must not quarrel but must be kind to everyone. They must be able to teach effectively and be patient with difficult people.

2 TIMOTHY 2:24 NLT

L inus goes to his teacher and says, "Thank you for recommending this book, Miss Halverson. I found it a rare experience, and feel that I am a better person for having read it."

He returns to his seat in front of Charlie Brown's desk. Charlie Brown asks, "How can you say things like that with a straight face?"

Linus turns and replies, "Is it wrong to make a teacher happy?"

Teaching can be quite satisfying when a student expresses gratitude for your help, your example, or the fun with which you introduced a lesson. But if you wait around for compliments, or rate your success based on positive student feedback, time for you could pass very slowly indeed.

A better gauge of your effectiveness might be the eagerness with which a project is tackled once you've assigned it. How much originality, creativity, and cooperative spirit of teamwork do you see, whether or not the results are necessarily what you hoped for? Children may actually be feeling grateful, but shyness, lack of words, or fear of their peers might easily get in the way.

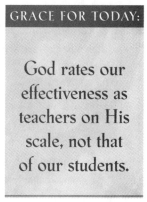

GRACE FOR TODAY:

God rates our effectiveness as teachers on His scale, not that of our students.

Better to watch for those signs in unguarded moments when positive attitudes and determined body language can speak louder than words.

It was not until Jesus had ascended into Heaven that Scripture speaks with verve of the disciples going out and preaching everywhere. In the last verse of the gospel of Mark it is recorded that "the Lord worked with them" and confirmed His Word by the wondrous signs that accompanied this activity. While He was with them on earth, we might more often than not describe them as hesitant and thickheaded. Some of the most meaningful evidence that they had gotten it did not come until they had been fully launched by the power of the Holy Spirit. God's power made them effective.

No, it is not wrong to make a teacher happy.

NO ROOM!

[Jesus said,] "Behold, I stand at the door, and knock: if any man hear my voice, and open the door, I will come in to him."

REVELATION 3:20 KJV

Mr. Christopher felt strongly that a class full of thirty juniors and seniors was full enough. So every year when his most popular classes filled, he sent word down to the counselor to close registration. Yet several times a semester, a student would specifically request his class or would move into town, ready for a brand-new start. The counselor would go upstairs and interrupt.

"Mr. Christopher," the conversation always began, "I know you said no more, but this particular student could really use your enthusiasm, your instruction, and your brand of caring." Mr. Christopher sighed, because he knew he would give in. Immediately, the prayers started . . . that he would make a difference . . . that people would see Jesus in him.

Why did Mr. Christopher always accept another student into a full class? Simple—because of the Christmas story. He just couldn't get past the phrase, "No room."

Have you ever thought about that part of the Advent story, or have you just dismissed it as a quaint little detail in a timeless, familiar tale? Read about it in Luke 2 again. "And she brought forth her firstborn son . . . and laid him in a manger; because there was no room for them in the inn" (2:7 KJV). Another version gets more to the heart: ". . . because there was no place for them in the inn" (RSV). No room. No place. However it's stated, it adds up to the same conclusion—rejection. Perhaps because of inconvenience. I don't want to give up my room! Perhaps selfishness. It is my room after all. Perhaps because the innkeeper had no idea whom he was turning away.

And there lies the crux of the matter. Neither do we. Like Jesus, be an example of tangible grace to that extra student who would crowd your classroom.

GRACE FOR TODAY:

God desires us to be examples of tangible grace for everyone you meet.

LEANING ON EVERLASTING ARMS

I will say of the LORD, "He is my refuge and my fortress;
My God, in Him I will trust."

PSALM 91:2 NKJV

The botanist lowered his binoculars and addressed his colleagues. "I concur. It's exactly what we came here for." They had been searching this remote area of the Alps for new species of flowers, and here was a find of incalculable value to science. It lay, however, in a deep ravine, walled in by steep cliffs. Someone would have to be lowered down to reach it. The botanist told a curious lad who had been watching their endeavors that he would be well-paid if he would agree to retrieve the flower. The boy peered over the edge, then said, "I'll be back soon." He returned shortly, followed by a gray-haired man. The boy told the botanist, "I'll go over that cliff and get that flower for you if this man holds the rope. He's my father."

Trust hinges on faith. When you trust someone to do something, that person's success earns your trust. Given that principle, God certainly deserves your trust in every situation.

Consider all of the times you have trusted God. Sometimes, it seemed like you had no other choice. Circumstances were beyond your control, and only God could have possibly helped you.

As you've grown in Christ, though, you've learned to put your trust in Him from the outset, knowing that He is sovereign. He controls the master plan for the entire universe, and He will never let you down.

Before you enter the classroom each day, put your trust in God's hands. Come what may, let Him be your guide and your help. God has blessed you with many talents and abilities, but your confidence comes from trusting Him to help you use them in the right way, at the right time, for the right reasons.

GRACE FOR TODAY:

God can be trusted to never let us down.

THE CANDLEWICK TRICK

Ms. Roberson stood in the back of the room watching the children enjoy their end-of-the-year party. One of the room mothers had arranged for an illusionist, and the kids were mesmerized by his tricks. As she watched, she observed him light a candle with a match, and then he asked Josh to come forward and blow it out.

First, the illusionist asked, "Tell me, son—if you blow out this candle, can it be relit without striking another match?"

"No way," Josh blurted. All the children began laughing.

"Well, watch this—I'll prove you wrong." The illusionist proceeded to light the candle with a match and then asked Josh to blow out the flame. Josh filled his cheeks with air and heaved a big blow. As a large puff of smoke rose from the wick, the illusionist quickly stuck the match into the smoke, and the candle reignited. All the children clapped, amazed that the candle relit.

Wish I was enjoying their fun, Ms. Roberson thought as the illusionist moved on to another trick. *It just makes me realize how burned out I am. I don't even know if I want to go on teaching next year. Is it really worth it?*

Then the Holy Spirit nudged her: You don't think you have anything left because you feel snuffed out, but God can rekindle your wavering spirit with His very presence. His light will never leave you.

Maybe like Ms. Roberson, the pressures of life have brought you up short, and you feel burned out as a teacher. God has not moved away from you, but maybe you've drifted away from Him. Turn your heart toward God, and He'll renew His Spirit within you. That's a promise!

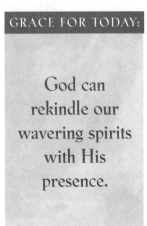

GRACE FOR TODAY:

God can rekindle our wavering spirits with His presence.

A bruised reed he will not break, and a smoldering wick he will not snuff out. . . . In his name . . . put [your] hope.

MATTHEW 12:20-21 NIV

COME JUST AS YOU ARE

By Charles Spurgeon

God's love for us never changes, but ours too often sinks to a low ebb. Perhaps you have become so cold in your feelings and desires toward God that it is difficult to be sure that you ever did love God at all.

Now, note well, that the cause that originated your love for God is the same that must restore it. You went to Christ as a sinner at first, and your first act was to believe God's love for you when there was nothing in you that evidenced it. Go the same way again.

God is as willing to receive you, now that you have played the prodigal, as God was to have kept you at home in the bosom of His love. Think about what kind of love it must be that can invite you still to return!

"Will God still receive me?" Does not God declare that God exists and changes not? (Malachi 3:6). Go to Christ himself at once. If you get the notion that you must pass through a mental state of torment or suffering before you may renew your faith in the Savior, you are mistaken. Come just as you are, bad as you are, hardened, cold, and dead as you feel yourself to be.

Believe in the boundless love of God in Christ Jesus for you. Then shall come the deep repentance, the broken-ness of heart, the sacred hatred of sin and the refining of your soul from all her dross.

—∞—

FATHER, I AM IN AWE OF THE LOVE YOU HAVE FOR ME. WHATEVER MY CONDITION, YOUR LOVE FOR ME NEVER CHANGES. I COME TO YOU NOW, LORD, AND ASK YOU TO RESTORE ME, FILL ME, AND GIVE ME PEACE. I CAN'T THANK YOU ENOUGH. AMEN.

[The Lord said,] "Yes, I have loved you with an everlasting love; there-fore with lovingkindness I have drawn you."

JEREMIAH 31:3 NKJV

A STARTLING THOUGHT

[Jesus said,] "It is the Gentiles who strive for all these things; and indeed
your heavenly Father knows that you need all these things."

MATTHEW 6:32 NRSV

Have you fallen for the lie that God is not personal, that He takes no notice of
you? That your classroom, your students, your daily teaching routine, concern Him not at all? Well, as Mary Poppins would say when unconvinced, "Pish
posh."

> **GRACE FOR TODAY:**
>
> **When we take Christ's hand, He will show us the scars endured for us.**

For some people, it is easier to believe in an
impersonal force far, far away, Someone who is really
much too busy to concern himself with us. But we
know better. God so loved us that He sent himself to
earth in the very personal form of Jesus Christ. The
Bible is replete with personal pronouns for God and
Jesus and the Holy Spirit. And every once in a while,
when maybe we've become too content with the notion
of a distant God, Scripture slides a startling reminder
right under our noses.

For example, the prophet Isaiah is going along just
fine recording the word of the Lord, when he suddenly
grabs you by the front of your shirt in Isaiah 42:6 NIV: "I, the Lord, have called you in
righteousness; I will take hold of your hand."

"In His grip" is scriptural! Not only that, but He watches over His people
(Genesis), has everlasting arms upon which we are invited to lean (Deuteronomy),
hears us (2 Chronicles), and rescues us (2 Timothy). More than once, His people have
been invited to take refuge in the shadow of His wings. God sees and God protects.
He cares a great deal about your hopes and dreams as a teacher.

It doesn't get any more personal than a babe in a manger.

THE TRAP

Because thy steadfast love is better than life,
my lips will praise thee.

PSALM 63:3 RSV

W hen you're tempted to quit teaching mid-year, what is it that stops you?
Well, assuming you have another way to pay for life's expenses, it's probably your contract. You have to honor it, or else pay the hefty consequences.

If you've ever wanted to give up on your marriage,
what stopped you? Possibly your contract. You gave
your word—made a vow. Until death do us part. And
you know how God feels about vows. He says, "It is
better not to vow than to make a vow and not fulfill it"
(Ecclesiastes 5:5 NIV).

Jonah didn't have a very good experience when he
chose to run away from God instead of answering the
call to preach at Ninevah. The prophet Jeremiah tells
God what it's like for him to try and wiggle out of his
calling to preach: "But if I say, 'I will not mention him
or speak any more in his name,' his word is in my heart
like a fire. . . . I am weary of holding it in; indeed, I cannot" (Jeremiah 20:9 NIV). Similarly, the apostle Paul

GRACE FOR TODAY:

God's grace
will help us to
keep our
commitments
and to continue
doing good.

feels a strong calling: "Woe to me if I do not preach the gospel!" (1 Corinthians 9:16
NIV). It's a burning, a calling, a vow, a passion. It is inescapable!

For many of us, teaching is that calling. It is a passion. The school is a mission
field where we may encourage the saints and plant seeds for the harvest. Pray for the
commitment to keep every vow and to continue doing good when it seems impossibly
hard. Ask for grace to love the unlovely and see the best in the worst.

Don't just go to school to do a job today. Rather go because you have a calling,
which you cannot ignore. Go because you desire what God desires so greatly that it is
impossible not to go.

THINK ON THESE THINGS

You'll do best by filling your minds and meditating on things true, noble,
reputable, authentic, compelling, gracious—the best, not the worst.

PHILIPPIANS 4:8 MSG

During World War II, Allied planes returning to England often found that a
thick fog had blanketed the airfields. Without a visible approach, many lost
their way—and their lives. Winston Churchill, deeply troubled, instructed his scientists and engineers to solve the problem. They protested, reminding him of their many
experiments and trial runs. They couldn't remove fog! Churchill wouldn't take no for
an answer, issuing a simply stated order: "Fix it!" In July 1943, they succeeded. A substantial fog was dispersed by means of a machine requiring the wattage of a small
power station, but it worked! Postwar calculations revealed that the invention saved
tens of thousands of airmen.

The world is a foggy place and always will be. Jesus is the light of the world and
He alone can disperse the fog, but you have to keep your eyes fixed on Him. The clut-
ter and clang of life conceals the Cross—your "landing strip"—and you, like Churchill,
must never give up seeking that one, true solution to all of life's ills.

Most children are educated in a secular school system where science and faith are
diametrically opposed. Your gentle, firm voice as a teacher who views science and faith
as compatible will ring out and resonate in your students' minds and hearts. Verse
yourself first and foremost in God's Word, but also make every effort to extend your
worldview into every aspect of life—relationships, politics, religion, culture, art, and
science.

Strive to be that Christian who embraces life, who ponders mysteries, who cal-
culates solutions, who counts the cost, and who believes Christ to be worth all of the
joy and heartache. In the foggy miasma of this world, you may be the only truly
enlightened person your students will ever know.

GRACE FOR TODAY:

When we keep our thoughts focused on God, He can
disperse the fog that blinds us.

SAFE HARBOR

A healthy spirit conquers adversity,
but what can you do when the spirit is crushed?

PROVERBS 18:14 MSG

Adversity, calamity, misfortune. Sometimes they seem to roll over us one after another, leaving us no time to catch our breath. It would seem that if anyone could speak from the annals of biblical history, Joseph would be the expert on this subject. He was betrayed by his brothers, thrown into a pit, sold into slavery, falsely accused by Potiphar's wife, and then spent thirteen years in prison for something he didn't do—that's true adversity!

Have you found yourself in a season of adversity or misfortune that just doesn't seem to end? Like Joseph, you may be tempted to think that God has forgotten you, but again, like Joseph, as surely as He had a plan for him, He has a plan for you. Joseph's adversity was his transportation to the future—and so it is for all who believe.

Adversity develops maturity and steadfastness in the face of the raging storm. It's never pleasant to have to lash yourself to the wheel of your ship just to survive, but when the waves subside and the wind abates, you realize that the experience was priceless. When the next storm comes, and it will, you won't be as afraid. Your faith will remind you that God was with you the last time, and He will be with you in the midst of this storm. Eventually, your ship will arrive safely in port.

The next time adversity tries to swamp your boat, refuse to be ruled by the storm. Elect instead to believe God and acknowledge that your misfortune is only a storm to be conquered on the way to God's safe harbor.

GRACE FOR TODAY:

When we suffer adversity, God wants us to remember
He has a safe harbor for us.

SOUL SEARCHING

You may think some of the names of the students in your class are quite unique. But probably there is not a single Horatio Spafford on the roll.

Mr. Spafford lived in the nineteenth century and penned the beautiful words of the beloved hymn "It Is Well with My Soul," which have comforted many a struggling heart in the more than a century since. A singular line of the hymn says that despite our circumstances, God has taught us to say that indeed, "It is well with my soul." Commend your class, your teaching, your all, into His great care this day and allow His soothing reassurance to carry you.

Though Mr. Spafford suffered financial ruin in the Chicago Fire and lost children at sea, he wrote those soothing words of strength out of the mercy he experienced from God in times of calamity. Eventually, he moved with his wife to Jerusalem to found a community that helped the poor, where he served out the remainder of his days.

Horatio Spafford lived a life of surrender to God. Like Job, he did not blame God for the loss in his life, but rather trusted God to give him the grace to go on. The final stanza of the hymn is a triumphant call to anticipate the day when Jesus comes again and all is made new.

Surrender your toughest problems to Him, whatever or whomever they may be. He loves to answer heartfelt prayer. In fact, why not sing "It Is Well with My Soul" while you wait upon Him in faith? He promises that you, too, will discover that "peace like a river attendeth my way."

> **GRACE FOR TODAY:**
>
> God can teach us to say, "It is well with my soul."

Bless the Lord, O my soul, and do not forget all his benefits.

PSALM 103:2 NRSV

FINDING CHRIST BY READING THE BIBLE

By Evelyn Christenson

An important fact to observe while studying God's Word is "to whom" a portion of Scripture is written. It makes a lot of difference who needs to be changed and also who is eligible to apply the Scripture to his or her life. At a Bible study in St. Paul, a woman observed "the eyes of your understanding being enlightened" from Ephesians 1:18 NKJV.

"My family is not getting along well. How can the 'eyes of my understanding be enlightened' so I will know how to run it better?"

"To whom did we learn this book was written?"

"To the saints which are at Ephesus, and to the faithful in Christ Jesus" (Ephesians 1:1 KJV).

"Are you a saint—one who knows Jesus as personal Savior? Are you in Christ Jesus?"

"No."

"Then you are not eligible for what Paul was praying for."

And at that she decided to accept Christ—right there!

A well-known Christian author and speaker said to me, as we were discussing the way God speaks so specifically out of His Word, "Do you mean to tell me that somebody can find Christ just by reading the Bible?"

"Yes, sir, it really works."[40]

—⁂—

FATHER, THE BIBLE IS A LIVING BOOK; IT IS YOUR WORD SPEAKING TO ME—ALWAYS RELEVANT, ALWAYS TIMELY. WHEN I READ IT, IT CUTS TO THE HEART OF THE MATTER AND THE CORE OF MY BEING. LEAD ME AS I STUDY TODAY. EXPOSE MY NEEDS, CORRECT ME WHERE I'VE ERRED, MINISTER PEACE AND HEALING TO MY SOUL, AND FULFILL MY NEEDS AS A TEACHER. AMEN.

The word of God is full of living power. It is sharper than the sharpest knife, cutting deep into our innermost thoughts and desires. It exposes us for what we really are.

HEBREWS 4:12 NLT

WHO'S GRUMBLING?

Be hospitable to one another without grumbling.

1 PETER 4:9 NKJV

It's an old joke written on a cartoon and shown to nearly every first-year teacher. A woman is moaning that she can't go to school because she doesn't like it, she never gets to do anything first, and everybody picks on her. Then comes the rejoinder, "Well, you have to. You're the teacher!"

"I hate this subject!" "I loathe pizza in the cafeteria!" "I don't feel like working today!" Why is grumbling and complaining so easy? Maybe because it's so contagious.

> **GRACE FOR TODAY:**
>
> God can exchange our grumbling for an attitude of praise.

It's probably also why Paul gave us a list of things to think on, none of which include grumbling. "Fix your thoughts on what is true and honorable and right. Think about things that are pure and lovely and admirable. Think about things that are excellent and worthy of praise" (Philippians 4:8 NLT). Hmm . . . sounds a lot like counting your blessings, doesn't it?

When we surround ourselves with people who grumble, moan, gripe, compare, complain, cast blame, and hold grudges, it's downright difficult to come up with anything positive to say, let alone think.

So examine your habits. Be honest with yourself and with God. Are you a grumbler? Do you have any habits that need changing? Perhaps you need to stay out of the teachers' lounge. Perhaps it would be beneficial to take out a yellow legal pad and physically list all of the things that you enjoy about teaching, about your room location, and about your students.

Maybe you could begin each morning by thanking God for the chance to start over, to begin a new day free of the old one. Pop in a praise tape on the drive to work. Sneak scripture snacks throughout the day. Post a few scriptures to memorize on your steering wheel, mirror, and computer screen. Fine yourself a quarter for every grumbling statement or thought. See what a difference an attitude makes!

MAKE THEM COUNT

Let your speech always be gracious, seasoned with salt, so that you may know how you ought to answer everyone.

COLOSSIANS 4:6 NRSV

A certain professor was known for spectacularly boring, cliché–ridden lectures, so much so that one particularly innovative class devised a method of surviving the semester. They assigned baseball plays to each hackneyed phrase. "On the other hand" was a base hit; "by the same token" was a strikeout; "and so on" was a stolen base. The center aisle of the hall divided the two teams, and the students played inning after inning of silent but focused baseball throughout the term. On the last day of class, the improbable occurred—with the score tied and the bases loaded, the batter hit a home run! The winning team stood and cheered loudly. The professor, though deeply appreciative, later wondered aloud why only half of the students had been so passionate about his lecture.

Few things carry so much power in so little a package as the tongue. In fact, it is only with God's help that you have any chance of taming it. God makes it clear throughout the Bible that the words you speak carry consequences, whether rash words of judgment or wise words of blessing.

Make your words count. The difference a few carefully chosen words makes compared with a deluge of ten–dollar terms is inexpressible. The best truths are conveyed simply, though not always easily. While a firm adherence to the truth should be the basis of your speech, season it with gentleness and compassion.

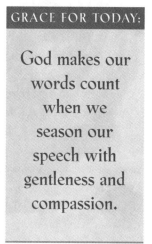

GRACE FOR TODAY:

God makes our words count when we season our speech with gentleness and compassion.

The most successful teachers are both effective speakers and listeners. Your goal isn't to impress your students with all you know, but to listen to their responses to what you've imparted. Your answers to their questions and concerns will make or break you as someone they can trust.

A LIFE-ALTERING POWER

Blessed are they whose iniquities are forgiven,
and whose sins are covered.

ROMANS 4:7 KJV

When Jason didn't make the basketball team, he was enraged and blamed Coach Todd for not being selected. Cursing, he heaved the basketball, shattering the exit light, and stomped off the court.

The next morning when Coach Todd backed out of his garage and closed the door, he saw that it had been splattered with paint balls, and he had a good suspicion who the culprit was. Coach Todd filed a vandalism complaint with the police, providing an account of what had happened in the gym the previous day. By the end of the day, the police had determined that Jason was the guilty party, and that night Jason sat alone in jail.

Coach Todd went down to the jail and used the opportunity to witness to Jason about Christ's love and plan for the young man's life. His words seemed to fall on deaf ears, but when Coach Todd ended the conversation, announcing he'd dropped the charges, Jason couldn't believe it.

"You've dropped the charges?" Jason asked, shocked he was getting a break.

"Well, I hope, Jason, that in dropping the charges, you'll learn a valuable lesson. You're not in jail because I decided to forgive you. Your attitude stinks, and you did vandalize my house, so you deserve the consequences. But a coach helped me out when I got caught cheating in college and could've been thrown off the football team. He took an interest in me when I didn't deserve it, and it turned my life around. So you might say I'm repaying the debt."

As a teacher, it takes wisdom to know when to forgive students and when to throw the book at them. However, when an opportunity comes to show a student forgiveness in a life-changing way, it can be an occasion to influence a life for eternity.

GRACE FOR TODAY:

God can give us the wisdom to know how
and when to forgive.

Take the Risk

Help us, O Lord our God, for we rely on you.

2 Chronicles 14:11 NRSV

Whenever Space Shuttle flights are grounded for precautionary reasons, astronaut families everywhere must breathe a huge sigh of relief. They probably have coffee mugs emblazoned with the words "Better to err on the side of caution."

All that brainpower, all that research, all that experience and still NASA officials will delay or even scrub a flight if they have any doubts about the mechanical integrity or safety of the next launch. Of course, they have paid a heavy price in the Challenger and Columbia tragedies. They are painfully aware of their own fallibility. Still more loss of life would be unthinkable.

Perhaps the question for the classroom is, what have we learned from the failures and the sacrifices that have led to milestones in innovation, discovery, exploration, and scientific and technological advancement? And when all is said and done, was it worth the risk?

On the other hand, how safe do you play it when it comes to faith? Do you see it as a risk? Are you reluctant to trust God with the daily malfunctions and occasional thorny problems that are standard operating procedure in most classrooms? Do you think, "If I risk too much, I may lose. Or risk too little, and I'll have to look back on a year with few strides in learning or personal growth?"

Faith is not as risky as it might sound. It is not blind trust. It is taking all you know about God and His faithfulness throughout the ages, and saying, "I know my Redeemer lives!" and then acting upon it. Remember, without faith it is impossible to please God. The world might see your faith and call it risk. But you know better. Faith is solid assurance based on God's flawless track record.

Grace for Today:

God wants us to trust Him with our daily needs.

PEARLS FOR PIGS?

Most of us don't own a string of genuine pearls, and if we did, we'd never think of taking them off and throwing them before pigs! So, of what was Jesus speaking? He was speaking of talking about the Good News, the saving grace of God—salvation. Remember the man who sold all he had for the Pearl of Great Price?

Neglected dogs and stray pigs probably often roamed the streets of Jerusalem. Jesus' audience would have been well acquainted with their disregard for anything precious or sacred. Jesus was warning them, and us, not to bother sharing God's story with those who are determined to mock it, ignore it, and hold it up to ridicule.

Knowing when and with whom to share requires discernment and reliance upon God's timing. Very often, taking matters into our own hands leads to disastrous results.

In a school where very few faculty members were believers, and a large number claimed to be atheists and agnostics, Charlotte wrote a public letter attacking some programs supported by a liberal teaching organization of which she was not a member. The backlash was tremendous. They taunted Charlotte, her "naïve" faith, and her judgmental attitude. For months almost no one spoke to her.

Isn't it an honor to share in Christ's sufferings? Yes. However, Jesus told us there was a time to shake the dust from our feet and move on. We cannot hold non-believers to Christ's standards. If you read the Gospels carefully, you'll notice Jesus' extreme patience with the sinners He came to save. His harshest criticisms were reserved for Pharisees who should have known better—whose hearts were far from what God required. We must not be surprised when sinners sin. Instead, we need to seek opportunities to share the reasons for our convictions and live in such a manner that people are drawn to seek Him.

> **GRACE FOR TODAY:**
>
> God advises we let the Holy Spirit lead us before sharing the gospel.

[Jesus said,] "Don't give pearls to swine!
They will trample the pearls and turn and attack you."

MATTHEW 7:6 TLB

RIGHT WHEN YOU NEED IT

By Evelyn Christenson

Many times God wants to change me when I'm reading or studying His Word, or when I'm with a group "reading until He speaks." But when I find myself in a situation where I need help immediately, then the Holy Spirit brings to my mind the Scripture that meets my need at that moment. One of the primary reasons for reading and studying the Bible is to provide Him with the Word to bring to our remembrance—*when we need it.*

We stay in the Bible, studying and reading devotionally, being taught by God so that the Holy Spirit can bring to our remembrance what He told us. We tell our children that they can't expect God to help them recall answers on a test if they have never studied the material in the first place. Neither can we expect God to bring to our remembrance answers to our needs if we have not stored His truth in our hearts.

A couple of years ago I was fretting because I was remembering less and less as I grew older. But in a moment the Holy Spirit kindly reminded me of this verse on His bringing all things to our remembrance—His way of dealing with old age! Then I thought back on the chat I had with quite forgetful eighty-two-year-old Corrie ten Boom the month before. "Evelyn," she said, "I never forget a spiritual thing."[41]

—∞—

GOD, THANK YOU FOR YOUR THE PRECIOUS HOLY SPIRIT. AS I STUDY AND MEDITATE ON YOUR WORD, I ASK THAT IT BECOME A RICH DEPOSIT FROM WHICH I CAN DRAW WHEN I NEED IT. DURING MY TIME IN THE CLASSROOM AND DURING EVERY OTHER PART OF MY DAY, I OFTEN NEED ANSWERS IMMEDIATELY. THANK YOU FOR BEING MY EVER-PRESENT, WELL-TIMED HELP. AMEN.

[Jesus said,] "The Helper, the Holy Spirit, whom the Father will send in My name, He will teach you all things, and bring to your remembrance all things that I said to you."

JOHN 14:26 NKJV

THANKFUL FOR THE THORNS

Let the peace of Christ rule in your hearts, to which indeed you were
called in one body; and be thankful.

COLOSSIANS 3:15 NASB

Scottish preacher George Matheson had a problem typical to most believers. He found it harder to praise God when things went wrong than when they went right. After his eyesight began to fail, however, he changed his thinking. Months passed as he struggled with this wearisome burden until he reached the point where he could honestly pray, "My God, I have never thanked You for my thorn. I have thanked You a thousand times for my roses, but not once for my thorn. I have been looking forward to a world where I shall get compensated for my cross, but I have never thought of my cross as itself a present glory. Teach me the value of my thorn."

GRACE FOR TODAY:

God develops in us thankful hearts when we rely on His grace during life's trials.

Have you ever thanked God for your weaknesses? It's hard to do so in this culture of self-sufficiency. It's easy to thank God when things are going well, but it's when you rely on His grace to see you through life's trials, heartaches, and difficulties that you develop a thankful heart.

Yes, God is good. That very fact enables you to get through the hard times, knowing that your loving Father in Heaven is working something good out of something bad.

As a teacher, when you rely on God's ultimate goodness and extend His grace to your students, your kindness, compassion, and offers of restitution to wayward students show your basic understanding of God's sufficiency.

Because He has seen you through your troubles, you do all you can to see others through theirs. That is the mark of a thankful heart—a heart contented by God's loving care.

FRIENDS IN DISGUISE

So from now on we regard no one from a worldly point of view.

2 CORINTHIANS 5:16 NIV

Janie was the new teacher at Memorial High, but it didn't take her long to notice that most of the female teachers wouldn't interact with Sammie, the girls' P.E. teacher. The woman was somewhat masculine and had a tough façade. One day Sammie went into the school cafeteria at lunch, sat alone, ate, and left in under five minutes.

"I wonder why she always sits alone," Janie asked Maryanne, who'd been a teacher at the school for years.

"Probably because she's smart enough to figure out she doesn't fit in with the rest of us," Maryanne said. "She's a breed all to her own."

"Oh," Janie said, puzzled at Maryanne's response, while thinking about how she could get to know Sammie. *I can't imagine anyone liking to eat alone,* she thought.

GRACE FOR TODAY:

God judges our hearts, not our appearance.

You can probably think of someone in your school who doesn't seem to fit in. However, if you take the risk to get to know that person's story, you might be surprised how much easier it is to understand where they're coming from and why they act as they do. Otherwise, you'll judge another teacher as a result of only looking at appearances.

Perhaps God may have unexpected blessings planned for your life through some gifting or strength that person might possess, but you'll never know unless you determine to overlook some rough edges and look at the heart.

Later on one wintry weekend when the city was blanketed in snow, Janie had a flat tire and no spare. She called several of her teacher friends to get someone to come help her out, but none of them wanted to chance driving on the icy roads. Guess who responded to the emergency? Sammie, and she bought and gave Janie a brand-new tire to boot!

ALL'S FAIR

When the crowd heard it, they were astonished at his teaching.

MATTHEW 22:33 RSV

Horace Mann once said that a teacher who attempts to teach without inspiring the pupil with a desire to learn is hammering on cold iron.

One teacher decided to end the lethargy of an afternoon class by loudly asking to borrow a student's ballpoint pen. No sooner had a student willingly surrendered his pen than the teacher broke it in two and threw it in the wastebasket. There was a collective gasp at this very unteacherly behavior, but the teacher ignored it and proceeded with the lesson.

After a few minutes, a hand hesitatingly rose at the back of the room and the lad whose pen had met so ghastly an end asked why. The teacher merely answered, "Because I felt like it."

When the young man protested that such wanton destruction of his pen was unfair, the teacher replied, "Not to me it isn't. In my world, I'll do what I want."

There ensued a lively discussion of how "fairness" is determined and who gets to decide the standard. The class concluded that unless there is an absolute standard—God's standard—then anything goes. The offended student was rewarded with a brand-new pen.

Sometimes for learning to take place, a shake-up is required. How often has God halted us through illness or loss, or rearranged the furniture in the carefully appointed living rooms of our lives, in order to gain our attention? Sometimes the best work emerges when you switch gears, tell stories, or get down on the floor for a different viewpoint.

Order, yes; calcification, no. Break a pen over your status quo.

GRACE FOR TODAY:

God often shakes up our lives to get our attention.

JUST WHEN YOU NEED IT MOST

Even if you do suffer for righteousness' sake, you will be blessed.

1 PETER 3:14 RSV

Corrie ten Boom was thrown into a concentration camp during World War II for the "crime" of hiding Jews in her home, saving them from certain destruction by the Nazis.

Much later, *The Hiding Place* was written, chronicling her faith and experiences during that time. In the book, as Corrie is being led away, frightened and trembling, she recalls a conversation with her father about what this sacrifice might entail. He reminded her of a familiar scene from her childhood. When they would ride the train into the city, he would hold on to the ticket, guarding it from little hands that might misplace it. When it was time to give it to the conductor at the end of the line, he would give the ticket to Corrie. In the same way, he assured her, God holds on to what we need, giving us the strength and courage for any situation.

To live life in this manner requires that we rely on God, not on ourselves, for the courage and strength to meet any circumstance that might come our way. We plan many things for our lives. However, none of us can predict what might happen to derail those plans. Neither do we know how displaying God's strength under fire might help others.

Ms. Dennison lost her home to a tornado during the last month of school. She missed one day, and then returned so that she could finish out the term with her beloved seniors. On the last day she received a note from a student: "Ms. Dennison, your conduct, optimism, and faith during these past few weeks have inspired me. You have taught me more than just history; you have taught me life lessons."

What about you? What life lessons are your teaching? Are you modeling qualities of courage, strength, and grace under fire for your students?

GRACE FOR TODAY:

When God is all we have, He is all we need.

PURE SATISFACTION

A man lived with his wife, two small children, and his elderly parents in a tiny, noisy, crowded hut. Worn down in spite of his attempts to be patient and gracious, he consulted the village elder. "Do you have a rooster?" asked the wise man. "Yes," he replied. "Keep the rooster in the hut with your family, and come see me again next week." The man returned and told the wise elder that living conditions were worse than ever, with the rooster crowing and making a mess of the hut. Over the next several weeks, on the advice of the elder, the man made room for a cow, a goat, two dogs, and his brother's children. At his wit's end, he finally kicked out all the animals and guests, leaving only his wife, his children, and his parents. Comparatively spacious and quiet, the hut became a haven and everyone lived in peace thereafter.

Lasting satisfaction is a matter of perspective. If all that mattered in life were fame, material success, and financial stability, why are so many rich and famous people miserable? When Jesus spoke of drinking living waters and never going thirsty again, He described living a godly life, drawing on God's infinite resources to provide both for today's needs and for a glorious future.

Certainly, you're not a teacher because of the money and fame, not because schools are an easy, stress-free environment, not because you can't do anything else. You teach because you love making an impact on children's lives.

Helping kids learn, guiding them toward being better people, and knowing that you are fulfilling God's plan for your life brings satisfaction. God wants you to be satisfied today as He shapes you into Christ's image and prepares you to enjoy the glories of Heaven.

> GRACE FOR TODAY:
>
> God gives deep satisfaction to those who follow His ultimate plans for their lives.

Fill us each morning with your constant love,
so that we may sing and be glad all our life.

PSALM 90:14 GNT

HIDDEN TREASURE

By Evelyn Christenson

Those of us who know the pain of trying to recall some of the information we stored in our minds there as a child, or even a recipe that seemed so simple twenty years ago, realize the inadequacy of our human memory systems. As human operators, we are frequently unable to bring forth even a tiny bit of stored information. But when we need to recall a particular spiritual truth, we have a supernatural computer operator—the Holy Spirit!

When I recognize there is something wrong in my life and I know God wants to change me, I feed the problem into the computer of my mind. Then, when I ask God to give me a solution, the Holy Spirit often *reminds* me of a portion of Scripture that shows me the specific sin that is causing my problem. Many times He flashes back: "pride" (Romans 12:3) or "worry" (Philippians 4:6).

Occasionally, before I'm even aware that something is wrong, my Supernatural Operator is already spelling out an answer to me. He knows the need or the problem before I ask, before I consciously formulate it into words. Jesus said in Matthew 6:8 that our heavenly Father knows what things we have need of *before* we ask Him, and the solution is recalled from my scriptural memory bank before I spell out my need. That's even less time than the fastest computer in the world takes to summon answers! Yes, before I even realize my sin, the Holy Spirit is reminding, prodding, reproving with His gentle nudge or stating in no uncertain voice, "That's SIN!"[42]

—⁓—

Father, YOUR WORD IS A RICH TREASURE THAT I HIDE IN MY HEART. THANK YOU FOR ANTICIPATING MY NEEDS—IN MY PERSONAL LIFE AS WELL AS IN MY ROLE AS A TEACHER—BEFORE I AM EVEN AWARE OF THEM MYSELF. I PRAY THAT YOU WILL BRING UP THE APPROPRIATE NUGGET OF TRUTH AT THE TIME I NEED IT MOST, AND I THANK YOU FOR IT. AMEN.

I have hidden your word in my heart, that I might not sin against you.

PSALM 119:11 NLT

DON'T BORROW TROUBLE

I always do what pleases him.

JOHN 8:29 NIV

P aula People-Pleaser was a popular teacher and could always be counted on to help, no matter what. One day Polly Procrastinator came rushing into school, focused on using her planning period to pull together a social studies unit she'd put off developing. Ms. People-Pleaser was in the workroom, and sensing Ms. Procrastinator's panic, she volunteered to help. Polly explained that she didn't have ready the new unit that her class was to start that day. So Ms. People-Pleaser set aside her own plans. Offering to help Polly, she raced back to her room and returned with pictures, handouts, and old quizzes.

> **GRACE FOR TODAY:**
>
> **God doesn't want us to fix the whole world— just our part.**

The bell rang, and Paula People-Pleaser returned to class with a sense of satisfaction that she'd made a huge contribution. You can just imagine her frustration when at lunch she overheard Ms. Procrastinator excitedly relating how, on the spur-of-the-moment, she'd come up with a brainstorm to teach about the Presidential election, since the country would be going to the polls soon, and how interested the class was with the idea.

Ms. People-Pleaser was so furious she felt like dragging Ms. Procrastinator into a circle of other teachers and having it out with her—especially considering the personal time she'd obviously wasted helping Polly.

Like most fables, there's a moral to this story—don't borrow trouble!

Do you ever find yourself volunteering to help on projects that God never intended you to take on? Yes, God wants you to reach beyond yourself to help others, but you need to seek His wisdom instead of trying to fix the whole world. He might be trying to teach a valuable lesson to the other person. Ask the Lord to lead and guide you as to how to distribute your time and effort so that your hard work furthers His kingdom and His purposes for your life.

THE GREATER GOOD

They are to do good, to be rich in good works,
generous, and ready to share.

1 TIMOTHY 6:18 NRSV

W hen you think of all the administrators, nurses, custodians, cafeteria workers, coaches, and yes, teachers, it takes to educate our children, it really is
quite remarkable. Add in the volunteers—chaperones, reading and math tutors, graduation committee members, and so on—and it constitutes an army of men and women
of goodwill who believe that education is that important.

Those who make a career of it inherently add
value to our culture. Teaching is a prime example. Not
only is it rewarding for you on a personal level, it is
beneficial for society on a universal one. Are there
more financially rewarding career paths? To be sure.
Are there any other career paths more worthwhile?
Not likely.

What you do, day in and day out, is for the greater
good. Paul in his letter to Titus said that the teacher who
sets a good example for their pupils and teaches with
integrity, seriousness, and soundness of speech, can
actually move those who seem to fight every inch of the
way. Now he specifically meant those opposed to spiritual teaching, but is it too far off to say that those who
resist common learning, or who misbehave and act out, can also be positively affected
by your example? No. The passionate teacher can, with heart, faith, and determination,
turn lives around right before his or her very eyes. That teacher is you.

> **GRACE FOR TODAY:**
>
> When we teach
> with the
> kindness and
> patience of
> God, He
> rewards us
> with His grace.

You see, the psalmist says that the Lord is good, that His love endures forever, and
that He is the greatest teacher of all. (See Psalm 118:1.) He instructs sinners and loves
justice and fills the earth with unfailing love. The classroom is your "earth," and daily
you fill it with love and mercy and truth. Actually, by your hard work and compassion,
it can be a little bit of Heaven in a child's life.

THE END OF THE STORY

Death and Hell were thrown into the Lake of Fire.

REVELATION 20:14 TLB

One evening at bedtime, a young boy sat huddled under his covers, reading a story. When his father walked by, he noted that his son was on the verge of tears. "What's the matter, Son?" "Well, I don't like this story. It's scary!" replied the boy. "Then stop reading it!" came the advice.

A little while later, the father again passed the boy's room and noticed that he was still reading the same story, this time with a huge grin on his face. Unable to resist, his father asked, "Son, how come you're still reading the same story? What's different about it this time?"

The little boy, with a huge grin on his face, answered, "Well, I read the end of the story. Now when I get scared, I just say to the bad guy, 'Oh, you're gonna get it! You're really gonna get it!'"

We, too, know the end of the story. When life scares us, feels out of control, too hard, too depressing, or too overwhelming, read it. It's in the book of Revelation.

If you're heartbroken, remind yourself that there will be no more tears in Heaven. If you feel like the struggle with temptation will be eternal, remember that you won't struggle there. If you're grieving, read again how death will be swallowed up and there will be no more sorrow there. If your nights are long and lonely, remember, Heaven will be lit by the glory of the Lamb, and there is no night there. Above all, remember that Satan, the Prince of this earth, is "really gonna get it" when Christ, the Prince of Peace, returns!

GRACE FOR TODAY:

God is the ultimate Victor and the Author of the best ending to the greatest story ever told.

LAY DOWN YOUR ARMS

Humble yourselves before the Lord, and he will lift you up.

JAMES 4:10 NIV

The ship's captain looked into the dark night and saw faint lights in the distance. Immediately, he told his signalman to send a message: "Alter your course 10 degrees south." Promptly they received the return message: "Alter your course 10 degrees north." Angry that his order had been defied, the captain sent a second message: "Alter your course 10 degrees south—I am the captain!" Soon came another reply: "Alter your course 10 degrees north—I am Seaman Third Class Hawkins." Immediately, the captain sent a third message, knowing the fear it would evoke: "Alter your course 10 degrees south—I am a battleship." The final reply came quickly: "Alter your course 10 degrees north—I am a lighthouse."

Submission is a stumbling block for most people. When colleagues find out that you're a Christian, their polite response is often how nice that is for you, although there's a part of them wondering how a reasonable, intelligent individual such as yourself can kowtow to such an intolerant religion, which says there is only one path to God through Jesus Christ.

Free will, seemingly pesky in its application, is by God's design the most beautiful part of being human. When you choose God, when you willingly submit to His lordship, you gain peace that the world cannot know, give, or remove. Hopefully, when others experience your peaceful nature, they'll want what you have.

It's easy to get too busy with school, lesson plans, meetings, and conflict resolution to hear what God is saying—too busy to remember His love, His mercy, and His grace. You can't afford to be that busy. God wants you to submit yourself to Him, so that you can show others who He is—the Savior of the world.

GRACE FOR TODAY:

God captains our souls, and the sooner we acknowledge it, the sooner we can get down to the work He has for us.

FOCUS ON JESUS

Do you find it difficult to make decisions for God at school, or when you're just hanging out with friends, or even when no one is looking? Is it hard for you to take a risk and step out in faith to do something that you feel God wants you to do? Take heart! God has an answer for you—fix your eyes on Jesus!

Hebrews 12:1-2 NLT has the prescription you need, and its power will help you to step out in confidence. It reads, "Therefore, since we are surrounded by such a huge crowd of witnesses to the life of faith, let us strip off every weight that slows us down, especially the sin that so easily hinders our progress. And let us run with endurance the race that God has set before us. We do this by keeping our eyes on Jesus, on whom our faith depends from start to finish."

So how does this Scripture translate into the twenty-first century? If you're running a race with a hundred-pound TV on your back, it will really slow you down. If you want to win the race, you'll have to dump the TV. The same principle applies to making decisions and taking risks for God. If your mind is weighed down and every thought is focused on your own needs, it will be difficult to hear God and receive His direction. That's what the writer of Hebrews is trying to say—get rid of anything that's preventing you from focusing wholeheartedly on God.

The truth is that you can't be focused on yourself, your weaknesses, your feelings, or your problems and be focused on Jesus at the same time. So make the switch today! He alone has the answers and resources you need, and He'll lead you in the right direction every time.

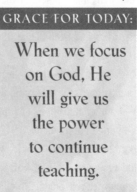

GRACE FOR TODAY:

When we focus on God, He will give us the power to continue teaching.

[You] who share in the heavenly calling, fix your thoughts on Jesus, the apostle and high priest whom we confess.

HEBREWS 3:1 NIV

A New Person

By Charles Spurgeon

Do you see that cat? What a clean creature it is! How cleverly it washes itself with its tongue and paws! Did you ever see a pig do that? No, cleanlinessit is contrary to its nature. It prefers to wallow in the mud.

Go and teach a pig to wash itself, and see how little success you would have. You may wash that pig by force, but it hurries back to the mud and is soon dirty again.

The only way in which you can get a pig to wash itself is to transform it into a cat; then it will wash and be clean, but not until then! And once that transformation is accomplished, then what was difficult or impossible is now easy. The swine will then be fit for your living room.

So it is with an ungodly person. You cannot force them to do what a renewed person does willingly. You may teach them, and set them a good example, but they cannot learn the art of holiness. Their nature leads them another way.

When the Lord makes a new person of them, so great is this change that I once heard a convert say, "Either the whole world is changed, or else I am." The new nature follows after right as naturally as the old nature wanders after wrong.

The Lord's working in this matter is a great mystery: The Holy Spirit performs it. God, who promises this marvelous change, will assuredly carry it out in all who receive Jesus, for to all such He gives power to become the Heirs of God.

—⁓—

HEAVENLY FATHER, THANK YOU FOR MAKING ME A NEW PERSON INSIDE. I SUBMIT MYSELF TO YOU TO CONTINUE THE RENEWAL PROCESS. I TRUST YOUR GRACE TO HELP ME CHANGE ANY PART OF ME THAT DOESN'T GLORIFY YOU. EVERY DAY I WANT TO LOOK MORE AND MORE LIKE JESUS. AMEN.

Those who become Christians become new persons. They are not the same anymore, for the old life is gone. A new life has begun!

2 CORINTHIANS 5:17 NLT

WHAT FLOATS THEIR BOATS?

To acquire wisdom is to love oneself;
people who cherish understanding will prosper.

PROVERBS 19:8 NLT

I n her no-nonsense guide to success for teachers, *If You Don't Feed the Teachers They Eat the Students!*, Dr. Neila Connors urges her readers not to waste time "fertilizing rocks or watering weeds." That is, you—the teacher—create a positive classroom climate in constant pursuit of improvement and advancement. You do not accept stagnation. Your students understand that their progress, and the progress of their neighbors, is paramount. Learning, growing, and improving are fun and satisfying. When one benefits from a breakthrough of the brain, all benefit.

GRACE FOR TODAY:

Because God believes in us and went to great lengths on our behalf, we can do no less for our students.

Do you care for your students? Do you love learning? Do you enjoy communicating? Yes? Then you are like Jesus who, even at His most footsore and heavyhearted, was passionate about those He came to redeem. Near the hour of His death, He comforted His disciples, told them to trust in God, and prayed for their protection from the evil one. And He prayed for all who would ever believe in Him, that they would continue to make God and His truth known throughout the world.

What a colossal waste of God's wonderful resources, including our time, if we persist in fertilizing rocks or watering weeds. Finger pointing, procrastination, nay saying, and self-doubt are paralyzers. Rather, commend the students who forge ahead. Celebrate their breakthroughs and milestones. Demonstrate a genuine excitement for learning and watch even the most reluctant students come alive.

God's ardor for us has never flagged. Just as you do not want one of your students to lose out on a life lifted by learning, God does not want to lose a single person through unbelief. For that reason, He is patient and long-suffering. When you do the same, by nudging along the doubters and the defeatists, not coddling them, all boats rise.

MY WAY

A man without self-control is like a city broken into and
left without walls.

PROVERBS 25:28 RSV

"DO NOT PICK (twist off, sever, cut, clip, snip, snap off, pluck, pinch off, pull, bend, crush, pare, cleave, divide, break, touch or take, borrow, steal, remove or otherwise harm, mutilate, or endanger) THE FLOWERS." So read the sign by a flower bed in a park. One wonders why the sadly humorous sign is even necessary. Until you consider that as a nation of egocentric individuals, we are incredibly selfish and seem to abhor delayed gratification. We want what we want when we want it. We are perpetually bombarded by an advertising media whose entire goal is to make us discontent with what we have and then immediately move to suggest a product that could help.

"You deserve a break today." "Because you're worth it." The phrases convince us that self-denial is outdated—old-fashioned. Self-promotion has all but replaced it. In an earlier time, we would have labeled it selfishness. Today, we're doing our best to call it leadership. A hundred years ago it was determined that the average American had about seventy "wants." A more recent survey discovered that their grandchildren have more like five hundred!

> **GRACE FOR TODAY:**
>
> To do great things for the kingdom of God, He wants us to do it His way.

What about you? How many things are on your want list? Ever blur the line between a want and a need? What's your disposition like when things aren't going your way? How do you act when you present your idea for block scheduling and the administration soundly vetoes it?

Isn't it marvelously easy to live virtuously when things are going your way? A secret stubborn streak in all of us secretly admires the old Sinatra tune, "I Did It My Way." But interestingly enough, no one who did great things for Jesus' sake ever did it their own way. They did it God's way.

IN HIS HANDS

The salvation of the righteous is from the LORD; He is their strength in
the time of trouble.

PSALM 37:39 NKJV

P astor Bruce Larson worked for many years in New York City, frequently counseling people wrestling with the decision of surrendering their lives to Christ.
Often, he invited them to walk with him from his office down to the RCA Building on
Fifth Avenue. A massive statue of Atlas adorns the entrance there, a beautifully pro-
portioned man who, with all his muscles straining, is holding the world upon his
shoulders. He would note that the statue, the most powerfully built man in the world,
could barely stand up under this burden. "Now that's one way to live," Larson would
point out to his companion, "trying to carry the world on your shoulders. But now
come across the street with me." On the other side of Fifth Avenue is Saint Patrick's
Cathedral. Behind the high altar there is a small shrine of the boy Jesus, depicted as
effortlessly holding the world in one hand.

God alone is strong enough to handle every difficulty you face. He allows challenges and trials to enter your life, not so you can show Him how strong you are, but
so you can learn to rely on Him to help you do the right thing.

True strength is more than mere survival; it is securing meaning and purpose
beyond the immediate obstacles of the day. Only God can provide both protection and
purpose. What awaits you today? A conference with a frustrated parent? A mediation
between hostile students? Let God be your strength, your confidence, and your wisdom.

Trust God to give you the right help in the right moment. You have Christ's mercy
and love working for you, which were not obtained by abolishing evil in an outright
show of power, but rather through His desire to do God's will. God's strength is
yours. You can count on it.

GRACE FOR TODAY:

God's strength is at its best when we're at our weakest.

A Great Plan

> May he ... fulfill all your plans.
>
> PSALM 20:4 NLT

Have you ever wondered how you could be more effective at school in communicating the grace of God? Maybe *The A-Team*, a television show from the early 1980s, can provide you with some inspiration. Colonel Hannibal Smith, leader of the A-Team, would end every show with the phrase, "I love it when a plan comes together." Wouldn't it be exciting if you were to hear God say to you, "I love it when you make a plan come together"?

Ask God to give you a vision—a plan—for how you can stay within the boundaries of your school and share His love and grace with the faculty and staff who need a touch of His love. Come to school having spent time in prayer and with the power of God's Word reverberating within you. Worship Him on the way to school, and expect that He will use you, whether you're aware of it or not.

Next, ask God to lead you to other teachers who have a similar passion to be used by the Lord. Probably you're not the only believer in your school. As He does, maybe you could organize a prayer group before or after school to intercede as He guides you all to pray.

God loves to see His grace spread around, and He can use you in powerful and inconspicuous ways to make a difference in your school if you're available for His purposes. In return, you'll experience great joy. Then one day maybe you'll hear Him say, "I love it when a plan comes together."

GRACE FOR TODAY:

If we focus on God's plan, He will make it happen.

GET TO KNOW "THE GO" INSIDE YOU

Motivation is an interesting concept. What stimulus, incentive, or drive makes us do what we do? For the small child, the promise of an ice cream cone might be sufficient motivation to clean up the bedroom. A teenager might voluntarily join the armed services if the educational benefits are generous enough. A man and woman might commit to one another for life if the love and attraction between them is deep enough.

Proverbs is heavy with motivation. Commit to the Lord, we are told, and our plans will succeed. Give heed to instruction and prosper. A laborer is motivated to work by the hunger in his belly. He who wishes to avoid calamity is motivated to carefully guard his mouth and tongue.

Some have likened teaching to a "community of truth." Entrusted to the community are great and immutable facts and realities of biology, history, mathematics, literature, art, and the list goes on. The body of knowledge that draws the community of truth together motivates us to impart that knowledge to others.

But it is not facts alone that compel us. We are also driven by the importance of how to live and utilize the knowledge gained. What constitutes good citizenship? What are our obligations as human beings toward other human beings? How best can we serve God? That we even ask these questions shows a powerful motivation, much of which comes from outside ourselves.

The Holy Spirit is our Teacher and Guide, motivated by the Father's will to equip us to live lives pleasing to God. Jesus was motivated by His desire to do the Father's will. When you teach, motivated by your desire to serve God by sharing all that He has made, you tap into the divine will and motivation to see all people reconciled to himself.

> **GRACE FOR TODAY:**
>
> God's Holy Spirit motivates us to serve Him.

Let the words of my mouth and the meditation of my heart be acceptable in thy sight.

PSALM 19:14 RSV

CONTINUALLY OPEN HEART

By William Law

Christ, after His glorification in Heaven, says, "Behold, I stand at the door and knock." He does not say, "Behold, you have Me in the Scriptures."

Now what is the door at which Christ, at the right hand of God in Heaven, knocks? Surely it is the heart, to which Christ is always present.

He goes on, "If anyone hears My voice. . . ." How do they hear but by the hearing of the heart, or what voice, but that which is the speaking or sounding of Christ within them? He adds, "and opens the door," that is, a living holy nature and spirit will be born within him, "and dine with him, and he with Me." Behold the last finishing work of a redeeming Jesus, entered into the heart that opens to Him, bringing forth the joy, the blessing, and the perfection of that first life of God in the soul, which was lost by the fall, set forth as a supper, or feast of the heavenly Jesus with the soul, and the soul with Him.

Now this continual knocking of Christ at the door of the heart, sets forth the case or nature of a continual imme-diate divine inspiration within us; it is always with us, but there must be an opening of the heart to it; and though it is always there, yet it is only felt and found by those, who are attentive to it, depend upon, and humbly wait for it. Now let anyone tell me how they can believe anything of this voice of Christ, how they can listen to it, hear, or obey it, except by such a faith, as keeps them habitually turned to an immediate con-stant inspiration of the Spirit of Christ within them!

—〰—

FATHER, I HEAR JESUS KNOCKING. THANK YOU FOR THE JOY AND BLESSING I WILL RECEIVE FROM OUR FELLOWSHIP. AMEN.

[Jesus said,] "Behold, I stand at the door and knock. If anyone hears My voice and opens the door, I will come in to him and dine with him, and he with Me."

REVELATION 3:20 NKJV

WHAT AM I DOING?

[Paul said,] "I do not understand my own actions. For I do not do what I want, but I do the very thing I hate."

ROMANS 7:15 RSV

Have you ever read through the conduct required of Christians in the Sermon on the Mount, and thought, "No way I can live up to that?" Have you ever thought about God's standards and known you couldn't measure up? Have you ever contemplated our awesome, omniscient, omnipotent, eternal God and thought, "I'll never be worthy?' Have you ever cried out along with Paul, "I don't understand! Everything good I want to do, I don't do; yet everything bad I always seem to manage."

GRACE FOR TODAY:

When we ask God for self-control, He will grant it.

We're much like kindergartners who have the entire district policy manual read to them on the first day of school and are overwhelmed, scared, and certain that they'll never remember or be able to do it all. On our own, we can't do it. There's no hope without Jesus.

God in His infinite mercy knew that when He created us for His pleasure, we were going to mess up. Big time. He gave us free will, and Adam and Eve used it to prove that none of us are long on self-control. So He made a plan. God reached down to us through His Son, Jesus. That Son was sacrificed for our sins. And He dwells within us through the Holy Spirit.

In Romans 7: 18 NIV, Paul says that he has the desire to do good, "but I cannot carry it out." Alone, neither can we. But the fruit of the Spirit, which dwells within us, includes self-control. We can ask God for it. We can stop living in the arrogance that makes us believe that on our own we can change our behavior if we simply try harder. We can do the hard work of surrender, and in the end, find that it yields the sweetest of fruit.

COMPASSION IN ACTION

What does the Lord require of you but to do justly, to love mercy,
and to walk humbly with your God?

MICAH 6:8 NKJV

In the early days of his presidency, Calvin Coolidge awoke one morning in his hotel room to find a cat burglar going through his clothes. Coolidge asked the burglar not to take his watch chain because it contained an engraved charm he wanted to keep. Engaging the thief in hushed tones, Coolidge discovered the bandit was a college student who had no money to pay his hotel bill or buy a train ticket back to campus. Coolidge loaned the young man thirty-two dollars out of his wallet—which he had also persuaded the dazed, would-be brigand to relinquish—and advised him to leave as unconventionally as he'd entered so he could avoid the Secret Service! Eventually, the loan was even repaid.

GRACE FOR TODAY:

God's ways are beyond our ways, but He loves mercy and wants us to share it.

When you don't get what you deserve, that's mercy. What justice demands, mercy forgives. It's a hallmark of God's character that time and again He gives you another chance to set things right. One reason He does so is that He loves you, but another is so that you can bear mercy's fruit by extending it to others.

The great challenges of loving your neighbor as yourself and loving your enemy both hinge on mercy. Before debating whether or not someone deserves mercy, consider whether more can be gained by exacting justice or by extending compassion.

When you work with young people, mercy is an almost daily requirement as you balance teaching what is right and letting your students learn from their own mistakes. Sometimes you need to show children that their failures aren't the final verdict on them as people. Every child's situation needs to be addressed individually as you rely on God to give you discernment.

CROSS OVER TO FREEDOM

It was for freedom that Christ set us free; therefore keep standing firm and do not be subject again to a yoke of slavery.

GALATIANS 5:1 NASB

There's no greater appreciation of grace than the personal freedom afforded to you through Christ. Apart from freedom, life can become a prison, as exemplified by the lives of many East Berliners once the Berlin Wall was built. Many East Germans risked their lives to reclaim their freedom, and many died in the process. It's estimated that ten thousand people attempted to escape to West Berlin, and only half succeeded.

Disney's movie *Night Crossing* portrays the desperation of two families, the Wetzels and Strlzycks, who in 1979 defied death in their determination to escape to freedom. They devised a plan to fly over the wall by making a homemade hot–air balloon. They cautiously bought nylon cloth in small amounts so as not to raise any suspicion, and when they had enough material, they sewed it together to craft a hot–air balloon. The night of their planned escape, they held their collective breath, hoping their limited amount of fuel would be enough to get them airborne. Then they desperately prayed that they'd float over the wall into West Berlin—to freedom.

Once the Wetzels and Strlzycks tasted freedom, do you think Mrs. Wetzel was at all concerned that the fuel bill was unpaid? Do you think Mr. Strlzyck was feeling guilty that he wouldn't be making his rent payment for the month? No way—they were free!

Picture the full impact of the freedom Christ bought for you with His life. Similarly, you've no need to be concerned about the things of the past; they're gone! Christ has lifted you over the prison wall to freedom—freedom from sin, shame, hate, and guilt. Enjoy it!

GRACE FOR TODAY:

Christ bought our freedom on the Cross.

GIVE THEM AN AXE

Teach the wise, and they will be wiser. Teach the righteous,
and they will learn more.

PROVERBS 9:9 NLT

SpaceShipOne was the first private-venture craft to leave the earth's atmosphere and enter space. The engineers who developed it are thrilled that their work, in part, has enabled space travel to become a possibility for the ordinary person.

You do that when you teach. You help level the playing field and give your students at least a chance of gaining the knowledge that will help them compete for jobs, raise a family, and enjoy life more fully. You encourage them to practice positive behavior and reject bad behavior. You stimulate their God-given consciences.

Jesus stirred the learned synagogue and government leaders. But the greater part of His ministry was reserved for the man on the street, the laborer who fished or collected taxes or worked retail. Such men and women lived closer to the ground and hungered for the mercy and grace Christ offered.

And so your students stand on the brink of space and dream of the day when cars will fly and home robots will do their bidding. They embrace science and technology as easily as a sheepherder embraces a newborn lamb. But who will teach them kindness and humility? Who will guide their attitudes toward life and what is truly important?

Parents, certainly. But given the number of hours you spend with your students, you have a huge role to play in how they treat themselves, their peers, and their ever-expanding knowledge. Jesus said, "I have come that they may have life, and have it to the full" (John 10:10 NIV). Teach your students to live abundant lives. Not only do you give them the axe with which to clear the way ahead, but you teach them the joy of swinging that axe. It is a joy that in its purest form comes straight from the heart of God.

GRACE FOR TODAY:

When we teach our students to live abundant lives,
God's will is done.

A LIFE INTERTWINED

The legendary Bicycle Tree can be found on Vashon Island, Washington, just south of Seattle. Apparently, the attraction began when a small child leaned a little red bicycle against the tree and never came back for it. (Perhaps it's another miracle that no one ever stole it, either!) As the tree grew, it wrapped itself around the handlebars, the banana seat, and rotten tires. The bicycle has even been lifted slightly off the ground, embraced by the tree. The tree and the bicycle dwell intertwined, one unable to live without the other.

What a visual image of how we live both as teachers and as God's children. We aren't really teachers without our students, are we? We need someone to be in our classrooms, ready, if not always eager, to listen. We need papers on which to write comments down in red or green ink. We need hall duty, lunchroom duty, and bus duty. We need the giggles from class parties and the powdery stuff that transforms vomit into a sweepable substance. Students can't learn everything required of them without us; we can't teach without them. Better still, there are so many days when they end up teaching us instead! Perhaps we don't need or want the degree of overlap like the Bicycle Tree, but, oh, what a feeling when we are first leaned against and then depended on!

Our lives with God, however, are to be exactly like that Bicycle Tree. Talking with God should be as natural and necessary to us as breathing. Worship should flow from our branches as we wrap our hearts, souls, and minds around the trunk—the vine that is Christ. We should not ever forget that apart from Him, we can't do anything. We can't even be a strong enough base against which a child may securely lean.

> GRACE FOR TODAY:
>
> God knows that apart from Him, we can do nothing.

[Jesus said,] "I am the vine, you are the branches . . . apart from Me you can do nothing."

JOHN 15:5 NASB

WAITING ON GOD

By Andrew Murray

In all our gatherings in any part of the work for God, our first job must be to be understand the mind of God. God always works according to the counsel of His will. The more that counsel is sought, found, and honored, the more surely and mightily God will do His work for us and through us.

The great danger in all such groups is that in our consciousness of having our Bible, our past experience of God's leading, our sound creed, and our honest wish to do God's will, we will trust in these and not realize that with every step we need and may have a heavenly guide. There may be elements of God's will, application of God's Word, experience of the close presence and leading of God, manifestations of the power of His Spirit, of which we know nothing as yet. God is willing to open up these in the souls who are intently set upon allowing Him to have His way entirely, and who are willing, to wait for Him to make it known.

When we come together praising God for all He has done, taught, and given, we may, at the same time, be limiting Him by not expecting greater things. It was when God had given the water out of the rock that they did not trust Him for bread. It was when God had given Jericho into his hands that Joshua thought the victory over Ai was sure, and did not wait for counsel from God. And so, while we think that we know and trust the power of God for what we may expect, we may be hindering Him by not giving Him time and not cultivating the habit of waiting for His counsel.

—m—

FATHER, OFTEN I AM IN SUCH A HURRY THAT I FAIL TO WAIT ON YOU. I WAIT ON YOU NOW TO GET YOUR MIND ON MATTERS. AMEN.

As your plan unfolds, even the simple can understand it. No wonder I wait expectantly for each of your commands.

PSALM 119:130–131 TLB

WHAT'S IN A NAME

A good name is more desirable than great riches.

PROVERBS 22:1 NIV

The Booth brothers both became famous in their time: the elder, Edwin Thomas, as an acclaimed Shakespearean actor, and the younger, John Wilkes, as Abraham Lincoln's assassin. Though Edwin was a consummate tragedian, his brother's murderous crime cast a pallor over his own name from which he was unable to recover. He retired in his prime, stigmatized by his association with a notorious sibling. Oddly, he carried a letter with him that could have vindicated him, a commendation from General Ulysses Grant's chief secretary thanking him for a singular act of bravery. Edwin, waiting to board a train in New Jersey, had saved a boy from an oncoming coach. Not until he received the letter of thanks did Edwin discover the boy's identity: Robert Todd Lincoln, the son of his brother's future victim.

> GRACE FOR TODAY:
>
> **When we are tested, God will uphold our reputation.**

Sometimes you may not be able to defend your reputation, but God will always be your defense. When you rely on Him to help you make right choices, He won't let you down, though the entire world should fail you. You're a member of God's family, bearing His worthy and honorable name. When you honor that name in all you do, God will uphold you.

A teaching career is shaped from tough stands taken on such issues as cheating, harassment, and plagiarism. Sometimes students, parents, and even administrators won't understand why you've chosen to defend what's right. However, when all is said and done, all of the personal attacks you have suffered won't matter, but only that you have followed God with all your heart.

A good name matters. You're representing not only yourself but God in all you say and do. Hold tight to His promises, rely on His wisdom, and speak carefully and prayerfully so that your reputation will shine His light in a darkened world.

UNDERSTANDING FROM ABOVE

Cry out for insight and understanding. Search for them as you would
for lost money. . . . From [the Lord's] mouth come knowledge
and understanding.

PROVERBS 2:3-4,6 NLT

Miss Laura, the kindergarten teacher, always got to school before anyone else so she could read her Bible and pray. She'd come from a dysfunctional family and so desperately wanted to show God's love to children, even though God was still healing her of her own past hurts.

She made it her daily practice to pray God's Word, seeking deeper understanding of Him: "Lord, I pray that You grant me, according to Your riches, to be strengthened with power through Your Spirit, so that Christ may dwell in me through faith. And I pray I'd be rooted and grounded in love." (See Ephesians 3:16-17.) She had prayed this verse ever since she had accepted Christ, and in her limited knowledge, Miss Laura interpreted her prayer to solely mean: God, use me to love others.

> **GRACE FOR TODAY:**
>
> When we ask, God gives us understanding.

However, one particular morning understanding came—like an epiphany—as Miss Laura prayed the verse that followed in Ephesians: "Lord, may I have power to understand how wide, how long, how high, and how deep Your love for me really is until I experience it for myself, though it's so great I'll never fully understand it."

Miss Laura paused a moment, staring out the window and allowing God to speak to her as she gazed at her beautiful plants, sitting on the sill. *I've been trying to show God's love to others, and I haven't even begun to understand it for myself,* she thought.

That day Miss Laura received a special measure of grace as she realized that to grow, her plants needed well-watered roots, and without water, no flowers would bloom. Even so, your roots need to soak up God's love until His love becomes an experiential reality in your life. Without well-watered roots—the ability to receive God's love and acceptance for yourself—you'll be limited in loving others.

STILL THE STORM

What a blessing was that stillness as he brought them safely into harbor!.

PSALM 107:30 NLT

There would be a lot less head-butting in the teaching profession if the Serenity Prayer were required recitation before every class and meeting: "God grant me the serenity to accept the things I cannot change, the courage to change the things I can, and the wisdom to know the difference."

Jesus, it must be noted, had a deep and touching serenity about Him that was surely one of the many traits that drew people to Him. Perhaps that is why we have idealized His birth. Every nativity scene, every herald angel, every card with shepherds watching over their flocks by night beams serenity into our lives. There is a serenity about the Messiah because He took the sinful world as it was and invited the whole ragtag bunch to drink the living waters of His love.

But, you protest, to teach is an invitation to trouble. The frog escapes from the terrarium. The classroom helper fails to show and doesn't find a substitute. Ralph calls Katie a rude name. Katie punches Ralph in the nose. Linda bursts into tears at the sight of blood and runs out the door right past the principal who chooses that exact moment to pay you a visit. Where's the serenity in that?

And yet the Serenity Prayer is said at the end of every meeting of Alcoholics Anonymous because a serene life is a life on the road to sobriety. The prayer was actually borrowed by a recovering alcoholic from an obituary in the New York Herald Tribune. Though the deceased person is unknown, the prayer has powerfully lived on.

The Irish pray the Serenity Prayer in order to be reasonably happy in this life and supremely happy in the next. It could do wonders for your teaching life.

GRACE FOR TODAY:

God knows that ships sink without tranquil harbors.

THE GROUCH IN THE MIRROR

Don't grumble about each other, brothers. Are you yourselves above criticism?

JAMES 5:9 TLB

One of the most well-known grouches in history was a man named William Claude Dukenfield. He was born in Philadelphia, Pennsylvania, on April 9, 1879. He was famous for such sayings as, "Anybody who hates children and dogs can't be all bad," and "I never met a kid I liked." He had a big nose, wore a top hat, and talked out of the side of his mouth. He starred in many movies during the 1920s, '30s, and '40s, including, *Never Give a Sucker an Even Chance*. Starting to sound familiar? You know him as W. C. Fields.

October 15 is National Grouch Day. Can you believe it? What a thing to celebrate! What a thing to be known for! The long-lived children's program *Sesame Street* has even succeeded in making the trash can–dwelling Oscar the Grouch a lovable, furry, if grumpy, character.

Undoubtedly, you've taught some grouches and you've worked with some grouches. But what about the grouch in the mirror? Are you quick-tempered? Do you blame others or circumstances for mistakes you've made? When you overhear students talking about you in the hallways, what do they say about your disposition? Do others want to be around you, or do they keep to the other side of the hall? When you catch the reflection of your countenance in the school-bus window, a downtown shop, the bathroom mirror, what does it usually look like?

It should radiate joy. It should be like a light set out to draw others into the circle of Christ's warmth. But sometimes it's so hard! The surface that should reflect His glory is dull, scratched, and disillusioned. We want a reason for joy, like a huge bonus for early retirement. How quickly we forget the depths from which He raised us up to be so much more than we could be.

GRACE FOR TODAY:

God's grace can cure our worst case of grouchiness.

BITTER PLANT, SWEET FRUIT

An ancient Jewish story tells of Abraham sitting outside his tent one evening. He saw an old man, weary from age and journey, coming toward him. Abraham rushed out to greet him, inviting him into his tent. He washed the old man's feet and served him. The old man immediately fell to eating without prayer or blessing. Abraham asked him, "Don't you worship God?" The old traveler replied, "I worship fire only and revere no other god." At hearing this, an infuriated Abraham grabbed the old man and forced him out of his tent into the bitter night air. When the old man had departed, God called to His friend Abraham and asked where the stranger was. Abraham replied, "I threw him out because he did not worship You." God answered, "Although he dishonors Me, I have suffered him these eighty years. Could you not endure him one night?"

Patience is one of the least-sought-after gifts of the Holy Spirit, which is perhaps why it is one of the most often required. Some people, it seems, naturally have more patience, while others battle much shorter fuses to attain it. Either way, while bitter to swallow, patience bears the sweetest fruit.

God allows opportunities for you to practice patience so that your faith may be perfected. Because God has provided you with everything you need to accomplish His will, it makes sense that He will grant you more and more patience as you grow in your relationship with Him.

When love and mercy mean more to you than the affront of the foolish and slow-witted, you'll learn patience. Each day at school provides ample opportunity to practice being long-suffering. Think of how much more you've accomplished with patience than frustration. Isn't that also true of the work God has done in your life?

> **GRACE FOR TODAY:**
>
> As we grow in our relationship with God, He grants us patience.

Let us lay aside every weight, and the sin which doth so easily beset us, and let us run with patience the race that is set before us.

HEBREWS 12:1 KJV

SEEING THE UNSEEN

By Hannah Whitall Smith

"**M**uch less" is the language of the seen thing; "much more" is the language of the unseen thing. "Much less" seems on the surface to be far more reasonable than "much more," because every seen thing confirms it. Our weakness and foolishness are visible; God's strength and wisdom are invisible. Our need is obvious before our very eyes; God's supply is hidden in the secret of His presence, and can only be realized by faith.

It seems a paradox to tell us that we must see unseen things. How can it be possible? But there are other things to see than those which appear on surfaces, and other eyes to look through than those we generally use. An ox and a scientist may both look at the same field, but they will see very different things there.

To see unseen things requires us to have that interior eye opened in our souls—that which is able to see below surfaces, and that which can pierce through the outer appearance of things into their inner realities. This interior eye looks not at the seen things, which are temporal, but at the things that are not seen, which are eternal; and the vital question for each one of us is, whether that interior eye has been opened in us yet, and whether we can see the things that are eternal, or whether our vision is limited to the things that are temporal only.

—◊—

FATHER, OPEN THE EYES OF MY HEART THAT I MAY SEE THE THINGS THAT YOU SEE. THANK YOU FOR THE HOLY SPIRIT WHO REVEALS THEM TO ME. AMEN.

It is written: "Eye has not seen, nor ear heard, nor have entered into the heart of man the things which God has prepared for those who love Him." But God has revealed them to us through His Spirit.

1 CORINTHIANS 2:9–10 NKJV

A SENSITIVE HEART

Since God chose you to be the holy people whom he loves, you must
clothe yourselves with tenderhearted mercy [and] kindness.

COLOSSIANS 3:12 NLT

Julie left school, thrilled spring break had finally arrived, and drove to the groomer's
to pick up her little Schnauzer before heading out of town to visit family.

The pet shop was crowded, so Julie had to wait. She couldn't help but overhear
another customer complaining and bad-mouthing the groomer because her poodle
wasn't clipped to her specifications. The customer grabbed her dog and belligerently
stomped out of the shop. It was Julie's turn, but as her
eyes met those of the groomer, her heart almost broke
inside as she saw an obviously sick, emaciated woman
who appeared to have radiation burns all over her body.
Wiping a tear from her face, the woman muttered,
"Excuse me, I've got to go to the restroom."

As she walked away, the owner came over and
apologized to Julie for the scene the customer had made
and then explained, "Our groomer has cancer. She has
no insurance, no family. She makes herself work just to
keep food on the table. Poor thing—I need to let her
keep working." The bell on the door jingled, and the
owner rushed to help another customer.

Obviously, the complaining customer either did
not notice or did not care about the groomer's weakened condition. If she were a
Christian, she'd apparently lost her sensitivity. It's so crucial as Christians to keep our
hearts tender before the Lord and not let them grow so cold that we can't even notice
another's pain.

Let God's grace wash over your heart today, and if you're losing sensitivity due
to callousness or life's trials, ask God to restore you and renew a tender spirit within
you today.

GRACE FOR TODAY:

**Let God's grace
wash over you
today and
restore your
sensitive spirit.**

ON THEIR OWN

While he was blessing them, he left them and was taken up to heaven.

LUKE 24:51 NLT

D o your students feel constantly under scrutiny? Possibly, since we often feel ourselves under the scrutiny of others. Aren't we always being tested, evaluated, and upgraded?

There's nothing necessarily wrong with those things. But when we micromanage our students and stand over them as if they are incapable of finding the solutions themselves, we only add to their apprehension—and ours—and to the likelihood of them perpetuating the same mistakes. Better to leave them to apply their own knowledge and to figure out their own applications, with you more as a resource than a police officer. Show them that you believe in their capabilities and that they can trust you to help them succeed.

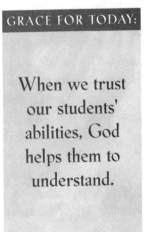

GRACE FOR TODAY:

When we trust our students' abilities, God helps them to understand.

Have you ever asked yourself why Jesus appeared to His disciples before ascending into Heaven? Couldn't He have said all His goodbyes and delivered the Great Commission before going to the Cross?

Though purely speculation, might His lingering a little longer have been His way of encouraging them, of lifting their sadness and shoring up their faith? How much more powerful was their witness after receiving the blessing of the resurrected Christ? It showed that He did not regret His choice of disciples and that He trusted their ability to act on all they had been taught despite His absence. Nothing less than the spread of Christianity hinged on it!

Let your students build on the confidence you place in them. Teach them how to fish and then allow them to go fish. They might tangle a line and lose a hook or two, but eventually they will come home with the big one that didn't get away.

WHO I AM

[He made] the stars also.

GENESIS 1:16 NASB

One evening at Sagamore Hill, the New York home of President Theodore Roosevelt, naturalist William Beebe walked outside with his host. Roosevelt looked at the expanse of star-soaked sky. Then he pointed out a small glow and said, "This is the spiral galaxy Andromeda. It is as large as our Milky Way. It consists of one hundred billion suns. It is one of a hundred billion galaxies." Roosevelt turned to Beebe and said, "Now, I think we are small enough! Let's go to bed."

As a child, Roosevelt was thin, sickly, asthmatic, and scrawny. He worked hard at overcoming these difficulties. Later in life, stories of him as a cowboy, a cavalry officer on San Juan Hill, and a larger-than-life president seemed to belie his shaky start. Roosevelt, however, never seemed to forget those obstacles. He kept before him the picture of what he had been, so that he would never confuse the identity of who he had become.

The Psalmist put it this way, "When I consider thy heavens, the work of thy fingers, the moon and the stars . . . what is man, that thou art mindful of him?" (Psalm 8:3-4 KJV). What indeed.

To recognize our lowliness as the work of the Creator is not to engage in false humility. Neither is it to flaunt our redemption or our knowledge that we share in His image. Rather it is to have a healthy confidence, secure in our identity. We are sons and daughters of the King—heirs with Him! We can be aware of our gifts, but not boastful. We can remember that our origins are dust, but not be downcast. We can also share this wonderful identity with our students by treating all of them as they truly are—precious children, who also belong to the King.

GRACE FOR TODAY:

God gave us our identity by making us His sons and daughters.

BEYOND UNDERSTANDING

The peace of God, which passeth all understanding, shall keep your
hearts and minds through Christ Jesus.

PHILIPPIANS 4:7 KJV

B erit Kjos told of a man who, seeking the perfect image of peace, announced a
contest to produce such a masterpiece. Paintings arrived from near and far, their
creators stirred by such a noble challenge. As the judges viewed each scene, the audience applauded and cheered, the tension growing with each passing moment. Two pictures remained. As the first was unveiled, a hush fell. A polished–mirror lake reflect-
ed soft, green birches under a pastel–blushed evening sky. Surely this was the winner.
The sponsor uncovered the last painting himself, and the crowd gasped. A waterfall
cascaded past a rocky precipice under a threatening sky. Lightning illuminated a spindly
tree jutting from the cliff, in the crook of which rested a humble bird's nest. Its occupant rested on her eggs, eyes closed, content in the midst of turmoil.

God's peace is beyond comprehension simply because God alone can offer it. The
world's peace rests on harmonious good will, occupational and financial security, and
altruism, none of which can be guaranteed.

In Jesus Christ, however, you have peace with God, salvation from sin, and a
future secured in Heaven by Christ's own blood. The Cross, violent and bloodied,
guarantees rescue, not condemnation. No wonder such peace can't be grasped, but only
received.

Most of the time, your classroom reflects God's own dignity and order. Everyone
and everything has its place, children work purposefully and pleasantly, and you
instruct briefly and redirect when necessary.

The true test of peace comes when your classroom descends into chaos, led by
rebellious students, or colleagues bicker over administration policies. As you continue to work calmly in the midst of these storms, it paints an amazing portrait of God's
peace at work in you.

GRACE FOR TODAY:

God grants us peace even in the midst of
turmoil and danger.

FRIENDSHIP WITH GOD

Teachers have the ultimate privilege of mentoring God's love to His precious children. A teacher may even be the first true friend some children ever make. So hopefully, you've personally discovered the ultimate grace that's been shown to you through the extreme favor of being called a friend of God.

A friend of God. Think of all that implies! It means God picked you as a friend just because He wanted to, and He knew exactly what He was getting. Sure, there may be times when He doesn't approve of things you do, but there will never be a time when He doesn't approve of you. He may discipline you, speak firmly to you, or even withhold something from you, but it will always be out of a heart of love because you are His friend.

> **GRACE FOR TODAY:**
>
> God has given us the ultimate privilege by calling us friends.

Friendship is more than benevolence—it's intimacy, relationship, closeness. To be friends with God means that you always have someone to listen to you, to be loyal to you, and someone strong that you can lean on. God is the kind of friend who will always be there when others may turn their backs on you, and He is a friend who'll always see your heart and not judge you by how things appear. He'll still love you unconditionally when all else seems to fall apart or even if you've lost the will to live. When you fall in a pit, He'll pull you out, and when you accomplish even the smallest of feats, He will cheer you on.

And the best part about being friends with God is that He is your friend—no matter what—forever!

So now we can rejoice . . . because of what our Lord Jesus Christ has done for us in making us friends of God.

ROMANS 5:11 NLT

ONE MAN'S PRAYER

By C. H. Fowler

We knew a preacher who was appointed to the charge of a church in Springfield, Illinois. The church seemed very much depressed. Its life was fading. It was in the midst of the harvest, in the hot weather, when things seemed most depressed. The pastor, a holy man of God, announced on Sabbath evening to a small congregation of under fifty people, "There will be a prayer meeting in this church tomorrow morning at sunrise for the revival of the work of God and for the conversion of sinners." The people wondered at the notice and went home.

The pastor went into his study by the side of the church and gave that night to prayer. Just as the East began to lighten up a little with the coming day, he had the assurance that his prayer was answered, and he lay down on a sofa for a little rest. Presently he awoke suddenly to see the sun shining on the wall over his head. He sprang up and looked out the window to see how late it was, and saw the sun just rising above the horizon.

Looking down into the church yard, he was overjoyed to see the church crowded with people, the yard full, and teams crowding into the street for a long distance. God had heard his prayer and had sent out His Spirit into the community, and there had been no sleeping in Springfield that night. People in the country who knew nothing of the meeting got up in the night, hitched up their teams, and drove into town and to the church to find out what the matter was. A good man had taken hold of God.

The prayer meeting began and was closed that night at eleven o'clock. Several souls were converted. A gracious work broke out, and the community was greatly blessed.

––––⁂––––

GOD, I LIFT MY SITUATION BEFORE YOU. THANK YOU FOR HEARING ME, FOR HONORING YOUR WORD, AND FOR MOVING ON MY BEHALF. AMEN.

When a believing person prays, great things happen.

JAMES 5:16 NCV

CAN YOU CHANGE?

Each of you is now a new person. You are becoming more and more like
your Creator, and you will understand him better.

COLOSSIANS 3:10 CEV

W e expect to see change in our students. We track signs of growth in understanding from month to month, week to week, and in the case of our more
mercurial pupils, day to day. We write about it in our progress reports, and we use it
to gauge our own effectiveness. Change in our students is a marker that tells us how
they're doing.

Change in you, the teacher, can be more complex.
You come to the job with an education and experience.
To suggest that you ought to change, that your students
would benefit from your willingness to modify and
reshape your own understanding, is for many of us an
uneasy proposition. We have our routine, and it feels
familiar and safe.

Winston Churchill said, "To improve is to change;
to be perfect is to change often." Some artists find that
there is nothing like radical change to give their work
fresh expression. Sometimes this is referred to as
"reinvention." In all cases, it is a willingness to take
stock and make adjustments where required. A seminar, a new approach, or even a
sabbatical might give your teaching new "oomph."

The Christian faith is all about change. We must be reborn. Our minds must be
renewed. When Christ returns, we shall be changed in the twinkling of an eye. All
these familiar biblical concepts require a radical, 180-degree turnabout in our lives.
Without it, we cannot share in the kingdom of God.

Don't fear change. See it as a way to fine-tune the gifts and talents you've been
given. Use it as a tool to model for your classroom what personal progress looks like.
If their teacher is willing to change, students will see it as a good thing for themselves.

WHAT'S IN IT FOR ME?

All the ways of a man are clean in his own sight,
But the LORD weighs the motives.

PROVERBS 16:2 NASB

During the Great Depression, when folks often lived with grandparents as extended families, there was a little boy who wet his bed every night. He slept with his grandmother. Each morning she would feel the sheet and groan. "Look what you did! You have to stop that!" And each morning he would counter, "I didn't do it—you did!" His parents tried reasoning, scolding, and spanking. Nothing worked.

Until his belatedly wise parents figured out that little Johnny had two wants: to wear pajamas like his daddy's and to get a bed of his own. His grandmother agreed to purchasing the new pajamas if he'd stop wetting the bed. His parents took him shopping to pick out his own bed. "Here is a little gentleman," the mother announced to the salesgirl, "who would like to do some shopping." The plan worked like a charm because they had discovered what motivated their son.

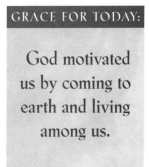

GRACE FOR TODAY:

God motivated us by coming to earth and living among us.

Humorous signs hang in Mrs. Simm's classroom as a motivational tool. "Attention Teenagers: 'No!' is a complete sentence!" "Teenagers—run away now while you still know everything!" She laughs at the signs, but more importantly, so do her students. Why? She has built a rapport with them by knowing their interests, perspectives, and the basics of what motivates each of them.

We can't expect elementary children to have the perspectives of high-school students. Neither can we expect high schoolers to have the perspective of a thirty-year-old. We must become students of human nature; we have to meet them at their level.

Jesus did it by becoming one of us. Even though He created us, He didn't just read the textbook; He lived our lives.

Dale Carnegie once wrote about human motivation, "Arouse in the other person an eager want." Jesus did this. "Thirsty? I'm the Living Water. Hungry? I'm the Bread of Life." What a motivation!

A HARD PILL TO SWALLOW

A man's pride will bring him low, but a humble spirit will obtain honor.

PROVERBS 29:23 NASB

P astor Michael Hartwig of Indiana told of a time when he was asked to speak at the funeral service of a man he'd befriended in a nursing home. Because the man had played a key role in starting the major industry in town, the church was packed with dignitaries. Despite Hartwig's nerves, the service went well. On the way to the cemetery, the funeral director interrupted Hartwig to compliment him on the service. Hartwig, soaking in the man's praise, stopped turning pages to the passage he planned to read at the graveside, 1 Corinthians 15, regarding the resurrection of the body. His heart swollen with success, Pastor Hartwig stood at the head of the casket, the deceased's family and friends alongside. He asked everyone to listen and began to read from the passage where he'd stopped earlier, 1 Corinthians 5:1: "It is reported commonly that there are fornicators among you!"

Pride comes with its own guarantee, backed by numerous scriptures: Inevitably, just when you think you've got it all figured out, something happens to remind you of your status as a mere mortal. It's a critical reminder that pride cuts you off from God, but humility restores you to Him. Acknowledging regularly, in every hour of trial and in every moment of peace, who God is and all that He has done for you, creates the necessary mind-set to live a humble life.

Pride works subtly, its first seeds planted by the simple act of forgetting God. All the hard work you've put into becoming an effective, moral teacher, all of the talents you've used to affect kids, are a tribute to Him. Any praise you receive in tribute of your efforts, redirect immediately to the Lord who loves you enough to save you, change you, and use you for His glory.

GRACE FOR TODAY:

God sends away no one empty except those who are full of themselves.

D. L. MOODY

THE HESITANT GENIUS

He calmed the storm to a whisper and stilled the waves.

PSALM 107:29 NLT

C elebrated painter, sculptor, architect, engineer, and scientist Leonardo da Vinci once said, "I have offended God and mankind because my work didn't reach the quality it should have." His love of knowledge and research, something we would wish on all of our students, resulted in both wonderful achievements and the melancholy of genius. The more he learned, the more he realized how much there was to learn and how little he had mastered.

Do you fret that many of your students won't grasp what you have determined to teach them in a year, let alone fathom what is yet to be discovered beyond the confines of the classroom? We all have those misgivings from time to time. Perhaps it would be more profitable to adopt the attitude of Christ in da Vinci's painting of "The Last Supper." In it, Jesus is the calm nucleus around which the emotional figures of His disciples agitate.

They ate, drank, and listened to His instructions and were stunned that He would wash their feet. It was the first celebration of the Eucharist, the lighting of the torch that the Church has since carried down through the ages. But why were the disciples so disturbed; why were their countenances so troubled? Because the painting captures the next few seconds after Christ dropped the bombshell that one of them would betray Him before sunrise. Their shock is plain.

It took da Vinci three years to finish the painting. Could he feel the distress the disciples felt? Did he doubt that he, da Vinci, understood the enormity of Christ's revelation? To be sure, all of us have more to learn about the faith, let alone the classroom. Look to the calm of Christ for steady nerves, and don't be too hard on yourself or others. Even the artistic masters had their misgivings.

GRACE FOR TODAY:

God can steady our nerves on the toughest of days.

A GOOD QUESTION

Your students have many questions and look to you for good answers. They may be surprised when you are stumped, but appreciate hearing you say, "That's a good question. I don't know the answer, but let's find the answer together." You might even incorporate a random curiosity question into your lesson plan. Perhaps it could be a "question of the week" that goes up on Monday and requires a solution by Friday. What a fun way to teach educational detective work and the value of library research!

The Bible poses some very pointed and colorful questions, from which spring some of the richest teachings in Scripture. The Lord asked Job, "Do you have an arm like God's, and can your voice thunder like His?" Or, "Can you pull in the leviathan with a fishhook or tie down his tongue with a rope?" God is able, He was saying, and His plan for us is in every way perfect.

Jesus asked, "What good is it for a man to gain the whole world, yet forfeit his soul?"(Mark 8:36 NIV). Those words were the gateway to many teachings about what is required of the faithful servant of Christ. When He asked the blind beggar of Jericho, "What do you want Me to do for you?" we learn volumes about what He is willing to do for us when we exercise faith.

The writings of Paul brim with excellent questions. To teach on unity in the body of Christ, he asked, "Is Christ divided?" and the wonderfully humorous, "If the whole body were an ear, where would the sense of smell be?"

Invite questions from your students. Guide them into understanding, as Jesus did, with questions both rhetorical and direct. And don't be afraid to ask your own questions. God loves a seeker of truth.

> GRACE FOR TODAY:
>
> **God asks us to be prepared for our students' questions.**

He shall call upon me, and I will answer him; I will be with him in trouble: I will deliver him, and honor him.

PSALM 91:15 ASV

DRAW NEAR

By Richard Baxter

B e of good cheer, the time is at hand when God will be near—as near as you desire. You shall dwell in His family. Is that enough? It is better to be a doorkeeper in the house of God, than to dwell in the tents of wickedness. You shall stand before Him, about His throne, in the room with Him, in His presence.

Would you still desire to be nearer? You shall be His child, and He your Father. You shall be an heir of His kingdom, and even the spouse of His Son.

And what more could you desire? You shall be a member of the body of His Son; He shall be your head. You shall be one with Him, who is one with the Father. For He himself has desired, "That they all may be one, as You, Father, are in Me, and I in You; that they also may be one in Us, that the world may believe that You sent Me. And the glory which You gave Me I have given them, that they may be one just as We are one: I in them, and You in Me; that they may be made perfect in one, and that the world may know that You have sent Me, and have loved them as You have loved Me" (John 17:21–23 NKJV).

—⁓—

HEAVENLY FATHER, I CRY OUT TO YOU WITH MY WHOLE HEART. THE LONGING IN MY SOUL CAN BE FILLED ONLY BY YOU. MY PARCHED SPIRIT CAN ONLY BE REFRESHED BY DRINKING OF THE PRECIOUS HOLY SPIRIT. I AM COMFORTED KNOWING THAT WHEN I DRAW NEAR TO YOU, YOU DRAW NEAR TO ME. THANK YOU FOR THE MIRACLE THAT I AM ONE WITH YOU. AMEN.

Let us draw near with a sincere heart in full assurance of faith, having our hearts sprinkled clean from an evil conscience and our bodies washed with pure water.

HEBREWS 10:22 NASB

THE POWER OF OPTIMISM

A cheerful heart has a continual feast.

PROVERBS 15:15 RSV

K aiser Wilhelm was probably the most despised man on the face of the earth during the last days of World War I. Even his native Germany turned against him as he fled to Holland to save his own life. Thousands would have loved to gloat at his public execution.

Still, one lone boy wrote to the Kaiser a letter glowing with optimism, admiration, and sincerity. He told the Kaiser that no matter what others thought, Wilhelm would always be his respected and beloved leader. The Kaiser was so moved that he invited the boy to visit him. The boy went along with his mother—and the Kaiser married her! Ah, the power of optimism, faith, and giving ourselves for others.

> **GRACE FOR TODAY:**
>
> God's grace can turn our heart's garden from a Gethsemane into an Eden.

Someone once said, "When life gives you lemons, keep them, because, hey—free lemons!" What's the difference between the person who ruminates on hatred of another person for real or imagined slights and the one who continues to believe in, pray for, and hope for the best? What's the difference in the student or colleague whose face puckers up in disgust at sour-lemon days and the one who adds a few ice cubes, a cup of sugar, and stirs up sweetness?

Perhaps the renewed popularity of gardening offers some lessons. You dig in some rather unpromising-looking dirt with the proper tools and throw in some seeds. Cover up the bulbs and seeds, weed out the undesirable elements, water as needed, and occasionally add some fertilizer. But what comes up depends wholly on what kinds of seeds you planted and how well you maintain your garden.

No, positive thinking won't solve all of life's problems. It doesn't replace our need for God. It won't automatically make us feel better. But it's a great thing to spread in the deep rich soil of our hearts. What about you? Does optimism grow in your heart's garden?

WITHOUT CEASING

The earnest prayer of a righteous man has great power
and wonderful results.

JAMES 5:16 TLB

The soldier stood before his commanding officer, accused of communicating with the enemy. He'd been seen returning from an area where enemy troops were known to patrol. The man defended himself briefly, stating that he had slipped away to spend an hour in prayer. "Are you in the habit of doing so?" asked his commander. "Yes, sir," he replied. "Well, you've never needed it more than you do now. Kneel and pray aloud so that we all may hear you." Expecting to die immediately, the soldier dropped to his knees and unveiled his heart before God. His prayer revealed intimacy, humility, fluency, and urgency, not only the words but the heart of one who came regularly before God. The officer dismissed him. "You may go," he said. "No one could have prayed that way without long apprenticeship. The fellows who never attend drill are always ill at ease for the review."

Forsake prayer only at the cost of your very purpose in life. It's that necessary—that urgent. Effective prayers are regular, habitual ones, filled with the urgency of wanting to know God more fully.

You never know all that a day may bring, but if you make prayer a regular habit, God will prepare you for every contingency. Prayer shakes off fear, casts away burdens, and trusts God to uphold you as He keeps His promises in your life.

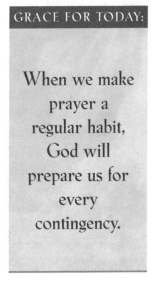

GRACE FOR TODAY:

When we make prayer a regular habit, God will prepare us for every contingency.

Daily, you build relationships with students, colleagues, family, and friends. How? You speak, you listen, you try to be useful or to get help. In the same way, share desires, disappointments, aspirations, and pleas for help with God in prayer. It's not always easy, but connecting with God strengthens you to face your own challenges and prepares you to help others face theirs.

SOUND ADVICE

Hold tight to good advice; don't relax your grip.
Guard it well—your life is at stake!

PROVERBS 4:13 MSG

As a teacher, you know that the advice you give students is as important, sometimes more important, than the subject knowledge and skills you impart. Since your sphere of influence includes not only students, but also colleagues, administrators, parents, and the general public, you want to be sure that the advice you're offering is biblically sound.

The best way to do that, of course, is to make sure you know what the Bible says about topics and issues relevant to those around you. It's important that they understand that while your advice may be filtered through your own experiences, it comes from God's standard of living.

If you've ever listened to your students, even some of those who call themselves Christians, talk about their beliefs, you know there's a buffet mentality at work—a dose of Christianity, a pinch of Buddhism, and a liberal dash of pragmatism. When they ask you what you think, you'll want to put forth a clear, gentle, loving statement that always leaves the door open for further discussion.

And as always, your advice will carry more weight if those around you know you to be just like your words: honest, encouraging, and always believing the best about others.

When people know that you aren't talking just to hear yourself speak, but because you take your principles seriously, and that your beliefs fuel the quality of your work and your demeanor, you'll be surprised at how many inquiries come your way. When that happens, know that God is working, that His light is shining in and through you, and trust Him to help you say the right thing at the right time.

GRACE FOR TODAY:

God can help us give sound advice.

THE SOUNDS OF SILENCE

[There is] a time to keep silence, and a time to speak.

ECCLESIASTES 3:7 ASV

S ilence in the classroom can signal a number of things. Your students aren't present. Or they're reading to themselves. Or there's a pause in the discussion. While silence may be rare among your pupils, it is not to be avoided. Especially in discussion, odd as that may sound.

Educator Parker Palmer says that we do not teach with words only, but with silence. "Silence gives us a chance to reflect on what we have said and heard," he writes in *The Courage to Teach*. "Silence itself can be a sort of speech, emerging from the deepest parts of ourselves, of others, of the world."

Do you panic at silence and interpret it as boredom or ignorance on the part of your students? Resist the urge to fill the void with talk. Time to reflect and dig down into our understanding is time well spent. It also gives those students who are more reluctant to speak the time to gather their thoughts.

We live in a society flooded with constant talk and the white noise of radio, TV, and cell phone chatter. But the good interviewer knows to allow pregnant pauses. It is in the pause that the one being interviewed sometimes gives more cogent observations than might otherwise surface in a rush to the next question.

Commander Joshua warned the Israelites to "not say a word" until the appointed time for bringing down the walls of Jericho. Had they jabbered on at an inappropriate moment, they would not have conquered. Talk at the appointed time will keep you from missing the great benefits of contemplation and rumination.

Remember the times when Jesus kept silent before His accusers. Isaiah prophesied that the Messiah would neither quarrel nor cry out. His silence was golden and of itself was a valuable teaching tool.

GRACE FOR TODAY:

The Holy Spirit will strengthen, teach, and guide us in the silence.

ME, ME, ME!

A detailed study of telephone conversations by The New York Telephone Company found out that the word most frequently used when people talk to each other is the personal pronoun 'I'. It was used 3,900 times in 500 telephone conversations.

Think about it. When you are introduced to a new group of students or colleagues, how much time do you spend regaling them with stories about you? How much time do you spend listening, really listening with interest? When you get your school class pictures back every fall, whose face do you look for first? When you attend a meeting or a party, do you gauge the success by how productive or what a good time everyone else had? Or do you measure by your own feelings?

Jesus advocated, taught, and modeled a completely different measure. We learned it in Sunday school, though its principles are often taught in public schools today. "Do unto others as you would have them do unto you." So simple. But it requires selflessness, a commodity that is more rare than crude oil these days.

To think of someone else's needs before our own seems unnatural somehow. *I'm cold,* we think. *Someone should turn that air conditioning down. I'm bored. I'm hungry. I hope we have a fire drill. I hope I don't have to be the PTA liaison this year.*

But what if we trained ourselves to think of others first—to put them at ease, to inquire about their dreams. President John F. Kennedy revived the Golden Rule sentiment briefly with his famous statement, "Ask not what your country can do for you—ask what you can do for your country."

Jesus said it another way. "Greater love hath no man than this, that a man lay down his life for his friends" (John 15:13 KJV) Daily, we can "give up our lives" for our students and make little sacrifices for those around us.

> **GRACE FOR TODAY:**
>
> When God gave up His life for us, He taught us how to be selfless.

In humility count others better than yourselves.

PHILIPPIANS 2:3 RSV

He Runs after Us

By Hannah Whitall Smith

A wild young fellow, who was once brought to the Lord at a mission meeting became a rejoicing Christian and lived an exemplary life afterward. Later he was asked by someone what he did to get converted. "Oh," he said, "I did my part, and the Lord did His."

"But what was your part," asked the inquirer, "and what was the Lord's part?"

"My part," was the prompt reply, "was to run away, and the Lord's part was to run after me until He caught me." A most significant answer; but how few can understand it!

God's part is always to run after us. Christ came to seek and to save that which was lost. "What man among you," He says, "if he has a hundred sheep and has lost one of them, does not leave the ninety-nine in the open pasture and go after the one which is lost until he finds it? When he has found it, he lays it on his shoulders, rejoicing" (Luke 15:4-5 NASB).

This is always the divine part; but in our foolishness, we do not understand it, but think that the Lord is the One who is lost, and that our part is to seek and find Him. The very expressions we use show this. We urge sinners to "seek the Lord," and we talk about having "found" Him. "Have you found the Savior?" asked a too zealous mission worker of a happy, trusting little girl.

With a look of amazement, she replied in a tone of wonder, "Why, I did not know the Savior was lost!"

—◈—

FATHER, I AM OVERWHELMED AND IN AWE WHEN I REALIZE THAT JESUS LEFT HIS HOME WITH YOU TO PURSUE ME TO BE HIS BRIDE. NOT ONLY DID HE PURSUE ME, HE LAID DOWN HIS LIFE TO SECURE MY PLACE WITH YOU FOR ETERNITY. HOW COULD I NOT RESPOND? NO ONE COULD EVER LOVE ME LIKE YOU DO. AMEN.

[Jesus said,] "The Son of man came to seek and to save the lost."

LUKE 19:10 RSV

DO THE RIGHT THING

The just shall live by faith.

ROMANS 1:17 KJV

A golf addict neglected his job, frequently calling in sick as an excuse to play. One morning, after witnessing the man's usual call to the office, an angel spotted him on the way to the golf course and decided to teach him a lesson. "If you play golf today, you will be punished," the angel whispered in his ear. The fellow dismissed it as his own conscience. "No," he said, "I've been doing this for years. No one will ever know." The angel watched from the first tee as the guy whacked the ball 300 yards straight down the middle of the fairway, bettering his previous best by 100 yards. His luck continued—long drives on every hole and perfect putting. Walking on air, he shot an amazing 61, about 30 strokes under his usual game. He couldn't wait to get back to the office to tell everyone! Suddenly, his face fell. He could never tell his coworkers or anyone else. The angel smiled.

> **GRACE FOR TODAY:**
>
> God's justice will bring us home on the wings of grace.

God's justice is a crucial but temporary thing, a means of drawing His children back to Him through His Son. One day, however, the demands of God's holiness will be met, and the day of grace will end in judgment.

Since judgment belongs to God, your role in life is to do the right thing as much as humanly possible. If you are led to show mercy, show it. If you are compelled to administer justice, do so calmly and firmly. Either way, you're merely demonstrating that there is a higher standard to which we are all held.

In your classroom, not every child is treated equally. One might need more individual instruction than another. You may then hear the rallying cry of youth—"That's not fair!" But as you maintain consistent boundaries in your classroom, your kids will learn that your justice helps maintain peace and provides fair opportunity for all.

RISK IT ALL

Paul said, "And why do you think I keep risking my neck in this dangerous work?. . . Do you think I'd do this if I wasn't convinced of your resurrection and mine as guaranteed by the resurrected Messiah Jesus?"

1 CORINTHIANS 15:30-31 MSG

"**D**amian, sit down," Mr. Nicholson said. "You might as well do your algebra if you're stuck in detention anyway."

"Ahh, get off my back," Damian grunted. "I can't understand it anyway."

"I've told you repeatedly, if you'd come in after school, I'd help you until you do
understand it," Mr. Nicholson coaxed. "I know I could help you get a handle on it."

"You just don't get it! Ain't nobody gonna help me learn," Damian smarted back.

"Didn't I hear that you won the rock-climbing
contest last weekend at Winter Park?" Mr. Nicholson
asked.

"Yeah, what about it?"

Mr. Nicholson sauntered over to Damian's desk
and got right in his face: "The same way you slaved,
accomplishing that feat, can also serve to help you scale
the heights of algebra. When you're climbing the ropes,
the harness doesn't give you the ability to climb higher
heights. It's your trust and dependence on the gear that
keep you from falling and allow you to develop the
strength, endurance, and perseverance to move slowly
up the wall. You're willing to take the risk because you
trust your equipment."

GRACE FOR TODAY:

If we stay close
to God, He
will enable us
to take greater
risks for Him.

Whether you've been teaching a long time or just beginning, it won't take you long
to figure out that God works the same way. He doesn't just empower you to barely
make it through life. He gives you the tools and keeps you safely harnessed so you can
risk the heights of faith—learning to trust and lean on Him.

As you come to trust the Lord, you'll develop confidence and take greater risks for
Him. Depending on God will enable you to be a better teacher, making it possible for
you to accomplish that which you initially thought impossible.

WAR NO MORE

We are human, but we don't wage war with human plans and methods.

2 CORINTHIANS 10:3 NLT

I t's hard to talk about war with kids whose lives stretch ahead of them. But it can't be escaped, not when the headlines blare and everyone takes sides and your students worry about over what it all means. Perhaps they come from homes that have been directly affected—a brother or uncle or friend is in military service, has been injured or killed—and it would be unkind to duck the topic. So you try.

But how do you foster hope and optimism and excitement over the future when you must talk of the guns and bombs and refugees of today's conflict? Or attempt to explain the equation of hate and greed and religious revenge? These are awful things and difficult enough for an adult to understand.

There they sit, watching you. Five or ten or fifteen years ago, they did not exist. Now they furrow their brows and talk of war and wonder if a few years hence they will be called to serve.

And you feel ill-equipped to help them struggle with their reality. In some ways, theory is so much easier and sanitary to discuss. After all, what teacher is smart enough, empathetic enough, and confident enough to explain the root causes of terrorism and the logic of warfare?

Yes, it is a difficult assignment. It means that you have to be rooted in the certainty of Heaven while living in the uncertainty of earth. You must be convinced that God will put an end to war one day and that your hope is in Him. And like Jesus, you must focus on the war within and redouble your efforts to vanquish the spiritual enemy that wants to take you captive. Only then will you have the right perspective to help your students grapple with war and peace in the human soul.

GRACE FOR TODAY:

God calls us to fight the good fight of faith and claim our victory.

THE ULTIMATE DELIGHTER

The LORD takes delight in his people.

PSALM 149:4 NIV

I f you've ever coached your students, whether on an athletic, musical, or academic team, then you know the feeling. They perform a piece for the school board, and your buttons pop. They win the state championship, and your heart swells with pride. They answer a difficult question or perform even beyond what you expected—what you trained them for—and you feel, at least for a moment, like they are your own children!

Our own children certainly delight, entertain, and amaze us, don't they? And wonder of wonders, God delights in us, His children, too. How do you know? The Psalmist assures us. The apostle Paul wrote, quoting from Isaiah, "No eye has seen, no ear has heard, and no mind has imagined conceived what God has prepared for those who love him" (1 Corinthians 2:9 NLT). We can't even imagine all that God has planned for us!

Can't you see Him, watching us make a right choice; master a difficult concerto; reach a recalcitrant student; meet and marry the love of our life; bring our first child into the world; celebrate autumn's harvest; trudge to school wearily; but lean on Him and do a great job anyway; share Him with a friend; bear up under a fierce trial? He is proud of us! He loves us! He delights in us! He wants us to spend time visiting with Him in prayer, chatting with Him over coffee, sharing with Him a wonderful passage from a book, just as we would with a beloved friend. That's what He is! He is also our Savior.

He supports us every step of the way. He has gathered the saints to cheer us home. Listen—can you hear it? The roar is getting a little bit louder every day. In just a little while, we'll hear those words—"Well done, good and faithful servant."

GRACE FOR TODAY:

As our heavenly Father, God delights in us as His children.

THE GREATEST OF THESE IS LOVE

As a teacher, you have the privilege of affecting students for time immemorial. Consider one teacher's lasting influence as you eavesdrop on this true account that twenty years later still communicates a powerful message:

"Without further fanfare, I introduce to you our keynote speaker, Ms. Laurajane Brown, who'll be speaking on the power of influence," the moderator announced, clapping to welcome her.

"As most of you know, I coordinate children's ministries, and tonight I want to encourage you—never underestimate how God can use you in the classroom. You're positioned in one of the most influential places of power known to mankind, and kids watch your every move . . ." Ms. Brown continued speaking, every person attentive to her compelling message.

" . . . and in closing I want to tell you about my eighth-grade math teacher who unknowingly helped shape my life

> **GRACE FOR TODAY:**
>
> When we love our students, God can influence them for a lifetime.

into what it is today. Mrs. Howorth had a practice of singing 'Happy Birthday' to students as they stood in front of the class on their birthdays. I've never forgotten Claudia's birthday. Claudia was a disadvantaged student on scholarship at this private school. Her clothes never matched; she always smelled, and she had no friends. Worst of all, she had mangy hair with lice. On Claudia's birthday, as everyone sang, Mrs. Howorth stood right beside her, hugging her close. As the singing ended, she leaned over and kissed her on top of her head. I remember the shudder that went down my back when she kissed her head, knowing Claudia had lice.

"You know, friends," Ms. Brown said, "what I learned in school that day, I've carried with me my whole life—I learned from Mrs. Howorth how to love people the way that Jesus loves people."

Like Jesus, love a child today and influence her for a lifetime.

Be imitators of God, as beloved children; and walk in love, just as Christ also loved you.

EPHESIANS 5:1–2 NASB

GRACE AND FAITH

By Charles Spurgeon

Grace is the first and last active cause of salvation. Faith, essential as it is, is only an important part of the machinery which grace uses. We are saved "through faith," but salvation is "by grace."

Grace is the fountain and the stream; faith is the aqueduct along which the flood of mercy flows down to refresh the thirsty people. The aqueduct must be kept entire to convey the current; and, even so, faith must be true and sound, leading right up to God and coming right down to ourselves, that it may become a serviceable channel of mercy to our souls.

We must not look so much to faith or exalt it above the divine source of all blessing, which lies in the grace of God. Never make a Christ out of your faith, nor think of it as if it were the independent source of your salvation. Our life is found in "looking to Jesus," not in looking to our own faith.

By faith all things become possible to us; yet the power is not in the faith, but in the God upon whom faith relies. Grace is the powerful engine, and faith is the chain by which the soul is attached to the great motor power. The righteousness of faith is not the moral excellence of faith, but the righteousness of Jesus Christ which faith grasps and uses. The peace within the soul is not derived from the contemplation of our own faith; but it comes to us from Him who is our peace.

Therefore, the weakness of your faith will not destroy you. A trembling hand may receive a golden gift. The Lord's salvation can come to us though we have only faith as a grain of mustard seed. The power lies in the grace of God.

———

FATHER, EVERY GOOD THING— INCLUDING MY GIFT TO TEACH—THAT HAS COME TO ME FROM YOU IS A RESULT OF YOUR AMAZING GRACE. THANK YOU! AMEN.

By grace you have been saved through faith; and that not of yourselves, it is the gift of God.

EPHESIANS 2:8 NASB

TRUE CONTENTMENTIT IS WELL WITH MY SOUL

If they obey and serve him [God], they will spend the rest of their days in prosperity and their years in contentment.

JOB 36:11 NIV

Fanny Crosby, author of some 9,000 hymns, including such classics as "To God Alone Be the Glory," "Great Things He Hath Done" and "Blessed Assurance," also taught English and history at what was then known as the New York Institution for the Blind, where she had become a student herself at fifteen.

Although many well-meaning people wished that God had included sight among her many gifts, she never complained, saying, "If perfect earthly sight were offered me tomorrow, I would not accept it. I might not have sung hymns to the praise of God if I had been distracted by the beautiful and interesting things about me."

For all the joys of teaching, there are also heartaches. Tragedy and misfortune strike within your school and community, putting not only ABCs and 123s in perspective, but perhaps also challenging your view of your own effectiveness.

During the course of the school year, you get to see children's lives change, mostly for the better, as they grow and learn under your nurturing hand. You don't do it for the money, but rather to make a differ-ence—to see God glorified in all you do. In Him alone it becomes possible to say that, despite the hardships, you are truly content.

> **GRACE FOR TODAY:**
>
> God wants us to be content with the knowledge that we are His children.

Working with children, you never know how far your influence extends. For each time you get the privilege of seeing the light bulb go on above their heads, there seem to be at least two other times when you wonder if you're having any impact at all.

However, just as you are faithful to make the best of available resources, to be a compassionate, humane voice in a topsy-turvy world, so is God faithful to help you. Let Him assist you in seeing the value of simply being His child on any given day.

THE HYMN OF YOUR HEART

Though he slay me, yet will I trust in him.

JOB 13:15 KJV

He shot himself on Christmas Eve, leaving behind a wife and two little girls. Having just lost his job, he doubted his potential to ever be a worthwhile provider again. He was too discouraged. They'd be better off without him, or so the note said. His children asked their teachers why their daddy would think that—they believed in him.

Another wife waved good-bye with an exaggerated thrust of her blossoming tummy, sending her husband off with a smile and a warm kiss. He left for a business trip from which he never returned. He was killed in a freak accident. She miscarried her twins just two weeks later.

Worlds shattered. Lives and plans changed in a moment—in the blink of an eye. And the terrible questions begin. Where is the hope?

Hope is found in the surety of God's promises. He never fails. He never changes. He is always with us. Always. Powerful, soothing words in the face of situations with unanswerable questions. Why, God? Of doubt. Are You really there? Why didn't You do something to stop this?

Doubt. It's an old emotion. It's at the root of Job's words when he cries out thirty-seven chapters' worth of hard questions for God. God answered. He said that we can't understand His ways. Even if He explained himself, we probably still wouldn't get it this side of Heaven. Doubt is present in some of David's anguished psalms. David wonders how long God will let his enemies get the upper hand.

At some point, all of us will struggle with doubt, asking our own hard questions. That's why we must determine in advance of our lives that God is good. All the time. Think of it. When confronted with deepest tragedy, what words would be written on your soul? What would be the hymn of your heart?

> **GRACE FOR TODAY:**
>
> God is bigger than our hardest questions and stronger than our deepest fears.

WHAT COULD BE

[In speaking of Abraham, Paul said,] "He is our father in the sight of
God, in whom he believed—the God who gives life to the dead and calls
things that are not as though they were."

ROMANS 4:17 NIV

When Guy Rice Doud was nominated as teacher of the year, at the small ceremony President Ronald Reagan read him a poem entitled simply,
"Teachers." Clark Mollenhoff, a former reporter for the Des Moines Register, had
written it as a tribute to his mother at her retirement as a country schoolteacher in
Iowa. There's a phrase in the poem that also inspired the later title of Doud's autobi-
ography—*Molder of Dreams*. You may not think of that often, but that's exactly who you
are.

One year a girl brought home a second-grade report card with this comment from
her teacher: "It is a real pleasure to have your daughter in my class because she adds
so much zest to it." The next year's card also had a comment about the girl, but from a
different teacher with a different perspective: "Your daughter talks too much."

Amazing, isn't it, how the reminder that we can mold, shape, destroy, or encourage dreams, reminds us of the wonder of how we affect the lives of those we teach—
those whose lives intertwine with ours in whatever capacity and however briefly.

Think back to the first time you were aware that someone believed in you—not
just polite lip service, but really saw your potential and believed in you. Do you realize that God does the same thing for us every day? He knows our weaknesses and our
frailties, but He looks past all of them to see what we can become.

This is grace at its finest—to look at someone, and rather than sighing and shaking our head, to look past what is, to envision what can be, and to gently nudge them
toward the sweet gift of becoming.

GRACE FOR TODAY:

**As we believe in our students' potential, God makes
us molders of dreams.**

THE ILLUSION OF CONTROL

"I am the LORD . . . I will also hold you by the hand
and watch over you."

ISAIAH 42:6 NASB

In your everyday life, how much effort do you invest in trying to control your circumstances? Life is full of uncertainties, and the truth is that control is just an illusion. No one knows when an unfortunate situation may arise: a problem with a child, a premature death, or a devastating illness of one you love. Truly, only God knows the times and seasons of your life.

The good news is that God's grace continually abounds toward you, and God is always in control, even when you can't be. His plans always prevail, but more importantly, His plans are always good. When something rocks your world and the illusion that you have control shatters, be assured that God is still on His throne, and He'll never leave you nor forsake you.

The real answer in dealing with life is to fall into God's everlasting arms and receive His comfort when you don't know what to do. The victory is always to be found in Jesus Christ. You see only through a veil dimly, but He sees the entire picture of your life, the scope of your situation, and the answer He has waiting in the wings. Yes, the victory is in Christ and comes when you continue to walk hand in hand with Him—both when times are good or when you experience the dark night of your soul.

If you're facing an uncertain future today, remind yourself that God's presence is always with you and that He is in control.

GRACE FOR TODAY:

When life threatens to overwhelm us, God reminds us
that He is in control.

THE LIVING WORD

How can a book thousands of years old—the Holy Bible—speak to a twenty-first-century culture? Is it still relevant today? Can it be understood? Yes! It takes time, but if you're willing, the Word will guide you in living a more meaningful life.

The first step in understanding the Scriptures is to develop a meaningful relationship with it's Author—the ever-present but invisible God. Sound impossible? Well, obviously, you can't just meet someone and know everything about them by the end of the week. Similarly, it takes time to grow close to God. But if you decide to spend time reading His Word, God will become as real to you as your best friend and reveal His heart to you, just as He did for David. Because David was a "man after God's own heart," the shepherd boy turned king took his joy, his pain, his sorrow, and his anger to God in the psalms that he wrote, and David records that God answered him.

As the apostle John revealed, God and His Word are one and the same, and spending time in the Word is spending time with Him. God is real, and He longs to be real to you. Our main problem today is that we most often seek to know God through our feelings, which can misguide us. The Word of God never will.

People today are not much different than people yesterday. We still love, get married, and work. We still cry, laugh, and speak angry words. God's Scriptures have something to say about all of it. Because the Word is living, God's Holy Spirit unwraps it for us like a Christmas gift to reveal how we can apply it to our lives.

Spend time in the Word today and allow God to flood your thoughts just as David did. It will make you a better person . . . and a better teacher.

> GRACE FOR TODAY:
>
> **When we spend time reading the Bible, God can make us better teachers.**

In the beginning was the Word, and the Word was with God, and the Word was God.

JOHN 1:1 NKJV

FOR THE JOY
SET BEFORE YOU

By John Bunyan

There was a king that adopted one to be his child, and clothed him with royal clothes, and promised him that if he would fight his father's battles and walk in his father's ways, he should eventually share in the father's kingdom. He has received the adoption and the king's clothes, but not yet his part in the kingdom. But now his hope of a share in that will make him fight the king's battles, and also walk the king's paths.

Yes, and though he may encounter many things that could discourage him from continuing, still thoughts of the promised kingdom, and hopes to enjoy it, will make him fight his way through those difficulties. His future hopes will, therefore, usher the child into a personal possession and enjoyment of that inheritance.

Hope has a thick skin, and will endure many a blow; it will put on patience as a vestment, it will wade through a sea of blood, it will endure all things if it be of the right kind, for the joy that is set before it. Hence patience is called "patience of hope," because it is hope that makes the soul exercise patience and long-suffering under the Cross, until the time comes to enjoy the crown.

—∾—

HEAVENLY FATHER, I CAN EASILY RELATE TO THIS STORY BECAUSE OF THE GREAT HOPE I HAVE IN YOU. STRENGTHEN ME SO THAT I MAY TRIUMPH IN MY STRUGGLES AND PATIENTLY ENDURE UNTIL I SEE YOU FACE TO FACE. WHEN I HAVE CHALLENGES WITH MY STUDENTS, HELP ME TO BE PATIENT AND KEEP IN MIND THAT EACH ONE IS SPECIAL TO YOU AND THAT YOU HAVE CALLED EACH TO DO GREAT THINGS. USE ME TO OFFER THEM HOPE. AMEN.

Let us fix our eyes on Jesus, the author and perfecter of our faith, who for the joy set before him endured the cross, scorning its shame, and sat down at the right hand of the throne of God.

HEBREWS 12:2 NIV

Topical Index

Author Index

Endnotes

1. *A Journey into Spiritual Growth*. Copyright 1999 by Evelyn Christenson. Published by Chariot Victor Publishing, a division of Cook Communications. All rights reserved. Pages 35–36.
2. Ibid. Pages 43–44.
3. *Found: God's Will* by John MacArthur Jr. Copyright 1973 SP Publications, Inc. Published by Cook Communications Ministries. All rights reserved. Pages 12–13.
4. *A Journey into Spiritual Growth*. Pages 45–46.
5. *Found: God's Will*. Pages 14–15.
6. *A Journey into Spiritual Growth*. Pages 169–170.
7. *Found: God's Will*. Pages 20–21.
8. *A Journey into Spiritual Growth*. Pages 175–176.
9. Ibid. Page 184.
10. *The Adequate Man: Paul in Philippians* by Paul S. Rees (Westwood, N.J.: Revell, 1959). Page 106.
11. *Anxiety Attacked* by John MacArthur Jr. Copyright 1995 by John MacArthur Jr. Published by Cook Communications Ministries. All rights reserved. Page 34.
12. *A Journey into Spiritual Growth*. Pages 189–190.
13. *Found: God's Will*. Pages 40–41.
14. *A Journey into Spiritual Growth*. Pages 207–208.
15. *Found: God's Will*. Pages 33, 35–36.
16. *Be a People Person* by John C. Maxwell. Copyright 1989, 1994, 2004 by Cook Communications Ministries. Published by Cook Communications Ministries. All rights reserved. Page 43.
17. *Found: God's Will*. Pages 23–24.
18. *Be a People Person*. Page 61.
19. *Be All You Can Be* by John C. Maxwell. Copyright 2002, Published by Cook Communications Ministries. All rights reserved. Pages 54–55.
20. *Be a People Person*. Pages 144–145.
21. *Found: God's Will*. Page 26.
22. Ibid. Pages 28–29.
23. *Be All You Can Be*. Pages 60–62.
24. Ibid. Pages 50–51.
25. *Found: God's Will*. Page 30.
26. *Lord, Change Me* by Evelyn Christenson. Copyright 1993, 2002, by SP Publications, Inc. Published by Cook Communications Ministries. All rights reserved. Pages 52–53.
27. *Be All You Can Be*. Pages 13–14.
28. *Be Encouraged* by Warren W. Wiersbe. Copyright 2004 by Cook Communications Ministries. Published by Cook Communications Ministries. All rights reserved. Pages 60–61.
29. *Stop Pretending* by Luis Palau. Copyright 1985, 2003 by Luis Palau. Published by Cook Communications Ministries. All rights reserved. Pages 63–65.
30. Ibid. Pages 9–10.
31. *Be Encouraged*. Pages 138–140.
32. *Be a People Person*. Pages 38–39.
33. Ibid. Pages 18–19.
34. *Handle with Prayer* by Charles Stanley. Copyright 1982, 1992 by SP Publications, Inc. Published by Cook Communications Ministries. All rights reserved. Page 56.
35. *Lord, Change Me*. Pages 53–54.
36. *Handle with Prayer*. Page 53.
37. *Stop Pretending*. Pages 95–96.
38. Ibid. Pages 45–46.
39. *Handle with Prayer*. Pages 57–58.
40. *Lord, Change Me*. Page 59.
41. Ibid. Pages 66–67.
42. Ibid. Page 68.

Additional copies of this and other
Honor Books products are available
from your local bookseller.

The following titles are also available in this series:

Daily Grace
Daily Grace for Teens
Daily Grace for Women

If you have enjoyed this book,
or if it has had an impact on your life,
we would like to hear from you.

Please contact us at:

Honor Books, Dept. 201
4050 Lee Vance View
Colorado Springs, CO 80918
Or visit our Web site:
www.cookministries.com

HONOR HB BOOKS

Inspiration and Motivation for the Seasons of Life